This portrait of the life and humanitarian work of Diana, Princess of Wales has been authorized by the late princess's Estate and her Memorial Fund.

ANNIVERSARY EDITION

DIANA
THE PORTRAIT

ROSALIND COWARD

FOREWORD BY NELSON MANDELA INTRODUCTION BY LADY SARAH McCORQUODALE

Andrews McMeel
Publishing, LLC

Kansas City

FOREWORD

When I heard about the death of Diana, Princess of Wales in a car crash in 1997, I was devastated. I was looking forward to seeing her again in South Africa, where I believe she could have played a major role in helping turn the tables on the HIV/AIDS pandemic. I grieved for the loss of such a remarkable humanitarian.

But this book reminds us that the value of a life is not ended by death. Princess Diana's example continues to inspire and challenge us. We can all learn from her example and embrace her legacy.

However privileged and famous she was, she had time for the most humble people—and made them feel special. She took time out of her schedule to talk at length to recovering alcoholics, young homeless people, the poor and the sick, and gave them hope. She often visited dying or desperate people, out of the public limelight. But she also knew how to transform public awareness with the help of her celebrity and beauty.

For example, who can forget those renowned images of the princess in protective headgear, walking through the minefields of Angola, or comforting the innocent victims of landmines? By doing that, she gave a massive boost to the international campaign to ban landmines, as public opinion, responding to her inspiration, demanded an end to hesitation and excuses.

When she stroked the limbs of someone with leprosy, she did more to break the taboos surrounding that disease than any number of books, articles and health education programmes. When she sat on the bed of a man with HIV/AIDS, held his hand and chatted to him naturally as a fellow human being, she struck a tremendous blow against the stigma and superstition which can cause almost as much suffering as the disease itself and makes it so much harder to prevent and treat.

We cannot all be a famous British princess. We can, however, all try to do what we can to insist that every human being is precious and unique, worthy of love and care. We can all insist, as she did, that nobody deserves to suffer from stigma and prejudice on top of their illness or disability. We can all try to follow her example in reaching out to people on the margins of society and welcoming them into our hearts.

It is good to know that the proceeds of this book will help The Diana, Princess of Wales Memorial Fund continue the princess's work around the world, while the photographs and testimonies included here will be a source of humanitarian inspiration and hope. I am proud and delighted to associate myself with this tribute to her remarkable humanitarian achievements.

May we never forget them.

Mandela

Nelson Mandela

INTRODUCTION

In the days after Diana's tragic death when my family was still deep in shock, the overwhelming public outpouring of grief was of real comfort. Although we had all been aware of—indeed had sometimes shared in—her humanitarian work, it was not until my sister died that any of us quite realized what an extraordinary personal impact she had had. The millions of tributes—letters, poems, flowers and gifts—that were sent from all over the world symbolized just how much she meant to people from all walks of life, most of whom knew her only from their television screens.

I take great pride in the legacy Diana has left behind, not only in William and Harry, but also the way in which she changed our view of what it means to be a human being. From HIV/AIDS to leprosy, from the victims of landmines to the profoundly disabled, Diana's informal, caring approach quietly broke down stigma, prejudice, and neglect.

Diana had the capacity to say the right thing to people. If they had a sense of humor, she would make them laugh. If they were incredibly shy, they would lose their shyness. It was an amazing quality. When she visited old people's homes or hospitals or hospices, she always went in with a smile and always seemed to find the appropriate word. As her lady-in-waiting on some of these occasions I was astonished at the effect she had. A joke, a gentle touch, an embrace, a sensible question, made everyone warm to her immediately and feel that her concern was genuine. Often she would keep in touch with those she met on her various visits long after the newspaper headlines had faded, maintaining her concern for their welfare for many years.

Many of the people whose lives were touched by Diana in this way have spoken for the first time in this book. I am glad that they should now wish to share their personal memories. Diana lives on in the lives of the many thousands of people whose lives she changed forever, and this portrait of her life and work stands as a unique celebration of her legacy.

I am delighted, too, that royalties from this unique book will go toward the work of The Diana, Princess of Wales Memorial Fund, the charity I have been associated with since its beginnings, just days after Diana's death.

An organization can never possess the personal charm and compassion of an individual, but the Memorial Fund can, and does, use its name, influence and resources to reach out to people on the margins of society. Following Diana's example of championing unpopular causes, the Fund supports many vulnerable and disadvantaged young people in the United Kingdom; whilst overseas it promotes the care of people who are dying unimaginably and unnecessarily painful deaths from HIV/AIDS in Africa; this in addition to its continued support for communities trying to rebuild lives after conflict living among landmines and other explosive remnants of war.

Like Diana, her Memorial Fund is prepared to speak out against the injustice and prejudice that make already vulnerable lives more vulnerable. This book is a reminder, not only of Diana's compassion, but also of her continuing legacy in leaving the world a better place.

Sarah McCorquodale

Lady Sarah McCorquodale
President
The Diana, Princess of Wales Memorial Fund

CHAPTER ONE – THE UNIQUE

... this distinction that her concern for other people all started when she married, and it's due to her being Her Royal Highness. It isn't. Becoming the Princess of Wales certainly embellished it all, but it was there, always ...

Frances Shand Kydd

Diana Frances Spencer was born on July 1, 1961 at Park House, a large country house leased from the Queen on the royal estate of Sandringham in Norfolk. Her father, Johnnie Spencer, was then Lord Althorp and would, on his own father's death, become Earl Spencer. Her mother, the Honorable Frances Roche, was the daughter of Lord and Lady Fermoy. The two married in 1954 when Frances was 18 and the couple's first daughter, Sarah, was born the next year. Another daughter, Jane, followed two years later and in 1960 Frances gave birth to a son who lived only a few hours. Diana was born shortly afterwards. Three years after her, the last child was born—a boy, Charles—who became heir to the Spencer title.

In keeping with the rest of her life, Diana's birth was recorded publicly. There was an announcement in *The Times* and a fuller report in the more parochial *Eastern Daily Press*. "Daughter for Lady Althorp" it announced along with her father's comment that "they had not yet decided on a name." By August they had, and the christening of Diana Frances Spencer took place at Sandringham Church. The local paper also covered the christening, with a photo entitled "Sandringham Baptism." This exposure in the local news reflected the social status of Diana's family in the area. Lord and Lady Althorp were titled gentry with close links to royalty in an area dominated by Sandringham, one of the royal family's homes.

At that time, Lord Althorp's father, the 7th Earl Spencer (Jack), was still alive, living at the family seat, Althorp House, near Northampton. Diana's parents took over the lease of Park House, Frances's family home, on the Royal Sandringham Estate, not long after the death of Lord Fermoy, Frances's father.

Diana's parents' families both belonged to the courtier class, people whose work and lives intersect closely with the royal family. Lord Fermoy had been an equerry to King George VI and had become a friend. Indeed, they had been shooting together at Sandringham the day before George died, coincidentally the day Frances was born. Lady Fermoy was a lady-in-waiting to the Queen Mother, and was one of her closest friends. The Fermoys had been given the lease of Park House—originally used to accommodate overspill from Sandringham—because of the close personal friendships that existed between the two families.

Like the Fermoys, the Spencer family also had close personal associations with the royal family. Diana's father became an equerry to the Queen and was acting Master of the Household at the time of his marriage. He even accompanied the Queen and Prince Philip on their first major overseas tour of the Commonwealth. They mixed socially, too. Johnnie Spencer joined shooting parties at Balmoral, and the Queen Mother had stayed at Althorp in his childhood. When Johnnie and Frances married the wedding was considered the social event of the year and was followed by a huge reception at St James's Palace in London, attended by several members of the royal family. All the Spencer children except, ironically, Diana, have one royal godparent.

The Spencer family was—in name at least—one of the grand families of England. Johnnie Spencer was heir to a title, a stately home, a significant art collection and a huge country estate of several thousand acres of park and farmland. Althorp itself is nearly 500 years old, bought by a Robert Spencer (1570-1627) who claimed descent from William the Conqueror. Spencer made his fortune from sheep farming and, it was claimed at the time, was the wealthiest man in England. Many past family members played key roles in British history. One forebear, Charles, 3rd Earl of Sunderland, was briefly Foreign Secretary and married to the Duchess of Marlborough, bringing together the two families of Churchill and Spencer. Another Charles became Leader of the House of Commons for the Whig party in 1830 and

afterward Chancellor of the Exchequer. In 1765 the specific title of Earl Spencer was created, coinciding with the beginning of Althorp's famous art and silver collection (est. 1670s).

At the time of Diana's marriage to Charles, various commentators noted that the Spencers' own ancestry was rather more impressive than the Windsors': she was the first British subject to marry an heir to the throne for 300 years and her ancestry could be traced directly back to the Stuart kings. Yet in spite of these apparently impeccable aristocratic credentials and the personal familiarity of the Spencers and the Fermoys with royalty, it would be wrong to conclude that Diana was already all but royal in name; there is a huge gulf between royalty and commoners. "The essence of being royal is you're not an ordinary person, and you don't grow up having ordinary relationships," says constitutional historian Ben Pimlott. "The psychology of being royal is that, apart from first cousins, people just treat you differently from childhood, and that's particularly true of the heir to the throne. But it's also true of other royal siblings. Adults treat them differently so they can't deal with people on the basis of equality and spontaneity."

Diana, by contrast, says Pimlott, "was from a very similar background to the Queen Mother. They were both daughters of earls and what they had in common was that they were non-royal, they came from outside and, to that extent, were ordinary people. But the key difference between them is that the Queen Mother came from a Tory family whereas Diana came from a Whig family. The Tory tradition in the aristocracy was deeply loyal to the monarchy; the Whig tradition was basically rather contemptuous. This difference can be exaggerated but there's a grain of truth, not necessarily in their traditions but in their style, and how they related to those traditions. The Whigs were individualists."

The personalities, social factors and values that surrounded Diana in childhood ensured that her upbringing and life were radically different from any clichéd notion of aristocratic privilege. She was born into a family already exposed to the social changes of post-war Britain, not least the difficulties and financial burdens of keeping large estates and valuable art collections together, an issue which lurked in the wings throughout all of Diana's life. Her four grandparents were each, in their own way, huge characters—complex, ambitious, philanthropic and eccentric—who made their mark on the family. Both Lord Fermoy and Lady Fermoy had been forceful local personalities. King's Lynn residents described Lord Fermoy as the sort of person who was just as likely to jump on the bus and go around the market picking up cauliflowers as come into town in his chauffeur-driven car. Lady Fermoy was an accomplished pianist and an enthusiastic supporter of the arts and, especially, music in the area. She initiated the King's Lynn festival, which has continued since to attract world-class musicians. After her husband died she moved out of Park House enabling Frances and her family to move in while she spent more time at Uphall four miles away.

On the Spencer side, Diana's father did not get on well with his own father who had devoted his life, obsessively, to conserving the extraordinary collection of art, furniture, and silver at Althorp, fearing it would be dispersed on his death. Maudie Pendry, the housekeeper and wife of the old earl's butler, remembers, "the preservation of the 500-year-old collection was his mission." The children didn't visit Althorp too frequently and Diana's grandmother, Lady Spencer (Cynthia), to whom many thought Diana bore a strong resemblance, usually visited the children at Park House until her sudden death from a brain tumor in 1972.

Relative impoverishment, social change, family conflict and the personalities of those involved meant Diana's family was open to experiences typical of the time and typical of society. It meant that the life that Diana experienced growing up was far closer to the ordinary citizens of England than her social background might first appear to suggest. Her experiences of her parents' divorce, a childhood marked by change, academic under-achievement, parental absence, illness and stepfamilies in many ways put her in touch—emotionally at least—with those less privileged members of society. It is the first of many paradoxes in Diana Spencer's life that when she married Prince Charles she was, in both senses, the real girl next door.

"Diana was born when a boy was much needed, much wanted, and not a girl," says her mother Frances Shand Kydd. "But then some horrendous doctor, a so-called therapist, or counselor—some ghastly woman—told her that she was a disappointment at birth. It took a lot of talking with me to realize her birth was very happy. And it took a lot of anger from me that people should write about her brother who died, who didn't know him or me. I'm sure we weren't doing bed and breakfast for journalists when he was born."

Park House, on the grounds of Sandringham, was Diana's home until she was 13 when her father inherited Althorp, the family seat. "She was more a Norfolk girl than a Northamptonshire girl," says Henry Bellingham, Conservative MP and childhood friend of Diana, "because she was born in Norfolk and she loved Norfolk. She went first of all to a governess at Park House and then she went to Riddlesworth School. You are molded by your early childhood and she looked back on the Norfolk years as being the lovely years, because her family was together and her mother, for some of it, was still around.'"

Diana's father described her as a sweet child who grew into a practical little girl. One of the children's first and favorite nannies, Judith Parnell, recalls there was nothing out of the ordinary about Diana as a little one. "The princess was very good and happy and contented. We walked a lot through the grounds at Sandringham, to feed the ducks on the lakes. And we would visit "John Chinaman," the Golden Buddha, there and walk to the stud to look at the foals in the paddocks. We used to go to the beach at Brancaster, where the family had a hut, to picnic and play in the sand and water. When Charles, her brother, was born, Diana loved to help with him, especially at bath time."

Charles Spencer loved Park House too. "It was the best place to grow up; it was beautiful and it was big. There was a huge garden and a swimming pool and a tennis court. It was a very lovely environment for anyone to grow up in; we didn't realize how lucky we were. But it was good fun for us. I'd say it was among the happiest years of my life, certainly."[1]

In many ways it was a classically privileged upper-class English upbringing, in a large house with staff and a nanny looking after the children. Like her older siblings, Diana was initially taught at home by a governess, Gertrude Allen, who had also taught her mother and other local children. But in 1967 Diana's parents separated and the subsequent divorce was accompanied by a custody battle over the children. "Actually for one term Charles went to the Young England Kindergarten and Diana went to Francis Holland when they were living with me in London," says Frances Shand Kydd. But in 1969 she lost the custody of the children who returned to Norfolk to live with their father.

Charles Spencer says "it's difficult to analyze" the effect of the divorce, "because I didn't know any different. In the holidays we did go between the two parents' houses, but in a way I think it was quite a balanced upbringing then because my mother lived in much more modest surroundings than this and I think that was probably a good thing."

Her father's cousin, Robert Spencer, recalls Diana as "a normal, busy, active child who one always wanted to be with. I mean, I loved all those children very much. Not having children of my own it was great to be with them. It was very sad their parents divorced and one was very sympathetic toward it, but I didn't notice any problems with them. All four seemed very happy children to me."

"She was outstandingly pretty as a child," recalls Anthony Duckworth-Chad who married Diana's older cousin Elizabeth Wake-Walker and knew the family well. "She was very, very pretty. And I remember going over to play tennis at Park House when the children were there: Sarah and Jane, and Charles was there, too, very small. Diana—she was sort of three or four years old—certainly stood out. You could always tell that she was going to be quite something. She had a sparkle, even in those days, and was always very sweet, very chatty, too."

Maudie Pendry and her husband kept house for the old Lord and Lady Spencer. "I first met Diana when she came to Althorp when she was about five and a half. She was a very shy little girl, very pretty, and very sweet. She loved music. She was a very caring little girl, very loving, always out with her grandma, giving her a hand. She used to go out in the garden picking grandma a flower or a rose to bring in. She was always dancing around, but she was very shy."

One thing everyone remembers about Diana as a child was her absolute passion for animals on which she lavished care and attention. "She was very keen on animals," says Robert Spencer, "you could tell she had a strong feeling for them. She loved to have her own pets and on her own bed she had lots of toy animals like a lot of girls do." "That was my family," Diana said later. Anthony Duckworth-Chad also remembers her as someone who was never squeamish and was really fond of animals. "When she was a small child, there were always guinea pigs and things like that sort of hurtling around the place, and they all had dogs and things like that, you know. All the children were very keen on animals. There was always quite a menagerie at Park House. When she used to come over to us when she was a child, we always had dogs and things, and she always loved the pets."

"She loved animals when she was a child," says her mother. "I think you want something to love, and she loved everything that's small and furry, or got feathers. She had rabbits, guinea pigs, hamsters; a long succession of animals to care for. She outgrew it and took on people, I think. But the animals were super-comfortable and rather well catered for—well looked after, well cleaned out. She had a great consciousness they were dependent on her. She did the dirty work.

"She didn't like horses very much. Well, she was quite happy with them, but she didn't ride them. She liked the miniature Shetlands I had because they were small. And she had one of her own. I bred the ponies when I had a farm but not any more. I had 29 at one stage. I had them because the children enjoyed them and when there weren't children there I sold them. But Diana didn't like riding. Sarah was very keen, the only one who was very keen."

"We weren't really alike as children," says Diana's sister, Lady Sarah McCorquodale. "I was completely obsessed with ponies and she wasn't. At Riddlesworth she used to run Pets' Corner—a great position of responsibility! She was made to check that all the animals had water, straw, food, whatever, and she was very diligent about that. And that's what I see as a first sign of the responsible person she became. But one of the things I find very odd, is when she was growing up in Norfolk she always had animals. She was always taking care of animals. She had guinea pigs and she had hamsters. We had a cat,

Marmalade. A lot of thought went into looking after that. When she married Prince Charles she didn't even have a pet. It is odd, and no charities connected to animals."

After a brief spell in London with their mother, Diana and Charles returned to live in Norfolk at Christmas 1967. Their father had enrolled them at Silfield School, a small family-run school in King's Lynn, not far from Sandringham. Mr. Walter Page who bought the school in 1960 when it had only a handful of pupils describes it at that time as "one of the last dame's schools in England" referring to the fact that his sister-in-law, Jean Lowe, who was headmistress, had formerly worked as a governess to aristocratic families.

Mr. Page kept the school accounts, his wife did the cooking and his own three children attended the school. By the time Diana started at the school, there were 40 pupils. "Some were the children of professionals like doctors, a lot were the children of local farmers, but by the time Diana started there was a fantastic social mix. There were children from the local Chinese takeaway and children from the caravan site nearby."

Diana was six when she started at the school and Jean Lowe remembers her as "very shy to begin with, but she settled in quite quickly. She was quite a pretty little girl, but she bit her nails. I tried to stop her, but it wasn't a lot of good. She was good at painting and she read fluently before I had her. I think she had had a governess; she'd obviously been well-taught. She was quite a bright child but there was nothing special about her, just a normal little girl. There was no side to her whatever."

Diana's sensitive and caring nature was obvious even at that age. Jean Lowe remembers she used to get concerned if other children were upset. "When her brother Charles started in the nursery," Jean Lowe can remember, "Diana was very anxious. In one lesson I was teaching I could see Diana was very restless and she actually kept saying, two or three times, 'Do you think Charles is all right? Do you think he's happy?' And I said, 'Well, why don't you just go and see?' And she went out and came back and said, 'He's fine,' and then she settled back to the lesson."

Jean Lowe was very struck by how much Diana's father was prepared to get involved. "He didn't put on any airs and graces. He was just like a lot of the families at the school at the time, farming folk. But he was an exceptionally good father." Her family all remembers Lord Althorp sharing the school run with other local families, including the Loyds, whose father was estate manager at Sandringham and whose daughter, Alexandra Loyd, was one of Diana's closest friends. "I remember the Land Rover coming with his lordship driving them. He would literally help the little ones into their classes, helping them take off their little coats and shoes, sorting out their wellingtons and hanging up their coats in the nursery.

"Perhaps Lord Althorp, as he was then, came from that generation where they didn't kiss and cuddle, but Diana obviously adored him. I did notice that she wanted physical contact. When she came up to read to me she would always lean on me. But he was wonderful with the children, very considerate and very humorous." On one occasion Jean Lowe remembers him coming into the classroom to find a little girl who had asked Diana to a party. "He said something along the lines of, 'Could you tell me where you live because I need to talk to your mummy about the party?' And the little girl in a very proud voice said, 'We live in a maisonette.' Lord Althorp enthusiastically responded, 'Do you? How wonderful!'"

Mr. Page also encountered Johnnie Spencer regularly at St Margaret's Church in King's Lynn where Diana became the source of one of the church congregation's favorite anecdotes. "Before the split-up of the family, Lord Althorp was a co-warden with me for a few years. And so he and his wife used

to come with Diana and Charles regularly. And there was one lovely episode. There was a lovely old choir man, who had been in the choir from the age of seven to 80-something. And he would intone, 'O, Lamb of God,' three times, just before the people go up for communion. And it must have caught her fancy or something, because on one occasion, he'd sung his little bit and he was leaving to go and play the organ in another church before the service finished. And as he was walking down the aisle, Diana pointed at him and said, 'Mummy, there goes the Lamb of God.'"

Johnnie Spencer was a large character. At Riddlesworth Hall, the boarding school in Norfolk where Diana transferred at nine, headmistress Patricia Wood said that all the kitchen staff and grounds people remembered him. "When you talked to the kitchen ladies they couldn't remember much about Diana because she was just one of the little girls, but they could all remember her father. He was—how can I put this?—a very conspicuous gentleman. He was very tall and noticeable and almost the first thing he did, when he brought her to the school after the holidays, was go down in the kitchens and talk to them."

Anthony Duckworth-Chad remembers Johnnie Spencer as someone who was "terribly good with people." A neighbor in Norfolk, they spent a lot of time together. "I was a great friend of his before I married Liz, and then because he was on his own with the children, I think he looked on Liz almost as a sister. My Liz was the eldest Spencer grandchild and Johnnie was always very fond of her, so we used to see a lot of them. Johnnie used to come and shoot with us, and he was terribly good with all the people on the estate. He knew everybody, and remembered people's names, which was something I could never do. And Diana was very good at that, too. When she used to come over and see us at home after she was married—she'd come over with the boys or something like that—and she would always say, 'Oh, where's Mrs. . . . ?' who was our woman who helps in the house, and she used to go and see her. Her father was just the same; he was terribly good like that. I think that was an hereditary thing."

Diana grew up with a father who was interested in everybody he met regardless of background. Diana's sister Sarah remembers that, like Diana, he used to get an incredible buzz out of just talking to ordinary people. "My father," she says, "had an instinctive way with people. We've all got an ability, my brother, my sister and I, we can all do it, you know, but Diana just did it better. I think it comes from my father. I'm not saying my mother doesn't have it, but he was brilliant, and he stood in this wonderful shop at Althorp selling wine and he would come in and say, 'I've had a really good day today.' So we would say, 'Oh, have you sold lots of wine?' 'No,' he'd reply, 'two divorces and a hysterectomy.' People would talk to him and he was gripped. He loved it. He loved people. And Diana did too. I don't think that kind of quality has got anything to do with upbringing. I think you've either got it or you haven't, and you can't find it. It's either in you when you start, when you're born, or it's not."

"Earl Spencer was very keen on everybody being treated in the right way," says his cousin Robert Spencer. "He would see and sense other people's problems straight away and that was very important because if you can put yourself into seeing what other people are thinking then you can help them. Johnnie certainly did that. And Diana certainly did inherit a lot from him in that direction, yes." "My father," said Diana, "always said: 'Treat every-one as an individual and never throw your weight around.'"

Johnnie Spencer was involved with the Boys' Club movement and was often away. But the life of the landlord left more time for his children than many fathers. But while many in that position would still not have involved themselves closely with their children's lives, Johnnie Spencer was pretty hands-on for his time. The first thing he did on moving to Althorp was to have a swimming pool built because of the enjoyment it provided the children, particularly Diana. He involved himself in organizing social exchanges for the children. He put on surprise parties including once hiring a dromedary for Diana's birthday. One of the nannies employed by Johnnie Spencer shortly after the divorce recalls how, after she applied for the job, he suddenly paid a surprise visit to her own home to meet her father. "I think he was checking what sort of background I came from and whether I would be suitable to be involved in his children's upbringing. It was a pretty unusual thing for a potential employer to do, but if you think about it, very sensible." "He was good with the children," says Robert Spencer, "although in some ways he let them do too much, he didn't control them enough. But he was a great father. He loved to do things with the children."

Both of these characteristics—involvement with his children and the popular touch came together in Johnnie Spencer's passion—photography. He was an enthusiastic photographer and amateur filmmaker. At the King's Lynn festival in 1954 all the seats were quickly sold out when he showed his cinefilm of the Queen's world tour on which he had accompanied her. Johnnie Spencer, "who sat by the projector with a microphone in his hand," gave a commentary. The local paper noticed that "in contrast to previous pictorial records of the tour, the film dwelt not so much on central figures but with the countries and their peoples, scenes on board ship, and informal shots of members of the household. Few indeed were the pictures of the Queen and the Duke and the glimpses of them were confined to official occasions—apart from one delightfully informal view of the Duke as he inspected a combine harvester while staying at a farm in New Zealand."

The most striking aspect of Johnnie Spencer's passion for photography—and one that may have had an effect on Diana's later life—was the record he kept of the lives of all his children. "My father," says Charles Spencer, "religiously kept photograph albums all through our childhood for each of us." They were presented to each child when they reached the age of 18. The albums chronicled everything: First parties, first steps, leaving for school, the family pets, any event of any significance in the children's lives however small. He also kept remarkably well-organized scrapbooks, recording even the smallest milestones and triumphs of his children. In Diana's case, hers included second prize for one of her pets in the "Fur and Feathers" section of the Sandringham Show.

Many were struck at the time of Diana's wedding and engagement that her father, a key player in the events, was seen photographing the crowds. "I've photographed all the other events in her life so I'm not going to miss the most important one," he said at the time. Quite apart from the fact they were taken by her father, the album of photos taken in London at the time of Diana's wedding are a remarkable record of how ordinary people responded to the event. They are photos of shops and ordinary houses decorated, of people wearing Union Jack hats.

Perhaps some of Diana's photogenic qualities came from the ease she acquired from becoming completely used to having a camera around. Her brother Charles has described how from a very early age Diana was "relaxed in front of a camera," something he never acquired. "Great posing. She loved all that. Always had a natural way."

On both sides of Diana's family there was an ethos of communication with, and care for, others. Her mother, Frances Shand Kydd, says, "I hate this distinction that her concern for other people all started when she married, and it's due to being Her Royal Highness. It isn't. Becoming the

Princess of Wales certainly embellished it all, but it was there, always; it was her entire life. She was motivated by these qualities for her whole life. She didn't just come down from a cloud and begin, which you'd think to read some of the books.

"She certainly was very drawn to vulnerable people, and that includes healthy youngsters as well as unhealthy youngsters. She was interested in anyone who because of their age was unable to defend themselves. Any form of deprivation, she was keen on. It is unusual. I think it comes from—and was instilled in—my family, and she certainly grasped it deeply in a personal way, a sense of you must care for others. That came from my father, and I passed it on to her.

"She believed, as I do, that everyone has gifts, and they sometimes don't know it themselves. You need a friend to tell you what they are, and what they aren't. If you think about it, the gifts you envy are the ones you don't have, but you do have some—everyone does—and it's finding what they are. I've tried to live by that.

"Diana was brought up to touch people, which she did a lot of, and also she used her eyes to look at people directly. There's nothing worse than someone who looks past you. I'd say: 'Look at them.' And she did have large eyes and she had this great appeal: 'Let's find out about you.' She was really interested in people. I'm sure she spoke to a lot of people and somehow found their names and addresses and followed up, at a tough time, and that is a very difficult thing to do. I know, because if you're in touch with people, it's quite hard to know how you let go when the bad times have relatively gone. But she was very good at it. She was marvelous even from a very young age.

"I think she was born with it, but it was certainly helped by upbringing, and then it came to fruition really in her life."

Robert Spencer says that a philanthropic attitude was part and parcel of the "aristocratic" ethos. "They all learned about how to care for people. We all did. It was just part of life. Goodness me, I remember all the things—even before the war as a small child—we had to do. We participated very much in village life. Even just a dance in our village I had to make sure I danced with Mrs. Crisps and talked to Mrs. Lewis. I had to make sure I knew if somebody's daughter was ill and if somebody was getting married. You had to know all those things and it was just automatic. It was duty, but I didn't not enjoy doing it. If you are somebody meant to be of some importance in a community you have to give the right example and you have to do your job.

"I want to emphasize we all grew up in that way. I was away at school, but during the holidays I played in the local football team and local cricket team. I went to the whist drives and bicycled to visit anybody who was ill in the village. It was just part of life, you just did it, and certainly Johnnie did. He was involved from a young age with a great number of activities in Norfolk and Northamptonshire, in fact he came back to be High Sheriff of Northamptonshire in the late 1950s. It was automatic: You got involved and you got on with it and did it."

One of Diana's relatives in particular seems to have been a role model for Diana. Many people, including Diana's family have commented that Diana's wonderful charm and beauty were characteristics she shared with her paternal grandmother. Lady Spencer (Cynthia) was considered very kind and caring and was also very popular. Diana even looked like her as a portrait at Althorp by William Nicholson shows. Lady Spencer's daughter, Lady Anne Wake-Walker whose husband suffered from Parkinson's disease was reminded of the similarities when Diana later involved herself in the Parkinson's Disease Society, "Diana was marvelous. She worked hard for them and they loved her. She wrote me a lovely letter when I told her that Christopher had

Parkinson's, really kind and caring. She was very distressed and longed to do something to help her uncle in her usual, caring way. She was a very wonderful young woman. She took on much more than she had to and approached it in a very human way."

"She came and stayed with her grandmother," says Robert Spencer, "and they were certainly close, although they didn't see that much of each other because Diana was still living in Norfolk. Diana was only 12 when her grandmother died, but certainly she looked back on what her grandmother had done and I'm sure it was some sort of inspiration to her. I saw quite a lot of my aunt and, yes, there were certain features where they were alike. They had a very similar smile. My aunt still had a lovely smile until she was in her seventies, so that's a similarity one can certainly associate with grandmother and granddaughter. Diana's was a wonderful smile, too." Yet for all these claims of hereditary influence, Robert Spencer acknowledges that no one else in the family had ever taken on issues "in the much higher sphere that Diana undertook. Her family has been well-known for undertaking works of all sorts, and therefore it was in her blood to do so, but that's rather different from the way that she managed to put herself in a position to change attitudes so much."

One area that seems to have had a huge influence in Diana's childhood is her schooling. It is standard practice for British aristocratic families to send their children to boarding school and the Spencer family was no exception. "The establishment view, written about by those who usually didn't know it, except second-hand," says Frances Shand Kydd, "was that you sent your children to boarding school not because they get the best education, but because you didn't want them at home, which I read time and time again. It's a fairly big myth." Diana certainly seems to have been very lucky in one aspect of her schooling. Even if she failed to cover herself in glory academically, the schools she attended were small and intimate and she seems to have enjoyed them. Indeed she made such strong bonds with some of the teachers that they were invited to her wedding and she revisited them and the schools later in her life.

Diana went to the boarding school Riddlesworth Hall near Thetford in Norfolk aged nine. She has described herself as feeling rejected at first because in the aftermath of the divorce she had been "busy looking after my father most of the time and then suddenly realized I was going to be away from him." But Riddlesworth Hall had a strong family ethos. The headmistress, Miss Elizabeth Ridsdale, was extremely maternal. Later Diana was to say she "adored" her time there. In return Elizabeth Ridsdale said, "I think she has developed into quite the most charming person. I am so proud."[2]

The Reverend Reginald Sweet, Latin teacher and chaplain, remembers "a super girl. We arrived virtually at the same time. I got there in the July/August of 1969 and then she came along. She was a sad and lonely little girl when she came, particularly at bedtime, because the break-up was quite a traumatic experience. But Miss Ridsdale immediately took her under her wing, explaining to us what a difficult time Diana was going through and asking if we would all try and make sure that she was OK. And she very quickly settled in, there's no doubt. Even in this first year you could see that she was beginning to look after other little girls in her form."

It was a school that encouraged an ethos of outside play and confidence building. The initiation test, which all the girls took at some point, was climbing up into an enormous cedar tree opposite the head's study. "Nowadays the health and safety people would put a stop to it," says Patricia Wood, who followed Elizabeth Ridsdale into the job when she retired. Particularly fortunate for the animal-obsessed Diana was the way the school positively encouraged children to bring their own pets to school. Diana

brought her guinea pig over from Park House for term time. "It was part of Riddlesworth that they'd bring pets. Not big ones—no giraffes—but little ones they could bring. We felt it was very important to encourage that because it was a link with home and, if a child was not getting on very well with other children or with staff, or finding it difficult to be away at school, which they all do to begin with, until they've settled, this was a kind of comfort blanket."

Of her time at Riddlesworth Diana said, "I won all sorts of prizes for best-kept guinea pig, but in the academic department you might as well forget that." "She was a great lover of pets, and the Pets' Corner which the girls had," says the Reverend Sweet. "She hated horses. They all had riding lessons and I think she fell off at some stage, whether at home or at school, not sure, but from there on she didn't really want to be involved with them. But the little creatures, yes, she was very much into them. She really took on the care of Pets' Corner, almost from the beginning of the first year that she was there. She was always there helping others with their pets."

The Reverend Sweet's own memories of Pets' Corner are rather more mixed. "We arrived in the August and had this lovely boxer dog called Louis who, unfortunately, used to go walk about and find his way across to Pets' Corner. I'd only been there a few weeks and the matron came tearing across one day to say that Louis had eaten one of the girl's rabbits. I mean I couldn't disprove it and we stood in the corridor in the school and she went absolutely berserk—and all these little girls were standing there watching this going on, including Diana. We had an awful set-to over that. Louis was never allowed over there again. Any sight of him and one of the teachers would call to say, 'Your awful dog Louis is over in Pets' Corner. Come and collect him.' Or I'd be teaching and the door would open and someone would be screaming, 'Louis is over here, get him out!'"

For Patricia Wood, Pets' Corner was also a headache. "It was absolutely crammed with guinea pigs and rabbits. We had rats and mice. Oh, the number of times I dosed them up with whisky when they were already dead! The children would say, 'I don't think he's very well.' And I would say, 'Well, you leave him with me and I'll give him some whisky on cotton wool!' This was about responsibility because nobody else was going to look after the pet if you didn't. And the toughest people were the elder children. So if a pet wasn't looked after they would slam into the owner in no uncertain terms, make sure that the pet was properly cleaned out and fed and watered. Diana organized the sweeping rotations and all that kind of thing—she was Queen of Pets' Corner at one stage."

"It was a very small intimate school," says Reverend Sweet, "so you really got to know them very well indeed. And she was one of the girls who really stuck in my mind. There were about half a dozen of them that I can still remember them for their particular idiosyncrasies and she was one of them. The first day that I went in to take a lesson, one of the members of the form said, 'Mr. Sweet, do you know who Diana is?' I said, 'What do you mean?' She said, 'Well, she is an 'Honorable.'" So I had to put them down and say, 'Well, I don't really care whether she's an Honorable or a Dishonorable, she is Diana.' But obviously the other girls were aware that she came from that background.

"She very rapidly seemed to settle in. I suppose it may have stemmed from the divorce, but she wanted to feel that she was useful, so that anything that she could do that proved her worth, she got involved in. I used to have the 'Most Helpful Girl' cup and I don't know how many times she won it. She was that sort of person. She would always remain behind to help clear up the form room, clear away books. 'Is there anything I can do, Mr. Sweet?' She was the same with all of the other members of staff as well—to the point at times you would say, 'Look, Diana, why don't you go off and play?' At times it felt the help that she wanted to give was almost over the top. But she wasn't a teacher's pet. She was really liked by the younger girls and the other members of her form.

"I used to teach first-year Latin and English, but it was very obvious that she was not going to be a Latin scholar. She went into 'Three Removed' which was the form for those who were not academically gifted and didn't continue with Latin. There were only about eight of them I think in the form. She was very quick to latch on to things and to people and situations. Whether she was simply bored or not interested in things academic and more concerned with doing things that she felt were practical and useful, I don't know. You can be very bright and not interested in academia and still be sharp. That was Diana.

"Diana was very keen on Prince Andrew. He was her great holiday friend. She had all these photographs on her desk and—I can see her now—she said, 'Mr. Sweet, when I grow up I'm going to marry Prince Andrew.' 'Really, Diana?' 'Yes, I'm going to marry him and he's my friend.' The impression I got is that they knew each other very well and used to spend time together during the holidays. When she got engaged to Charles I wrote to her and it crossed my mind to say 'Haven't you got the wrong chap?' But I did write to her tongue-in-cheek to say how delighted I was she was getting married, especially as it was to a Naval chap, but I was a bit fed up that she hadn't asked me to conduct the wedding. So she wrote back and said she was awfully sorry, but who married her was out of her hands! Then she said, 'The thing I'll always remember about you is you were always catching me posting my letters to my boyfriends.' So I wrote back and said, 'Well, actually it wasn't quite me catching you. You used to bring them to me.' They were only allowed one letter a week, which they had to write on a Sunday after church. The duty member of staff had to read the letters to make sure that they weren't putting anything wrong in—which I thought was terrible. I was virtually the only male member of staff there and they knew I was a soft touch so all these girls would come to me during the periods that I took them, and bring me their letters. You know, 'Please would you post these, Mr. Sweet?' I used to go out with these things hidden in my jacket, because I was equally terrified of the deputy head. And Diana was among the worst. She used to have loads of these letters for me to post.

"She did occasionally talk about feeling lonely. The divorce obviously deeply affected her. And she was very torn. At that age you love both your parents and it's very hard to see objectively what has happened. She had a little cry on several occasions about why doesn't Mummy love Daddy? And why doesn't Daddy love Mummy? It's something very difficult to explain to a child. The only thing I could say was 'Well, they do both love you and that's what you've got to remember, so whenever you go to Daddy or you go to Mummy, they love you.' There's not a lot else at that age that you can say. . . . She had to work it out for herself more than anything."

Diana was always happy to help get things ready for the church services, says Reverend Sweet. "At the time I just put it down to her again being helpful, but I suspect that it was probably even then a latent spirituality. I don't know whether it sprang out from her domestic situation—when people go through that sort of trauma, it can either make them very bitter and anti the idea of God and religion, or it can make them much more receptive and open to spiritual development. And I think that was true of Diana in a quiet way."

Frances Shand Kydd says, "She was brought up, yes, Church of England, and she went to church. I think that there was a latent desire to join in something, but also she did believe she'd be happily married, again, to

someone and have more children, so she was not keen to join anything that might be a hazard. So, she really embraced every faith, and knew a fair bit about them. She was spiritual, yes. Not very obviously and not joined to any branch of Christianity particularly, but she was spiritual. When things were going unhappily for her in her married life, she consulted horoscopes, doctors, all kinds of alternatives, thinking there was some sort of answer—which there wasn't. So she threw her efforts more into what she was doing. I certainly encouraged her to live each day at a time.'"

"She retained a childlike need for approval," says Charles Spencer. "It was always important to Diana, from earliest memory, to feel appreciated and I think I also said in the [funeral] speech about her having a childlike quality and that is it. I see it with my children and they're just aching to be approved of, whether it's by me or their mother and their teacher, whatever, or their friends. And that's a quality Diana never lost and I think that's a very endearing quality really, wanting approval. Not in a sort of egotistical way, but just, you know, am I doing OK? She wanted to know—and it's a fair question. We look and we see the cheering crowds and the Union Jacks and all that stuff and say, 'Well, of course you're appreciated!' but for her it was much more complex than that. She would go home at night and think, 'Well, were they just doing that because I'm the Princess of Wales?'"

❋ ❋ ❋ ❋

WEST HEATH SCHOOL ~ After Riddlesworth, Diana followed both her sisters to West Heath School in Sevenoaks. Piano teacher Penny Walker was Diana's form mistress when she arrived. "Sarah had just left when I got there, and then Diana came. I wasn't necessarily aware that she'd only just arrived, because she seemed to fit in quite quickly. It was a jolly lively group anyway, and she was just part of the lively noisy lot. I sort of noticed her about the school just being naughty and things, but nothing spectacular. She started learning the piano with me when she was 14, and I think she could have done really well, but I think it was just a bit late to start.

"I think she had a real musical talent there, unrealized at school. She had a lovely singing voice, but we couldn't get her to audition for the choir. She was just too scared, which was a real shame. We tried every trick to get her to come and just sing just a scale, but she wouldn't. It was a lack of confidence and shyness. Her year was also a very musical year. There were lots of high grades in singing, piano, everything, really, so I think she felt she wasn't going to be able to compete with that.

"It was amazing that she was able to go on and speak on the world stage because she didn't have any of that sort of confidence at school. But she took Grade One piano and she passed it, which I thought was fantastic. Then she just said, 'I don't really want to take exams,' which is fine. She said she'd love to play some ballet music, which obviously tied up with her dancing, and anything else that sort of appealed to her. So we played lots of bits out of *Swan Lake* and things, but she went on to a piano duet by Dvorak, one of the *Slavonic Dances*, which actually is about, I should think, between Grade Four and Five in standard, and because she liked it, she learned it. It was never note-perfect, but the essence of the music was there, and she managed to play it and that was really fun. We got lots of laughs and giggles, as you do with duets. I just remember thinking 'Gosh, if she can do that, she could have really done something with it.'"

Dance, however, rather than music, was Diana's earliest and most passionate interest. All her family remembers the role it played in her childhood. Her mother recalls, "She loved dancing, absolutely loved it; she practiced forever. She was too tall. Ballet was her first love, and then tap dancing, and any dancing, really. She danced once at Covent Garden—do you remember?—with Wayne Sleep. She certainly loved her dancing. And there isn't one photograph of her getting into a car, or whatever, awkwardly, because ballet helped her posture enormously."

Her brother Charles Spencer also remembers that when they moved to Althorp Diana used to dance in the entrance hall to the house. "She was a very keen tap dancer. She was a very keen dancer altogether actually but the entrance hall has a wonderful marble floor so for a tap dancer it has wonderful acoustics. She would spend hours practicing there and I think one of the early disappointments of her life was realizing she was going to be too tall to be a proper dancer. But she really did adore it, it was one of her passions actually."

Anyone who encountered Diana through her adolescent years knew about this passion. At West Heath School, she often got up before breakfast and practiced her dancing, drawing all the curtains. The school had a new performance hall built two terms before Diana left and the headmistress, Ruth Rudge, recalls how Diana immediately started using it to practice. "Anyone who came down before breakfast would see her leaping about in great swoops and whirls. She used to practice her bar work on the window bar. It's just the right height."

Penny Walker noticed how Diana, who struggled with academic work, found dancing so easy and so satisfying. "I think she was someone who found doing something practical easier than mental exercise. She was always very keen on swimming. She was amazing, particularly at diving. And she was always practicing her dancing in the hall. She shut all the curtains so no one could see in—this is at half past seven in the morning—and went through all her ballet routine. She was really graceful, but she always said she was too tall, that was her cry: "Too tall for a dancer!""

During her engagement and in the early years of her marriage, Diana asked Wendy Mitchell, accompanied by Lily Snipp on the piano, to give her dance lessons. Dancing herself and supporting dancers became and remained absolutely central to Diana's life. Her first charitable activities included the London Festival Ballet, which later became English National Ballet (ENB). She often used their studios and continued to dance through her marriage. "She danced from when she was a little girl and I think, maybe, at some point in every little girl's life they dream of maybe becoming a ballerina, a dancer," says Peter Schaufuss, former Artistic Director of ENB who knew Diana well and danced with her. "She must have gone through that. But her future suddenly became different, and I don't think there was a lot of time to think. It all happened very, very quickly. I think she would return to that feeling that she had maybe when she was a younger girl and wanted to be a dancer. I think it was a kind of moment of relaxation and a moment of freedom, a moment of non-pressures, maybe."

"I don't think that she would have been the patron in the way she was, had she not had a true love for dance. She loved many art forms and culture, but ballet had a special place in her heart. Dance is a language without words. It is a language you can perform anywhere throughout the world, across boundaries, across everywhere. It's a universal way of communicating. And movement is something that is, of course, perhaps the oldest art form in the world, because humans have danced for thousands and thousands of years— dances, rain dances, war dances, so it's all in us. And that's why people dance at parties and discotheques, as a way of expressing themselves. Maybe it was a way for Diana to express herself without any words."

Derek Deane, who became ENB's artistic director after Peter Schaufuss and to whom Diana was close, also experienced her intense passion for ballet when she quietly came to watch rehearsals. "She just loved being lost with the rosin box and the piano playing and the girl in her practice tutu with a bun and spinning and hitting an arabesque and suddenly being lifted off the ground. You could just see her going 'ah' and getting romantically lost in it really. But she was interested in all different types of dance. It wasn't just *Romeo and Juliet* and *Swan Lake*, no it wasn't. She loved tutus and she loved tiaras and the prince's costumes, but if I put half a dozen dancers out there in leather and tights, which I did sometimes and they were doing very modern contemporary stuff she loved it."

The young ballet dancers of ENB always experienced Diana as incredibly supportive and encouraging about their lives and aspirations. Alice Crawford says, "I think she could tell we were all striving for perfection even when we were here and it's all a bit grubby and a bit whatever, we're still all trying to make something as perfect as we can. Even though ultimately we can't ever be completely perfect, that's what we are trying to be."

Perfection may have been what Diana was striving for later on, but teacher Penny Walker remembers that "the year she was in was naughty. Not malicious naughty—I suppose 'lively' is the word. That always borders on naughtiness because, inevitably, they're going to go over the top, but she was part of a huge group of really strong characters. They used to go down to Sevenoaks for Voluntary Service to do visits or whatever was asked of them. She was down one day and came back past the pet shop, saw a kitten in the window that she absolutely fell in love with, bought it and brought it back to what's called the 'cowsheds.' This was a sort of corridor where the sixth form were, and it was all partitioned off. She kept it for about a fortnight before it got discovered. The school basically found it amusing and, actually, one of the ground staff wanted it, so it stayed as a West Heath School cat.

"There was another thing they all did but only she got caught— although she never knew it. The girls used to have tea at four o'clock, and they had bread and jam and tea. The staff, in the staff dining room, would have lots of cakes and things, really fantastic stuff compared with the girls. So if there were things left over, and the girls were passing the door, they would nip in and grab whatever was left, and then flee with it. On one occasion Diana looked in, saw that there was something left, and she nipped into this small room. But unknown to her, at the end of the corridor, there was a member of staff just approaching through the swing doors, and she saw Diana go in. The teacher came along the corridor and made a lot of noise and when she heard her coming, Diana dived under the table. The member of staff then sat and had about 20 cups of tea, slowly, so that Diana was stuck there through the next lesson, which she got into trouble for. I don't think Diana ever knew that she'd been rumbled; she just thought that it was coincidence that this member of staff had come in to have their tea late. The staff had a laugh about that. But she was no more high-spirited than others in that particular year."

Friends from West Heath remember Diana as a lively girl who had a lot of friends. She was an exceptional swimmer and made a lot of her own clothes. "It was a very tempestuous year, because they were all strong characters and they did bicker and argue and fall out with each other, so you never knew who was friendly with whom," says Penny Walker. "But, in the end, they did all keep in touch. She was popular but they were all up and down, as girls are at that age. She'd be popular one minute and not the rest. It was a big group and they were always swapping friends. She was never called 'Di' at school. Her peers called her 'Spencer,' because there were three Dianas. Diana was always very pleasant to look at. They weren't sleek and groomed at school; it was always baggy cardigans. But there were lots of really pretty girls and there were five in that year who were really top music students. They did A-level music and five out of a year of probably 16 is amazing. The whole year was pretty talented musically. One or two went on to become professional musicians.'"

"I remember one of the little cameo plays we used to perform as a dormitory at the end of term. Diana was dressed elegantly in silk while Laura Greig played the housemaid—a situation replicated later when Laura became one of her ladies-in-waiting," says Belinda Knox, who was in Diana's year at West Heath.

As at Riddlesworth, staff at West Heath were aware of a very bright girl under-achieving academically. "I was aware that the other staff felt she was struggling," says Penny Walker. "I could never understand that because, although the response in her piano lessons was sometimes slow, it was her wit that struck me and the speed at which she could give me an answer. I could never quite work out why we got that lovely fast sense of humor and, yet, she could be slow in other ways. She was unusually witty. There are lots of people who just don't do anything at school, for whatever reason and I think she was one of those. They get into their twenties before suddenly everything comes together and they really fulfill all their talents. Unconsciously, I think she was distracted because what was going on at home and in her outside life was just totally absorbing all her mental energy, so there wasn't anything left for school. There probably was an underlying sadness, but that wasn't so obvious at school, because she was quite close to quite a few of the staff and so she did have people to go and talk to. She was close to Miss Rudge, but in that position of authority, I don't think she would have spoken at length, intimately, until after she left. But there were other members of staff, and the matron, I think she could go and just chat to. I think she needed to be drawn out all the time, and she was quite difficult to draw out. She didn't actually talk to me in a personal way in the lessons, and that's unusual in music."

Even at that early age, however, Penny Walker remembers Diana as unusually caring, trustworthy, and kind. "She threw herself into the Voluntary Services Unit at school. She went to the local mental hospital, Darenth Park. We also used to have parties for the elderly at West Heath, and she was always a big part of that. She didn't have to do it; it was by choice. I also remember she was equally able to go along and chat to the kitchen staff and the people who were there working at West Heath as she would have been to the other children's parents or the academic staff. She was always in the kitchen, after tea. Actually, she came back to school the term after she left, and she was in the scullery or the washing-up place, chatting to one of the people in there, and Miss Rudge walked past, and she said, 'Diana, where are you supposed to be?' And Diana just turned around and said, 'I'm not here any more, I'm not supposed to be anywhere.' She had been ticked off because she was always in there talking when she should have been at a lesson or something."

An aspect of Diana's later character already stood out at West Heath. She was the only child in the school Penny Walker asked to babysit her new-born child. "In 1977, my son was born in the holiday. And the first day of term she was on the doorstep with a cuddly toy for him. Well, that says quite a lot, you know, it was not an inexpensive toy she brought. And she just stood there and said, 'Quick, take it, before I have to keep it, because I think it's lovely.' Then she kept coming over saying, 'Can I help? Is there anything I can do?' And she became the babysitter. This is from nought to four months, because she left at Christmas that term. But there was certainly nobody else of her age in the school that I could possibly have trusted with a newborn, but she knew exactly how to hold him, what to do with him, completely OK. So she wasn't shy when it concerned something sort of practical." "I remember Diana used to look after a baby at West Heath," says her mother. "It's quite a recommen-dation that the teacher said she was the only girl she would have trusted."

Interestingly Diana retained close links with all her schools. She returned to Riddlesworth and she retained especially strong ties with West Heath where many of her significant adult friendships were formed. "It was a very cohesive school," comments Penny Walker. "It didn't pretend to be academically fantastic; the emphasis was really on the feel of family, the fact that it was a secure, safe place for them to be. Miss Rudge in particular was a quite remarkable head. Her study door was always open. If pupils wanted to be away from the noise of the school, they could go up there with a book or some sewing or something and there would be classical music on quite low and Miss Rudge would be just sitting reading, writing, or whatever. You could just go and be in there. They trusted her so utterly and most of them keep in touch. Diana was not any exception to that and kept coming back, sometimes just to see the school, but as she got older, she would come back and go to Ruth's flat and just sit and chat and I imagine home in on the normal again.

"When Ruth left the school in 1987, we did a surprise concert with all the members of the Madrigal Choir over the last 13 years. We had secret rehearsals and then we did this huge concert. I wrote and asked Diana if she'd like to sing and she said she couldn't possibly sing with all those people, and she couldn't come, either, because she'd got another engagement. And then I had a message from Carolyn Bartholomew saying, 'She wants to come.' So we had complete uproar at school because I had to then say to her, 'You can't come as Princess Diana, because I can't cope with all that that means, this has got to be a private concert, you're coming back as an old girl.' And she said, 'Oh, absolutely, absolutely.' And that was fine until the night of the concert, just before Ruth was going to be delivered at the door, we had somebody come rushing up and saying, 'Maidstone Police are on the doorstep—they've found out!' It was an absolute palaver. But Diana came in and said, 'Oh, it's lovely to be here,' and walked in, through the audience and sat down in the front row. She chatted to everybody around, came back to the common room quickly afterwards to the buffet supper that we'd got for Ruth, and then she disappeared. Her bodyguard had lost her. Because she knew the school so well, she'd nipped up the back stairs and she was up in the dormitory telling stories to the juniors. And the matron, who'd seen her coming, had rushed down the dormitory saying: 'Quick, quick—tidy up! The Princess of Wales is coming to read you a story.' And they'd all said, 'Oh, yeah.' And then in she walked. And they just couldn't believe it, they were just grinning from ear to ear."

Muriel Simmons worked for Sevenoaks Voluntary Services and was responsible for organizing the voluntary work for the girls of West Heath. "Darenth Park was a very large Victorian institute—a classical asylum with huge turrets and a great big wall. It had a really formidable appearance. People just didn't want to come inside. It had 2000 residents and it was its own closed world. One of the first things I did when I joined the voluntary service unit was organize a dance on Tuesdays and Thursdays. It was an enormous, echoey hall and the mentally ill make all sorts of weird and wonderful noises that get amplified. The first time I heard it I almost had to hold my ears. The dance seemed a good idea and we explained to a couple of the local schools what we were trying to do. They agreed to send a minibus. I did have some reservations. It might have been one thing for the kids for the local estate, but the West Heath girls came from a different world.

"It was a scary thing for girls of that age to do. I remember the minibus arriving in this place with these bright smiley girls tumbling out. I had to explain to them they were going to hear a lot of noise and there would be people rushing up and touching them, they didn't have any restraints. They might hug, they might slap. So I taught them to stoop down and told them touch and feeling were important, but also that if you get hold of someone's hand it can stop them from having a slap as well as establishing warmth and contact. I remember talking about the mentally ill and how they are excluded. The school visits were the first steps in breaking down the barriers symbolized by the huge walls of the hospital. I discussed with these girls how important it was to include all strands of life: There's so much to be learned from the sick and the handicapped.

"Diana took to it like a duck to water. She was extremely agile. The music and dancing suited her. We had a mixture of pop and some old-time music. Most people who dance with wheelchairs would get hold of the handles and push but Diana did something rare which was get hold of the arms so she was facing the patients and danced backwards pulling them along. It's difficult to do; you have to be fit. I thought, 'Goodness me, that's athletic.' But it was wonderful to see the complete communication and the joy on the patients' faces being danced with like that. She wasn't self-conscious at all. It took some of them longer to get the hang of it but they were a very good group of youngsters, very much of Diana's ilk, brave enough to do this.

"She also used to do some visiting of old people. She used to go in each week and make a cup of tea. It was typical of her, an almost natural way of knowing what makes people feel comfortable. It was her laugh that made me notice her. It was a very joyful sound, a very fresh sound. It's hard to describe but it made you want to laugh, too. Her star qualities didn't stand out then. She was ordinary, but that's what's remarkable. What came over was warmth, and humour and natural empathy. Otherwise she had the normal worries and fears of a youngster, but she had the courage to overcome this."

Diana's family also remember how important voluntary service was to Diana. "At West Heath" says her sister, Sarah, "there was a strong and perhaps unusual emphasis on community work. We all went to Sevenoaks and we did shopping for the old ladies or sat and talked to them and comforted them. I think the first time Diana came into contact with charity work was at Darenth Park.

"Darenth Park was absolutely terrifying to me. Horrendous. It smelled of disinfectant and pee. I remember them opening enormous wooden doors, like in a medieval castle—you know the ones you would have had to take a battering ram to. And what you saw was this sea of ill people just coming toward you. Basically we were there to dance. If you didn't get several proposals of an evening it was a pretty poor do. And you tried to dance in a circle and all the men wanted to do was to dance with you close up. It was quite a daunting experience as a 14- or 15-year-old, because they were all people with mental problems, serious mental problems. We had never seen places like this before—we were all sheltered little girlies, we didn't know about places like this. It was frightening."

"Some of the nurses put on music and you were meant to join in. I did it, but I don't remember particularly enjoying it. But apparently with the people in wheelchairs Diana actually got down and danced at their level, face to face with them. It was noticed that she was unusually good as a teenager in that kind of intimidating situation. I think this kind of experience was forma-tive because now I am as keen as my sister on forgotten causes and mental health is definitely one of these. Diana was extraordinary for the way she broke down these stigmas and prejudices. She broke it down on AIDS completely and she'd done a pretty good job on leprosy and landmines the same."

"Diana also did voluntary service in the community," says her mother. "She had one old lady she visited and one day she announced, 'I'm going to wallpaper her walls,' and the thought of Diana wallpapering was unlikely, to say the least. But she loved it. She felt fond of this woman and she wanted her to be happy, a good environment, just happy, comfy."

When Diana was 13, her grandfather died. "One morning," says Penny Walker, "she came rushing down the corridor saying, 'I'm Lady Diana!' Rather naughty but she was really, really excited. They're not allowed to use titles at West Heath, so it was only that it happened while she was there during the term that we knew. If it had happened in the holidays, she would have just remained plain Diana Spencer. It didn't affect other people's treatment of her. It wasn't that sort of school and, anyway, she wasn't that sort of person. She didn't change at all, she was just really excited that that was her title."

Title aside, the move to Althorp was not particularly welcome. According to Charles Spencer, "It was a huge wrench. We had a very relaxed upbringing despite the privileged background. So coming here was actually quite a shock because suddenly after my grandfather's death, we both had titles and the staff here called us by that, whereas before we had just been Charles and Diana and had a much more easy-going lifestyle. I mean this house is fantastic, but it's great if you're an adult really. It's not much of a family home inside, or it wasn't then. I hope it is now—I've made parts of it very child-friendly, but it was always a bit daunting coming here so I think we found refuge really in the park outside which we both adored."

Raine Spencer, who would become Johnnie Spencer's second wife, was already in evidence in his life, so in spite of the privileges of background, the swimming pool built by their attentive father and the staff attached to a stately home, Diana was never very settled. "When Diana moved to Althorp, her father got remarried and the relationship with Raine was pretty difficult," says Henry Bellingham. "I think it wasn't a very happy situation to be honest. And when Johnnie had a stroke, he wasn't really the robust individual that he had been, so it wasn't a cozy home to go back to. Probably that's why she sought the security of marriage at such a young age. Diana saw her mother, whom she adored, but she had got remarried, and was living in Scotland, a long way away."

Her father's illness was a particularly difficult time for Diana. Immediately after his stroke Johnnie Spencer was transferred to what is now called the National Hospital for Neurology and Neurosurgery. It was one of the few types of strokes that was operable but needed specialist facilities and skills. "Raine was exceedingly protective of her husband," says Norman Grant, the neurosurgeon who operated on Diana's father. "I remember two of the girls as pretty young teenagers, but I never spoke to them. Raine really took over, left, right, and center. And Diana, even if she had been older, more mature, wouldn't have had much of a look-in. I quite enjoyed looking after Diana's father the way things worked out—although it was worrying at times, anyway, without Raine getting her oar in all the time. Once he recovered, yes, he was very hale and hearty. At the party at Althorp he'd certainly recovered his form, and bonhomie, by then."

Althorp under Raine's regime was devoted to serious socializing and it was during this period that Diana began to mix again with the royal family. "She was always talking about Prince Charles," says Penny Walker. "I can remember the weekend she came back after she'd met him, because she couldn't talk about anything else. She said: 'I've met him! At last, I've met him.' She'd met him in a ploughed field on a shoot. I think he was with Sarah at that time. She had pictures of him up in her cubicle. It wasn't entirely unusual for a girl from that kind of background, but it was unusual because it was so consistent all the time she was at school. Her only talk was of him and meet-ing him. I'm not sure there was any talk about marrying, but she just seemed completely besotted, dreaming of escape, I should think, into fairy tale."

In spite of difficulties, staff and family found Diana both down-to-earth and very special. Housekeeper Maudie Pendry says, "When she came to live at Althorp she was always shy. She used to blush ever so easily too, used to go scarlet. My husband adored Diana, we all did. She would come and see her father about every six or seven weeks. When we knew Diana was coming for the weekend my husband would get her all her favorite food in and make sure she had everything up in her bedroom. She used to sleep in the nursery, in a little black iron bed—real old iron, old fashioned. When she used to come home to Althorp the first thing she did was come and find my husband, because she was a very lovely, very polite little girl—always called him Mr. Pendry—but she always found him first, I don't know why. Of course he used to spoil her.

"After her father remarried, she used to come and talk to us quite a lot. She sometimes used to come and have lunch with us. She never had airs and graces. Diana was just an ordinary lovely girl. She was very sweet and all the staff loved her. They used to put flowers in her bedroom when she used to come to Althorp. We used to make a fuss of her and made sure she was someone important. My husband said to me, when he saw her start growing up, he said, 'You wait. She's going to be someone very special.' But we never thought she would marry Prince Charles."

Diana "stayed one term into what would be the lower sixth," says Penny Walker. "I don't know when the decision to go to Switzerland came, whether she came back to school to retake O-levels or what, I mean, that's not an unusual scenario. As far as I remember all her friends went on to do A-levels." After leaving West Heath, she went first to finishing school, taught briefly at Madame Vacani's, the ballet school, and then ended up helping with the children of friends. These included her cousins Liz and Anthony Duckworth-Chad and the Whitaker family. "She looked after two small children quite soon after she left school," says her mother, "and that was very happy. She was a complete natural with children. She felt on an equal level with them. And she didn't have any inhibitions about her, to be a pied piper, she just was. You can't hoodwink children."

"We always saw Diana a lot," says Anthony Duckworth-Chad. "She was absolutely smashing. She came and helped us—I should think when she was 17. She might have just left West Heath. I think that would have been about 1978, just after my daughter was born. She always had a fantastic way of talking to children of all ages and they loved her. Everybody loved her. She had—I don't know if 'sparkle' is the right word. Later in life obviously it was 'charisma,' but I think she had charisma in those days, too. You knew she was special with the kids because they all loved her. You could tell that Diana was popular with all children; she just always used to go up and chat with them. And, of course, small children always love it when an older person takes an interest in them.

"She was bright, she was quite sharp, as I say, it was there, and she was quick with an answer. But not cuttingly, I mean, nicely, you know. I think she probably was a late developer. People said she didn't get many GCSEs or whatever they got in those days, but I think lots of people didn't get many GCSEs and then went on to become very, very bright people. She certainly didn't give you the impression of being stupid, ever. She was a very good storyteller too; she could make you laugh. She was a fund of stories, and loved them too, and was also extremely good at telling them."

People began to notice how attractive she was. "She had lots of admirers," says Maudie Pendry. "I loved it. She was so beautiful and when she used to come down to dinner at night with all this jewelery on, everybody had eyes for her. My husband always said that she'd be someone very special one day because she was so pretty and she had a lovely personality with it. She'd talk to everybody and everybody loved that."

"I knew her from a young age—five or six," says Henry Bellingham. "She used to come and stay in the holidays and when she moved over to Northamptonshire she used to come and stay with my sister. They used to go riding together and that sort of thing and I went on holiday with her as well before she got married, once. She had a very good sense of humor, always playing pranks and that sort of thing.

"As a teenager, she had that certain star quality. As she grew into a superstar, her looks changed—I mean she went through a hell of a lot—and, you know, the sort of innocence from early on went. But she certainly had a star quality that very few people have. Although she had no academic qualifications, she had a lot of instinctive practical common sense and this extraordinary ability that not many people have of being truly captivating on a one to one level. I could see the effect she had on other people: you didn't forget seeing her. She was immensely popular."

Even her siblings began to notice how Diana was blossoming, although it took friends and relatives to point it out. "She suddenly became very sort of magnetic and people were interested in her as a character when she hit about 16," says Charles Spencer. "Before then she was quite quiet—I mean always up to something, you know, never dull—but quite quiet and shy. But I think as she started to become a pretty, young woman as opposed to a girl, she got some confidence then. That started to open her up quite a lot and I think she realized then that she had a knack for being the life and soul of the party. People really enjoyed being around her."

"I didn't realize when she was a child that she was going to turn out so beautiful," says her sister, Sarah. "But all my friends, male and female were talking about—not exactly the ugly duckling—saying she's going to be stunning. They could see it. But you don't notice it in your siblings. In pictures of her at my wedding, she was a bit plump, but then it all came off."

"I do remember her smile particularly though in the summer of 1980," says Robert Spencer. "It was about a year before she got married and we all went to a dance. I hadn't seen her for a year or so and there was a big change between 17 and 19. Instead of being a child she was a beautiful girl. She was a woman, a lady."

In 1979 Diana moved to London. "In every book that's ever been written about Diana, it says that her flat at Coleherne Court was given to her by her father," says her mother. "It wasn't, it was given by me. All three girls had a flat from me, and only one, Sarah, sold hers. I bought that one and Jane's one. It was a very happy time for Diana when she was in that flat. She loved being a working girl."

According to her mother, Diana's concern for others was very much in evidence even in this exciting new life as a single working girl in London. "For instance, when she was 18 in London, she shared my flat with another girl, and one night, the occupant of the ground floor was burgled. Anyway, Diana rang me in the morning and said, 'She's very upset, and there's a frightful mess in her flat, do you mind if we make her comfy?' And then she rang in the evening and she said she'd tidied the whole flat and she'd taken down my telly, and kept her company and fed her. It was all quite natural to her."

All Diana's sisters were imbued with an ethos of self-sufficiency. "By the time I was 19 I was living in London, holding down a very good job," says Diana's sister Sarah. "My father owned a house which I ran and I had tenants. I took money from them, I paid the bills, got the insurance, changed the plugs, you know. I was desperately practical. That's when Diana worked as my cleaner. We paid her whatever the wage for dailies was at that time. She was living in Coleherne Court and I lived in Elm Park Lane and she would walk round. She had a nannying job in the mornings only, and she wanted extra money. She was very diligent and hard working.

"It's a misconception that Diana didn't have to work. She had to have a job. We both had full-time jobs and were pretty much self-sufficient, Jane and I, but Diana's job, the one she wanted to do, was only half a day, so she was semi-supported by my parents."

James Colthurst met Diana on a skiing holiday when he was a medical student. "She slept on the sofa bed. It was fun. There were a lot of pranks—Diana was great company—lively, outgoing and frivolous and she enjoyed practical jokes." Colthurst was part of a small circle of friends to whom Diana confided her increasing intimacy with Prince Charles. "She was in love. You could tell. When the engagement was announced it wasn't much of a surprise. We knew it was going to happen."[3]

Kay King who ran the Young England Kindergarten in Pimlico had been at West Heath and she and her sisters knew the Spencers from school. "When Diana left school, Jane asked my sister whether there was any chance that we needed an assistant. Jane said to Janie, my younger sister, 'She really wants to work with children. Do you have a vacancy?' Initially she helped us for three afternoons a week, but she was obviously a natural with children. She had a wonderful sense of humor and made them laugh. So we asked her if she would like to do three full days with us, because she was also doing her nannying job and all the other various things she did. She was with us for just under two years.

"She was very much the youngest of the team and she was incredibly willing. She helped with the things that she really enjoyed, like painting and music, but she also did a lot of other rather boring things like taking children to the loo and wiping noses and she was very happy doing that. She never minded that side of things at all. She was very kind, very thoughtful, very generous—a very nice person to work with.

"She was very good with people and even at that age she had great charm. She was also very thoughtful and kind: she would be the first one to go to a child if they were crying. I have always thought that she would have loved her own children, because she loved children so much. She always got down to their level, not in a patronizing way, but just getting down to their level. She definitely had a natural affinity with kids."

Clementine Hambro, who was a pupil at Young England and one of Diana's bridesmaids says "I think she had an incredibly magic way with children, which sort of made you feel like you didn't want her to go away, you really loved her doing what she was doing. When I fell over—it was just after the wedding lunch—she bent down and she sort of teased me and she was incredibly sweet."

Perhaps some of Diana's acceptance of people of every background and type came from her experience of working in a nursery. "It's the best training anyone could do, whatever you do in life," says Kay King. "It teaches you how to entertain children constructively. But you also see how incredibly different children can be—you can't just lump them together. Every human being is different, and from an amazingly young age, you can see the personality traits beginning to show through. And everybody's interesting: Some have skills in some direction, some in others, some need much more nurturing and help than others, some, even at this very young age, are very independent."

When news of Diana's romance broke, Kay King's nursery was under siege. "I'd been away on holiday and I came back to find a load of photographers outside. 'So, what's going on?' I asked. Someone said, 'Haven't you seen the papers?' Of course, I hadn't. And they said, 'Oh, Diana was spotted with Prince Charles.' She was very embarrassed about it. We didn't know what to

do, actually, because they were becoming pests. They were ringing up and knocking on the door. I said, 'What do you think we should do? Do you think if you go and have a photograph taken, then they'll go away?' This was in our very naïve days, both of us thinking that that would keep them happy. She said, 'OK, well, I suppose we could try that, but can I take a child out with me?' And I thought, 'Well, of course, if I'm going to do that, I've got to get the permission of the parents.' So I rang up a couple of mums and said, 'Look, we've got this rather unusual situation, would you mind if your child was borrowed to have their photograph taken?' I remember laughing and saying to them, 'You never know, she may be the Queen of England!' So fairly unwillingly—she used to blush incredibly easily—she disappeared out into the garden with two little boys and two little girls. Photograph taken, she came back in, and we got through the rest of the day. Just as we were about to go home, the doorbell rang, and a hand came in with a copy of the *Evening Standard*. So, I opened it up, and there, on the front, was this picture of poor Diana in her see-through skirt. She was wearing one of those floaty skirts, which were absolutely fine as long as you didn't have full sun behind you, and I'm absolutely sure they positioned her just where they did deliberately. I remember her standing there with her hands over her face and going bright red, and me thinking, 'Oh, dear. I think I've rather blown her romance.' Knowing how sensitive the palace was about things like that. There was this poor girl and the first picture of her was in a see-through skirt. She laughed about it, but it was quite an embarrassing moment.

"The force at which it happened was all rather overwhelming. It went from nothing to suddenly a television crew front and back every day. It was the Christmas term—after that she was unofficially engaged.

"She was undoubtedly apprehensive before the wedding, but I think we all are. She was obviously well aware of the fact that the eyes of the world were upon her. The exposure she had was a nightmare because, while she was here, there was no guidance from the palace because they couldn't be seen to be endorsing. So she was left to do her own thing. We didn't know what to do, or who we should be talking to. It was very, very difficult.

"The great thing about her was that she never gave in to them. She was always here, every day. We did say to her in the end, 'Look, if this is getting too much, we will quite understand,' but she was determined—and, actually, there was an element of enjoyment. Quite often, at lunchtime she'd say, 'I'll go and get the lunch,' and I would think, 'You really want to run the gauntlet.' And she used to belt out there. It was a bit of cat-and-mouse. There's a lovely picture of her running back here, wearing one of our smocks, looking over her shoulder. The local Indian restaurant still has it in the front."

Jayne Fincher was a young photographer in her father's business when stories started to circulate about a new girlfriend of Prince Charles's. She was sent to photograph a ball. "We were all standing there and this young girl walks up behind us, and the way was blocked with all our ladders. She said, 'Oh, excuse me, can I get through?' She was all hunched up in this funny little coat, big pink cheeks—pretty girl. Someone said, 'I'm sure that's that girl.' But someone else said, 'You must be joking! She looks like a farmer's daughter who's come up from the country for the evening.' But later on someone else said, 'No, I'm sure that was her.' It was a freezing cold night, and it was a really late party, but I thought, 'Well, I've got to get this girl,' because I'd missed the whole story for the last few weeks. At about three in the morning she came out, huddled in this coat, and walked along the edge of the Ritz Hotel to her car. As soon as she walked out she saw us, and she just went absolutely like a little beetroot—she was so embarrassed. I literally just took a couple of pictures—she seemed such an unlikely candidate. I'd photographed other girls in the previous years, and they had all seemed quite sophisticated women of the world. She just looked so different from them. They all had very coiffured hair and were obviously very much part of a social set and had the confidence with it. She looked as if she'd just been allowed up for the night from the country. She had hardly any make-up on, and she'd obviously done her hair herself. There was a complete lack of sophistication.

"I thought she was pretty and I liked her because she was giggly. Although she was shy she didn't clam up. Sometimes when you photograph famous people, some of them are very arrogant and rude, but she took it in very good humor although she obviously hated every minute of it. Even toward the end when she was obviously getting fed up she was never rude, so we instantly took a liking to her. On one occasion she couldn't get her car out of its parking spot. She just sat there giggling and then she got out and said, 'All right, one of you are going to have to get it out for me now.' The photographer from the *Daily Mail*, who was a cheeky little Cockney bloke, moved her car out for her. It was all good-natured.

"The strange thing was that there was a sort of magnetism about her. Whenever she walked into the room, something would always draw your eyes to her, whether you were male or female. You couldn't put your finger on it: It wasn't sophistication; it wasn't classic beauty. She had some sort of style that was difficult to define.

"If you photograph a normal person you'll probably get one or two shots that you really like from a whole roll of film, but with her, you'd take a whole roll and probably only have two that you didn't like. I've photographed a lot of film stars and famous people and she stands out. Often even if they're trying not to show their conceit, they're still very worried about what they look like. You can tell that from their mannerisms, and the way they're always touching their hair and worrying about their lipstick. I never once saw Diana put lipstick on or worry about it or her hair. You would never catch her checking herself, which was actually quite astounding, really. Even the Queen you see sitting there putting her lipstick on. You never saw Diana doing that."

Diana's natural instinct with the press was obvious from the outset. "On one occasion—probably only about a couple of months into this madness—Diana came out of the house where she was working as a nanny for American businesswoman Mary Robertson. She was pushing the baby. There were a couple of television crews and a lot of media there. She looked around and said, 'OK. I want to go for a walk, and I don't want you lot all running after me. So I'll go for a walk, and when I come back, if you will behave yourself, you can take some pictures.' She learned how to do the deal, straight away. Off she went. We all waited on the corner. She went for her walk. Nobody followed. Half an hour later she came back. 'All right, you can all do it now.' So we all went down to the end of the road and she walked toward us with the pram, and we all got the pictures we wanted. She used that technique all her life, but it was quite a thing to clock for someone that young and inexperienced."

As the public announcement of the engagement became imminent, Diana re-visited her old haunts to share her excitement. "The week before the engagement was announced, she came back and had tea with me," says Penny Walker. "She burst through the door and I said, 'I've got to ask you about all these rumors. You probably can't tell me but what's going on?' She just grinned and said, 'I can't say.' But I felt that the grin must say that it was true, but you couldn't be sure enough to tell anybody."

"When she got engaged," says Maudie Pendry, "she came to show us her ring and she said, 'You'll come to my wedding?' I said, 'Will I be able to see you in St Paul's?'—because St Paul's has got all those pillars around—and

she said, 'I promise you you'll see all of me.' I could have touched her when she went up with her dad. She's never forgotten, that girl, and she used to write me lovely letters, especially when my husband died. She was the most caring girl and she said she never would forget me, never."

The engagement and wedding of the person who was fast becoming the world's most famous nursery teacher was celebrated very personally in her old place of work. "We had a mug made which had 'Miss Diana' and the years that she was here, on one side, and then 'HRH Diana, Princess of Wales' on the other. Just before she got married," says Kay King, "we had a royal wedding party, along with everyone else in the country, and I remember saying at the time, 'Well, we're lucky because the bride came.' It was a children's party with lots of red, white, and blue. She brought a little present for everybody. She wrapped up a little present for all the children, and one of the teachers made this wonderful cake and she wore a paper crown.

"We all went and watched the fireworks the night before and Diana invited all of the teachers who worked here to the party, and then to the wedding. It was enormously exciting. I was thinking, 'Gosh, this is going to be a bit like being part of a play,' because you knew that, quite literally, the eyes of the world were on this event."

For David and Elizabeth Emanuel the royal wedding was as much a fairy tale for them as it was for the bride. During her engagement she had fallen for their romantic designs and much to public surprise, chose them as the designers of her wedding dress. "She was very sweet," says Elizabeth Emanuel, "very nice and easy to get on with, not at all demanding, but quite shy. Fashion wasn't her thing at all; it was something that was really forced upon her because she had to dress up for the part. And we were just out of college, quite inexperienced at the time, so we felt we were sort of in it together. We had a giggle, we really did.

"As soon as we knew we had the commission I started to do a lot of research, going through all the books on royal weddings. The dress had to be something that was going to go down in history, but also something that Diana loved. And we knew it was going to be at St Paul's, so it had to be something that would fill the aisle and be quite dramatic. I'd done loads of designs for her, and we all sat on the floor and went through the sketches. Her mother came in as well. So the designing actually didn't take that long, especially because we knew the kind of look that she liked. It was the making of the dress that took forever—and the fact that she did lose a lot of weight.

David Emanuel says, "I do not understand it when people say she was nervous before her wedding. At the time she was absolutely ecstatic. And why shouldn't she be? She was a bride. She was so excited. What she was saying was, 'Oh, do you think the train is big enough?' 'Darling, I think it's more than big enough.' 'What's the largest train?' 'Oh, we're going to make it bigger,'—and then having made it bigger, 'Do you think it should be bigger?' It was a joke. It was magic. And the sessions with the bridesmaids were great as well. My God, did they adore her! Getting them coordinated in the diary wasn't easy but when it happened we'd get Diana there first and they would burst into her salon and kiss her. And one or two of them would come in jeans and roller skates, skating through the carpet here at Brook Street. 'This is different,' I thought, 'this is extraordinary.' But she was wonderful with them."

In spite of the enormous pressure on her, and the fact that she was isolated in Clarence House in the run-up to the wedding itself, those involved remember Diana through this period as informal, considerate, and fun, especially with the children. Bridesmaid, Sarah Jane Gaselee who was 11 at the time remembers the fitting sessions and what led up to them. "We used to have a great time when we came up for all the fittings, because Diana used to have her wedding dress fitting at the same time as the bridesmaids, so most times we were all there together. One time we went shopping in South Molton Street, and people started seeing her and following her. And we were trying on jeans and she was just in a cubicle, and people outside were going, 'Isn't that Diana in there?' We were laughing. She was really fun.

"The fittings were fun. I had a pair of roller skates, red roller boots that I dashed around on. I don't think she was that stressed by it or anything; it didn't appear that way. What I do remember is that she and Charles were really in love as far as I could see, at that age. I saw them cuddling on the sofa and during the rehearsals they had their arms linked and they were skipping down the aisle. It was all really happy, or so I thought."

Sarah Jane had met Diana through Charles but it was Diana who invited her to be a bridesmaid. "I was ten; she was only 19. But even though there was a big age difference she was really easy. We got on really well. I'd only just started boarding school and I hated it. I used to ring her. She gave me her phone number and said, 'Call me whenever you have a problem.' And she sent me little presents to school, cards and that sort of thing. I remember once my headmistress saying, 'You can't write a letter back like that!' I'd drawn pictures all over it and love hearts, you know as you do when you're that age. And I said, 'Why not?' I did in the end. Diana's letters were just asking which teachers were nice and saying it's not too long until you come home again, just ordinary stuff. There used to be a phone box at the school so all my friends would cram into the box and say, 'We're going to go and phone Diana!' It was all really exciting. She wasn't as famous then but it was still exciting for everyone at school.

"The day she asked me to be a bridesmaid we were walking around a race course. We were with Prince Charles, Mum and Dad and I think a security guard or something. I was about to go back to school that evening, and she was giving me a piggyback ride, and we were separated from the others. She said, 'Come here, I want to ask you something.' I said, 'What?' And she said, 'Do you want to be a bridesmaid at my wedding?' I think the invitation obviously came from her rather than him, because he's obviously got lots of godchildren and people, but we just got on really well. So I said, 'Yeah! Great! Of course!' So we went over to Charles and she said, 'I've asked her,' and then I said, 'Am I going to be on TV?' And they laughed. I wasn't allowed to tell anybody for a long time."

India Hicks was another bridesmaid, who had been chosen because of her associations with Prince Charles—he was her godfather and had had a close relationship with her grandfather, Lord Mountbatten. India remembers Diana's unusual ability to empathize with the young girls and help out with them even on her own most significant day. "It was the days leading up to and the day itself that I knew her the best and, as you say, it was a very childlike recollection I have. I was 13. I was a complete tomboy with a sort of severe haircut. I remember being thrilled at the idea that it would get me a day out of school, and then, of course, it happened to be during the school holidays, which was an enormous disappointment. I also remember the horror of realizing I was going to have to wear a dress—not only a dress, but that frilly dress with those big puffy sleeves. I was horrified by the whole thing. It's so obvious to portray Diana as a sort of angel from the start, but, funnily enough, I really do think that she was thinking of others at that point and certainly she always had a very nice attitude toward me, even though I wasn't someone she had chosen. I was very much from Charles's camp, as it were, but there was never any suggestion that she wouldn't have perhaps chosen me.

"At the time I wasn't aware of the magnitude of the event at all. It sounds awful, but my grandfather had been so close to the Queen and to

Prince Charles that I had been on the balcony before and I had been to quite a few of the Trooping of the Colours and all the rest. I had been a bridesmaid several times before, as well. I remember Diana being very hands on when we were having fittings and things, helping the little ones get dressed, very much advising about what she liked on the hair and how the dresses should look. Of course I have childlike memories of it all—about things like the shoes coming from a company called Ivory. Mine were very tight—everyone's were very tight for some reason—but the excitement of the shoes was that they gave us a credit in the store, which meant we could then go and get something for free, afterwards.

"She was very sweet about everything, but I think there also was the feeling that she was going to become a princess and one was quite aware of that. Thirteen is a sort of awkward age, and I was a complete tomboy, and yet I was obviously quite enthused about the idea of going to a ball. But Diana was very good at handling me exactly as one would have liked as a 13-year-old, neither as a child and neither as a complete adult. Sarah Armstrong-Jones and I were given the job of dealing with the veil, so we felt slightly more grown up.

"Sarah and I were given a lot of practice with a big long sheet. At one of the rehearsals I remember, it was a white dustsheet. It was measured out and tied around Diana, who was wearing jeans at the time, so Sarah and I could practice how to get it in and out of the carriage, because I think the train was something like 25 feet, which was the longest ever. The Emanuels always said they needed something enormous and grand to fill the cathedral.

"The night before, there was a huge firework display which I went to with my sister who was great friends with David Linley, Princess Margaret's son. We all went together and after the royal fireworks I was meant to go back to my parents' house at Albany. But the crowds were so enormous we were literally unable to get back to my sister's car and she was beginning to get very nervous that I would be very tired and not get to bed early enough. So Princess Margaret said, 'Well, don't be silly, I'll take India back to my house.' Since Sarah was also a bridesmaid it was easy for me to go with Sarah the next morning. We rang my parents and my mother said, 'Absolutely,' thinking, how lovely, India in the lap of luxury at Kensington Palace. In fact, Margaret put me in the sort of old nanny's room, and I remember her distinctly offering to lend me her toothbrush. In retrospect it sounds very strange, but these are the funny things that stick out in a child's mind. All I really wanted to do was to be at home, especially the night before this day.

"The next day, Sarah and I went to Clarence House. Diana had her own enormous dressing room, full of the hustle and bustle of people coming and going, flowers being delivered and all the rest of it. I distinctly remember there was a small television on the side of this dressing table, and Diana was seated in front of it, again, dressed in her jeans, and the tiara was being put on her head. She started to shoo anyone who got in the way of the TV screen out of the way because, obviously, she was very interested to see herself on television. It was all very new and very exciting to her. And the TV was obviously reporting on her early life and all the rest, and she was watching this fascinated, with her tiara and her jeans on. And then the commercials came on and, there was the 'Just One Cornetto' ice cream commercial. Diana started to sing and we all started singing along, too. It sort of indicated, I think, the sort of mixture of feelings around getting dressed—she was obviously intrigued to see herself on television and relaxed enough to be able to sing, but yet sort of nervous enough that we're all laughing and joking along.

"When it came to the time to leave Clarence House, we had to go ahead and wait in one of the side chambers in the cathedral. There was a sort of incredible hush around the cathedral. As the carriage drew up, Sarah and I went down the steps to help Diana get out, and the cheer that went up when she got out—I have seen crowds and listened to applause and things, but I have never heard anything like that noise when Diana got out of that carriage. It was absolutely extraordinary—the cheer and the cries of people. Then Sarah and I went to work on straightening out that train before she went up the steps with her father, who at the time was extremely wobbly. I think she was more concerned for him, which probably, in a way, was quite a good thing, so she didn't realize the enormity of it all.

"He had an aide who was helping him, but I do remember that she just kept looking at him the whole time until they got to the top, and then she moved in and took his arm and they began down the aisle. But when we got to the top of the aisle, she did something unusual. She turned around and looked at us all, standing behind her, which I think was very nice, because a lot of brides take it for granted that the bridesmaids are there and doing what they should be. She actually turned around and looked.

"We'd been given little stools to sit on. I remember the King of Tonga was sitting five rows down, and he had his own chair brought in, because he's so vast. So he had this sort of huge gilt chair, and we were perched on tiny little stools. And the King of Tonga came with a wife and several ladies-in-waiting, and they had these sweets that they opened up and passed down the line to me.

"At the end, I had to fold up that whole train and put it back into the carriage. One extraordinary memory for me, talking very personally, is riding in this horse-drawn carriage through the streets of London. I was with Catherine Cameron [one of the other bridesmaids] and Prince Edward, and Catherine got dreadful asthma from the horse. She was allergic and her eyes started streaming and her face puffed up completely. One of Lichfield's photos in one of the grand corridors of Buckingham Palace shows the Queen standing and Diana bending down because Catherine's face had swollen up so much in the carriage, she was checking to see if she was all right. She was only five or something.

"Another strong memory is coming out onto the balcony and seeing all those millions of people below. The police had been holding them back and then as we came out onto the balcony, they literally pushed forwards and you saw these swarms, and it was literally like ants swarming forward. It was so wonderful to see a crowd like that all gunning for the same thing, no hostility whatsoever, and just everyone euphoric. It was a very, very strong image. And I remember the crowd was shouting: 'Kiss, kiss!' Obviously we all turned and thought that was great fun. They were very much prompted by the crowd to kiss.

"Afterward, at the wedding breakfast, I remember Diana being very relaxed and relieved that it was all over. The dress by this stage was incredibly crumpled and she picked up Clementine [Hambro] and put her on her dress while they were eating lunch, and it was a kind of total abandonment and great fun. There were all the official photos—Charles on his own, Diana on her own, Charles with the best man, the whole family, and then one of us with the crowned heads of Europe, just on and on. And finally Andrew was telling one of his jokes that made everyone laugh, and Diana just lifted up her arms and flopped onto the floor. 'I am exhausted!' she said, or something, and just lay there. At that stage everyone sort of crumpled around her, and Patrick Lichfield took a wonderful shot of everybody just in a heap on the floor.

"After the lunch, Diana had to get into her going away outfit. Again, Sarah and I went up to help her. But afterwards, it was much less organized, much more chaotic. Diana's sisters were around, helping her get dressed and changed, and there was much more of a family feel by that stage.

She was very giggly by that time. Then we went downstairs to see them off, and they got into that carriage and Edward and Andrew had tied lots of cans with string to the back of it. They were clunking off as they went and I remember, again, being very struck by the fact that, as they drew out, the courtyard was filled with, you know, intimate family, but, obviously, if you're English royalty, intimate family goes to about 300 people. The carriage took off and the Queen started running behind waving, and then everyone started to run. Obviously for me, aged 13, the Queen is very much the Queen and to see her run behind the carriage was great fun. We'd all been given confetti to throw and everyone had their boxes of confetti and we're throwing and tossing, and the Queen running in the courtyard. It felt just like a family wedding until they pulled outside the gates and it changed."

For make-up artist and style expert Barbara Daly, Diana's wedding was the start of a friendship that lasted through the years. She had been introduced to Diana by *Vogue* and, after a trial run, was invited to do the make-up for the big day. "I can remember meeting her for the very first time. I was in the room and she walked in and she grinned at me and put her hand out and said, 'Really pleased to meet you.' She and I are exactly the same size and she looked at me and said, 'It's not often I can look a woman straight in the eye,' and we both cracked up. She had a great sense of humor, very witty actually, very funny. She was never hurtful, just very funny."

She was impressed by Diana's consideration for others even through such a long and stressful day. "She was only 19, which is very young to get married. When I got to Clarence House that morning it was quite early—I think I met her about half-past six, quarter to seven. We had the television on when she was getting ready and we were watching the crowds on the television as well as outside. I remember her turning round and grinning to me at one point and saying, 'Gosh, it's a lot of fuss for a wedding, isn't it?' She asked me if I'd had breakfast and when I said no, she said, 'They brought me loads of strawberries and things. Have a bit of mine—we'll share it.' She didn't appear to be particularly nervous—I would say she was more excited than nervous and, let's face it—it was a very big day.

"We were on a pretty tight schedule. There was the frock to put on and the hair to do so we were all very aware of the time: Make-up first, then the hair, then the dress and then touch-ups. So she and I were alone doing our bit at the beginning and I remember at some point the Queen Mother popped in. After that, she had her hair partially done and then David Emanuel put the dress on, which was a large dress if you can remember and there was lots of it. And then she came back to me because we were then going on walk-about to get the bridesmaids and obviously Patrick Lichfield was around taking lots of behind the scenes pictures at that stage. She didn't have heavy make-up, but it had to be enough because there were a lot of lights, a lot of television, everybody looking at her, but on the other hand I wanted her to look her very best but not overly made-up. This was not some Hollywood starlet, this is the future Queen who was also very young and a very, very pretty girl in her own right, so I certainly didn't want to give her the kind of look that would overwhelm her.

"One thing that happened that Liz and David Emanuel never found out about was Diana saying, 'I've just put my perfume on and I've just spilled some on the front of the dress. They'll kill me.' I said, 'They'll never know, there's so much fabric it will evaporate.' She said, 'Do you think if I just tuck the front in they'll never notice?' I said, 'Yes absolutely—you and every bride in the country has done that.' We put her in the coach and off she went. I went with a little entourage including the guy who was doing her hair—the Emanuels had already left—and we had to go with our motorcycle escort through London so we could beat the carriage to the door. We had to be seated before she came in and, obviously, the Emanuels had to be there to arrange the dress. I had to go into the vestry to do touch-ups before she came out to be seen again by the cameras.

"It was going really well apart from the boob she made with Charles's name, which was very sweet. She did mention it to me, but I just said to her, look, it really doesn't matter. Everybody was so enthralled with that day.

"She was very concerned about her father on the day. We were speaking about him earlier in the morning, she was hoping he was going to be OK—and in fact he did splendidly well, but there was all of that to worry about, too. The whole day was really very arduous. I don't think she was out of the limelight for very long at all and even at those moments when she wasn't being seen on camera she was still with other photographers and meeting people. I thought she coped brilliantly, always with good humor and, I have to say, kept everybody going. She was absolutely terrific with the bridesmaids and the little pages and some of them were really tiny. She was great with them."

For photographer Lord Lichfield, who took the famous pictures of Diana's wedding, it was also a day of tension and elation that left him with what still remain as some of his most treasured photos. In particular he, too, recalls Diana's tenderness toward the bridesmaids. "I was in the room in which I was going to take the photographs, and I went out to the next door corridor where they were all assembling and I saw Diana walking toward one child who was beginning to look uncomfortable. And I just pulled a little camera out of my pocket and I snapped, and that is how I often work. I always have a camera, and I don't always just concentrate on the main job in hand. I tend to always look out for the unusual snaps that might make an informal picture.

"I noticed that she was extremely quick to comfort the child. She had a lot of other things to think about: She had to be on the balcony, do the waving, she had to go and do the group photographs again and again and again, you know, so the whole thing was ahead of her, and yet she found time to make this gesture, which was in itself touching. And I did nothing cleverer than to have a camera in my pocket and whip it out quickly and take the picture. It wasn't a particularly smart camera and nor was it anything that I would have used for an official job, because it's the sort of thing that I just take snaps with. But it was a snap that worked.

"I took some other shots, formal ones and informal ones, and there was a back view of them all waving to the public from the balcony, which is a picture that's not often seen. By then, I knew that they were all exhausted, and I still had one more frame left in my camera, and I just said, 'OK, I've finished now,' and they all collapsed on the floor, and I still had one more shot. That's another photographer's trick, I'm afraid.

"I felt elated when I took those photos and I still treasure them among my most precious. I knew that I'd got something special, but, of course, I was terribly worried. We didn't have instant replay then, we had to wait for three or four hours while the processing people developed the films. I had three hours of anxiety while everybody else was having their lunch and I was sitting outside the labs on a motorbike waiting to see the results. I missed the lunch but it was worth it. Absolutely."

For make-up artist Barbara Daly, there was a very surprising end to the day. "The phone rang at about a quarter past ten that night. It had been a very long day for everybody. I answered it and I said, 'Hi, who's this?' and she said, 'Diana.' And I said, 'Good grief, why on earth are you ringing me now? You must be exhausted!' 'I just wanted to say hello and thanks for today,' she said and we had a little chat. After I put the phone down, I thought how remarkable that was, because I wouldn't have been the only person she phoned. I thought, gosh, I bet she's rung the Emanuels, the hairdresser, she's probably rung the flower lady and the caterer and God knows who else. It's the sort of thing she would do in those circumstances. She was motivated, I think, by general thoughtfulness and very good manners. I can't imagine many people doing that after a day like that. There are many beautiful people in the world, but Diana had that extra thing, which is really a very genuine warmth because she had a very loving and compassionate heart."

Diana was brought up to touch people, which she did a lot of . . . And she did have large eyes and she had this great appeal. . . . She was marvelous even from a very young age.   *Frances Shand Kydd*

Dear Mummy and Daddy

I hope you had a
nice journey and that
you are enjoying your
holiday.

We had a power
cut on Monday and I went
to bed with a candle in
my room.

Lots of Love
Diana

I first met Diana when she came to Althorp when she was about five and a half. She was a very shy little girl, very pretty, and very sweet. She loved music. She was a very caring little girl, very loving, always out with her grandma, giving her a hand. She used to go out in the garden picking grandma a flower or a rose to bring in. She was always dancing around, but she was very shy.

Maudie Pendry

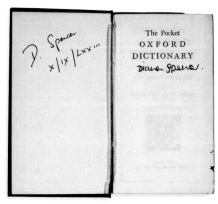

Report

Summer Term 1967   Diana Spencer

Stars : 3

	Exam. %	
Scripture	-	Diana takes a lively interest in this subject.
Arithmetic	85	A very definite improvement this term.
Reading	-	Much improved. Sound progress made.
Writing	75	Very good.
Grammar	80	Diana has made a good beginning
Dictation	-	Diana is working better with good results.
Geography	.	Good generally.
History	-	Diana shows great interest in this and makes lively comments.
Nature Study	.	Very good.
Drawing	-	She works with enthusiasm.

General Remarks: Diana is beginning to gain confidence in her work. There has been a noticeable improvement during the latter part of the term.

Autumn Term begins on Monday, 18th September

SILFIELD SCHOOL
GAYTON ROAD
KING'S LYNN

Head Mistress:
Miss J. M. S. LOWE, C.M.T.

Telephone:
King's Lynn 4642/4737

SCHOOL REPORT

Term Ending Dec. 18th 1969.

Name Diana Spencer.   No. of days absent   1.

Age 8 years 5 months   Form Upper II

Religious Knowledge
Good —

Tales
Good. —   Has worked much

History
Fairly good. — better in these subjects

Geography
Good. — Diana's written work

Natural History
Good. — is more factual + accurate

Writing Very good but must be careful where she puts 'Capital Letters'

Reading
Ex

P.T.O.

She was a very keen tap dancer. She was a very keen dancer altogether, actually, but the entrance hall has a wonderful marble floor so for a tap dancer it has wonderful acoustics. So she would spend hours practicing there and I think one of the early disappointments of her life was realizing she was going to be too tall to be a proper dancer. But she really did adore it, it was one of her passions actually.

Charles Spencer

As a teenager, she had that certain star quality. As she grew into a superstar, her looks changed—I mean she went through a hell of a lot—and, you know, the sort of innocence from early on went. But she certainly had a star quality which very very few people have. Although she had no academic qualifications, she had a lot of instinctive practical common sense and this extraordinary ability that not many people have of being truly captivating on a one-to-one level. I could see the effect she had on other people: You didn't forget seeing her. She was immensely popular.

Henry Bellingham

Just before she got married we had a royal wedding party, along with everyone in the country, and I remember saying at the time, "Well, we're lucky because the bride came." It was a children's party. . . . She wrapped up a little present for all the children, and one of the teachers made this wonderful cake and she wore a paper crown.

Kay King

I have seen crowds and listened to applause and things, but I have never heard anything like that noise when Diana got out of that carriage. It was absolutely extraordinary—the cheers and cries of the people. Then Sarah and I kind of went to work on straightening out that train.

India Hicks

With all my love, your devoted
daughter. Diana. July 29th 1981.

Another strong memory is coming out onto the balcony and seeing all those millions of people below. The police had been holding them back and then as we came out onto the balcony, they literally pushed forwards and you saw these swarms, and it was literally like ants swarming forward. It was so wonderful to see a crowd like that, all gunning for the same thing, no hostility whatsoever, and just everyone euphoric.   *India Hicks*

CHAPTER TWO – THE COMPLEX

She very much touched people's lives. I think when she died, I gather that a lot of people felt "what happens to me now?" And they felt all their difficulties. But she had some difficulties, major difficulties, in fact, and she was able to cope, so they could too.

Frances Shand Kydd

Princess Diana's early marriage was a time of rapid and extreme change for her. It started with the fairy-tale wedding—an event on a grand scale, marrying into the grandest family in the land, stirring up almost archaic popular expectations of a happy ending. In itself this was a potentially overwhelming event for a 20-year-old. But within a year Diana was also a mother. At the same time she found herself required to undertake public duties, all under an intense public and media scrutiny that sometimes bordered on complete hysteria. Under this public gaze the gauche teenager began to transform herself into a glamorous woman whose fashion choices were a source of continuing fascination. When Diana developed an eating disorder as a result of the stresses and strains of her situation, few people realized what was happening. As far as the public was concerned, she was still part of a glamorous couple, a young mother and an increasingly hard worker for the various charities she took on.

By the end of this short period, though, it appears Diana had lost all hope of a happily ever after life or even a comfortable life as wife, consort, or mother. It is only hindsight that has revealed just how hurt she was by the failure of her marriage. At the time, only a few knew that the couple, celebrated everywhere they went together, were desperately unhappy with each other. Yet as the fantasy began to crumble something more interesting began to emerge. In that era of female self-discovery, Diana, too, was a young woman forced into creating a working life and identity for herself. As mothers increasingly entered the workforce, Diana also emerged as a modern young mother trying to combine her children with a more public existence. And in that period where celebrity journalism came of age, models became supermodels and high glamour preoccupied the soap operas, Diana emerged as the most glamorous woman of the era.

This was also a time when Diana was beginning to show the qualities that made her work for charities exceptional. Beautiful, hardworking, intimate with the people she met and self-deprecatingly humorous, she was quite unlike anyone else before in the British royal family, and it was deeply unsettling, especially for her husband. This personal evolution had constitutional implications. According to William Rees-Mogg, former editor of *The Times*, Diana's life could be seen as "three stages of a constitutional argument in which she was largely right but the court usually opposed her. The first stage was the period of her early marriage, down to the birth of Prince Harry, in which the young bride saw increasingly clearly how the monarchy ought to develop but was brushed aside as an inexperienced girl trying to influence an ancient institution which was determined to go on doing things in its own way. There was some jealousy of her celebrity status. The people loved her."[1]

The wedding had been an enormous strain for the young Diana and immediately afterwards she seemed greatly relieved. "After her engagement and up to the wedding," says royal photographer Jayne Fincher, "we hardly saw her, but when we did, she looked stressed out. Then when she came back from the honeymoon and had that famous photo call up at the River Dee, the expression on her face seemed to say, 'Phew, thank goodness.' She looked really relaxed that day, as if all the pressure had suddenly gone and she was taking a deep breath."

Anna Harvey, then editor of *Vogue*, also remembers "looking at those pictures of her sitting next to Prince Charles by a stream at Balmoral on the honeymoon and thinking that she'd transformed completely from the girl I'd met eight months earlier. She was wearing a tweed suit with those bare brown legs and she looked great. It wasn't just the weight loss, which was dramatic and the blonde hair—she was I think very happy at that time."

But within three weeks Diana was undertaking her first major tour, being "presented" to the people of Wales and Fincher noticed how worried

she was looking again. "It was a big tour and everyone was out because the princess was coming to meet the Welsh people. And the crowds were so huge, huge crowds, unbelievable, everywhere." One thing that was almost certainly worrying Diana was what she was expected to do as a new princess. Probably her thoughts had not gone much further than the wedding itself. Kay King, for example, who ran the Young England Kindergarten where Diana had worked until her marriage, thought she would have been thinking mainly about becoming a wife and mother. For those in her own social circle it wasn't immediately obvious what she would do with herself or that she would fall into charity work. "I don't think anybody really knew what she was supposed to do when she got married," says family friend Lucinda Hall. "You know, because she didn't seem very horsy. She wasn't going to start hunting or that sort of side of things, so we were all wondering what she was going to do . . . She had to work out her own role, in relation to Prince Charles, too. We're always reading or hearing about how they clashed, one had more photographs taken than of the other, and all that. I suppose she had to sort of work out her own little half, you know, as to what she was going to do. The people she liked were the sort of slightly theatrical people, ballet dancers and that type of person, rather than the National Hunt."

An office was assembled to deal with Diana's as yet unspecified role. Oliver Everett had been Prince Charles's assistant private secretary, seconded from the Foreign Office to which he then returned. "I was called on March 16, 1981 by the Prince of Wales to come back from where I was staying and look after one Diana Spencer. It was a month after they got engaged. I wasn't called her private secretary, because she didn't qualify for one at that stage, but that's what I was. And just before they got married she asked if I wanted to stay on."

Diana's staff at this stage was a small hastily assembled team charged with sorting out the general correspondence and setting up systems to deal with it. One member of staff from that early period remembers that, "She was just 20, exceptionally young, but very well organized for someone of that age.

"Three months after the wedding, there were still 20 mailbags of unopened letters, cards, parcels, from the wedding and then it was announced that she was expecting her first child, and everybody started knitting. People were incredibly generous, and thoughtful as they felt they had to knit for this baby. There were the most wonderful knitted jackets, mittens and hats, in every color under the sun. It was such an extraordinary phenomenon. But she looked at everything and anything that really was exceptional was put to one side."

Meanwhile, Oliver Everett was receiving all the more formal offers for her patronage, and there was an immense amount of pressure right from the word go. "Patronage of worthy organizations is part of the responsibility," he says. "It's not written down as a responsibility but it's an expectation. I'd been involved very much in Charles's life and from that realized that it was very much part of the position." By the Christmas of 1981 Everett had sorted out a range of "suitable" charities for Diana.

"Those first charities were charities that had approached the office and they were put into categories," says a former staff member. "Oliver selected a cross section: Children, charities to do with Wales, and music. She danced but she was also very musical, too.

"I don't know how much she felt pressurized into doing it and how much of it was by choice. In retrospect, she might have preferred not to have taken on so many, to find her footing a little bit first, because she needed to adjust to the whole situation. I don't think she objected, because she cared about people."

It was only a matter of weeks after the honeymoon that Diana began to undertake public appearances, the first being her "introduction to the people of Wales." That visit was a sign of things to come with the public and the media. Jayne Fincher says, "There was press from all over the world—Japanese television crews, American television crews—everyone was descending on these little Welsh villages. The Welsh Office was very good; we all had these big plastic passes they issued, and if you didn't have this pass, you would not be allowed near the event. But we all worked out that the rain made all these passes soggy. So we were all putting them in puddles to make them smudge so that they couldn't read what they said. We would all turn up, and the police would go, "Yes, go through, go through." The Welsh Office couldn't work out why they'd have this pen for 12 people and there were 100 in there. The tricks that were going on behind the scenes to get access to her were amazing. And I can't tell you what it was like among the photographers. There was no one else in the royal family they felt like that about."

"The first official engagement the Prince and Princess of Wales did together was a three-day visit to Wales," says a former member of staff. "On day one she did two remarkable things. The first was when talking to children, she would crouch down. She wouldn't just bend; she put her whole body down. Luckily she was young and strong enough as well as a ballet dancer and she could do that. Anyone else would be wobbling. But she got down on the level of children. The second thing was the way she was with the elderly. She was confronted by people who had been sitting in their wheelchairs in the cold for hours, waiting for the Prince and Princess of Wales. And there was an elderly man who had been in the army, and he was in floods of tears because he was meeting *his* Princess of Wales. And all she did was put her hand out and touch him. She didn't need to say anything. She just held on to his hand and talked to his carer pulling the rug around him as she talked. It was just instinctive, nobody had taught her, it was something you couldn't teach."

There can be little doubt that Diana's pregnancy was a time of turmoil. She was suffering from morning sickness, which was difficult enough. She was under pressure working out the way to handle the already large public demand on her time. She was under intense public scrutiny for her appearance, her dress sense and her decisions. "Couldn't sleep," she later said. "Didn't eat. Whole world was collapsing around me." Her friend Rosa Monckton tells how, in the last year of her life, Diana described those first moments of her marriage. "At just 20, she was totally unprepared for life in the royal court. When we were at our Greek cottage she talked about those early days—about her love for her husband, about her total exhaustion after the wedding, the escape from being on *Britannia* and then returning to the realities of her new position at Balmoral after only two weeks away. How she was suddenly Her Royal Highness and how people were hanging on her every word—'only I had none.' We talked about how she 'learned to be royal' and how, even then, she understood intuitively the importance of the human element to it all."[2]

As far as the public was concerned none of these doubts were apparent. In the first year, Diana's engagements were general visits, mainly to town centers or opening new buildings but everywhere she went she delighted and interested the crowds. Wherever she went the press followed her in droves. "With her," says Jayne Fincher, "everybody wanted to go to everything. So because of the huge demand we had a rotation system where you take it in turns and those who get to go inside share their pictures with the others who don't. But with her there would be just as many press outside because you knew that she would never just come out and get in the car. She'd be off on a completely unscheduled walkabout so you would never dare miss an event."

One of Diana's first public appearances after William's birth was at a fashion show for the charity Birthright. This was the fund-raising branch of the Royal College of Obstetricians and Gynecologists, devoted to improving research on all aspects of women's health but especially childbirth. Vivienne Parry who worked for the organization then, and later became a friend of Diana's, remembers her being extremely nervous. "The event was called 'The Brilliant and Beautiful Evening of Fashion,' at the Guildhall. It was November 1982. For six months after the birth of William she hadn't done much at all. This was one of the first, really big events where she was carrying the show. And there was huge interest in her.

"It was a bit of a shock for her to get back into the world. Diana was sort of wheeled into this, and she was looking terribly thin—she was wearing an off-the-shoulder evening gown. She was incredibly nervous, and she kept coming up to me and saying, 'Oh, Vivienne, am I doing the right thing?' And I was as green as she was. She was very, very hesitant, not sure of what she should be doing. In fact everyone was in absolute awe of her; this was the beginning of 'Diana Mania,' really. She was immensely charming to everybody and there were lots of lovely frocks. It was a rather soppy event but she was extremely nervous about it. But at this stage the main interest in Diana was as a clothes-horse and this was the time when speculation about anorexia started. Everybody was saying, 'Isn't she appallingly thin?'"

✻ ✻ ✻ ✻

DI-MANIA ~ It was in Australia that "Di-mania" took hold of the world. Media attention to the royal couple's tour of Australia and New Zealand was unparalleled. "A royal trip never had so much attention," says Jayne Fincher. "We had a hundred or more press from the UK alone. We were away for six weeks and had something like 140 flights." "The rules were changing,"[3] says photographer Ken Lennox. "Instead of seven photographers being there, there were 70. Before, there was one from each paper and a couple of freelancers. Now they were coming from France, Germany, America, and Japan. For us it was a bit of a nightmare because we'd had a fairly easy time until then, but when you have 70 photographers all squeezed onto one spot, trying to climb up ladders, pushing and shoving with each other, elbows were what you kept yourself safe by."

"Because they had William with them," says Fincher, "they decided to base themselves at this outback station, and then fly off. So, they were leapfrogging here, and we were leapfrogging there. We had all these chartered planes, hundreds of them, landing everywhere. The organization was astounding. I'd seen the crowds in Wales but the crowds in Australia were incredible. It was Di and Charles mania, at complete fever pitch. We went to Sydney and we wanted to photograph her with the Opera House, but when we got there it was like the whole of Sydney had come out. It was just a sea of people as far as you could see, not just on the land, the harbor was full of boats and people. And all you could see was the top of this little pink hat bobbing along.

"The huge interest was because it was all three of them," says Fincher. "It was historic taking William on the trip. At that point it was both of them, the glamorous couple, the future King and Queen. But it was very noticeable that the crowds were keener on Diana. They were desperate to see her, and when the two of them walked down the road you would hear these huge groans from one side to the other, because she was that side and the others would go, 'Oh, no, we want Di!' Charles was good-humored with it. He would laugh and call her over, and they'd all moan that side. You didn't feel he was upset by it at that stage. He seemed proud of her. There were lots of little touches like he would put his arm round her, and say, 'Here's my wife.' He seemed very proud showing her off and I think she was a bit overwhelmed by it sometimes, because the crowds were so big."

"She was terribly shy at first," says royal photographer Tim Graham. "And, of course, nobody had the slightest idea that she would turn into this massive, worldwide, kind of iconic figure. But the six-week tour of Australia with William was such a hit for her and was probably when she grew more confident. I've never done a tour like it. And just to show you the power of the interest in her—and that was only two years after their marriage—there wasn't a single day in six weeks when we didn't get a photo in the papers, which is quite remarkable. And that was probably the start of the hysteria."

With the benefit of hindsight it was also the start of Diana's journey toward the more informal and modern approach to royalty that so endeared her to the Australians. "Significantly," says Patrick Jephson, later Diana's private secretary, "that journey started on her first visit to Australia with Charles and, definitely, the infant William. She was just 21 and the gesture of taking baby William with her, despite pressure to leave him behind, told anyone willing to see that here was a woman who took her duties as a mother as seriously as her position as future Queen of Australia. That ability to be both emotionally approachable and innately royal touched a chord with skeptics who, even then, were unsure if they wanted their existing monarch, let alone another. Watching her triumphant progress, who could be surprised that her overshadowed husband felt the royal landscape begin to shift beneath his feet?"

"The things that struck you about her were her youth—she was a very young lady—and her beauty, her vivacity, her joy of life," said Bob Hawke, former Prime Minister of Australia, in a television interview in 2001. "I liked very much her skepticism about the pomp and ceremony. It was obviously a steep learning curve and I thought she did it well when, as I say, she had this skepticism about pomp and ceremony. She was inclined to have a little bit of a laugh about it, which I enjoyed, but she nevertheless was responsible. She knew her duties and handled it well. I thought it was going to be a tough job for her—because she was so young—but let me say that as I saw her in later years, it strikes me that she'd acquired a maturity."[4]

It was also hard for the press to miss that they had a bit of a star on their hands. "She was very easy to photograph," says Tim Graham. "You had to be a pretty useless photographer if you didn't get a good picture of her." And the public couldn't get enough of her: What she was wearing, where she went, whom she talked to. "We wouldn't think twice about flying to the north of Scotland and covering one small engagement, because we knew it would make a picture and we knew that the magazines would want it." The press were getting used to another phenomenon as well. Diana was fun. Unlike any other royal on the circuit, Diana joked with them, related to them as human beings and had a great sense of humor.

"The royals, have all been brought up to think, 'Oh, those awful press people, you mustn't talk to them.' But Diana hadn't had that experience, so she just made her own assumptions and built up a relationship with them, without any preconceived ideas about it. She was also a good communicator and had them on her side very quickly. When Diana walked into the room it was like being with somebody you went to school with. She'd say, 'OK, what gossip have you got? What's going on? Heard any dirty jokes?' She would just chat with you about anything, naturally. She was so different from the rest of the royal family."

Like many of the others, photographer Arthur Edwards loved working with her. "The thing about Diana was you could never predict. I remember being at a dinner in Melbourne and she walked in and I was

expecting a fantastic dress and she was wearing a necklace with a headband, emeralds, amazing picture. And, you know, another time she walked in and she was wearing the pearls back to front down her back. You could never ever predict what this woman was going to do. I loved working with her. I loved tours, I loved the fact that she was hard working and she gave me some great pictures, she gave me some great laughs.

"She had a great sense of humor. I was in Tokyo with her once and we were looking at a car—a Honda-McLaren racing car. Ayrton Senna had just won the World Championship in this car and I remember that she'd just been stopped for speeding before we left and I said to her, 'I'll never catch you in that, Ma'am, on the M4.' And she said, 'I'll tell the jokes, Arthur.' That was the name of my book. She was like that, full of quips. I remember once she had her hair cut short. We were at an RAF base in the north of England somewhere. I said, 'God, if they cut your hair much shorter you'll look like Sinead O'Connor.' She took one look and said, 'At least I've got some hair.' Then she laughed and got in the car and she said to her chauffeur, 'I soon told him, didn't I?' She had a sort of a wicked side. She used to torment a number of the royal back-up policemen when they had to do duty on state occasions. They had to put on footmen's gear and ride at the back of the coaches, pretending to be footmen. For that they've got to put pink stockings on and she'd often take the mickey out of the policemen saying 'Ooh, got your pink stockings, dear.' I think she liked to bring laughter and happiness to most things. Yeah, she was great to work with, there's no question." Says Tim Graham, "At the end of the day, when you were actually out working with her and you met her at press receptions, we all used to love having a joke."

In spite of her obvious style and her apparent ease with the people she was meeting, underneath Diana was insecure. Her mother says she was much less confident going into social situations than she appeared and often sought out those who held back because she could relate to their insecurities. "She didn't speak to confident people half as easily as those who weren't. And this was, in her case, a kind of battle that went on. She wasn't all that confident herself, she knew she had this gift with people, and she used it, wisely and generously. But, in fact, she felt, going into a big room of people rather drawn to those who are feeling a bit nervous, rather as she was herself. It's quite hard going into a room and everyone stops talking and you know, 'Hell, I've got to break the ice myself'." "She was one of the more insecure people of this world," said her friend Rosa Monckton. "She achieved a veneer over her natural shyness but found walking into a room full of people an ordeal."[5]

Jayne Fincher noticed Diana often made a beeline for children for much the same reason. "It wasn't a deliberate thing. I think it was actually to help her overcome her feelings of self-consciousness more than anything. If she could find a child that she could touch or bend down to, she didn't feel she was standing feeling all self-conscious with her hands by her side. It was obvious right from early days that she really enjoyed children. She found it easy to go and chat to them, but to talk to the mayor, she wasn't quite sure of what she should say to him, at that stage."

In later years Diana told Jayne Fincher about her fear in those days: "She said, 'When I first came, people thought I had loads of advisors and this and that. I didn't. I used to walk into a room and, for instance, if the Queen was there everybody else would know where they were supposed to stand and what they were supposed to do. I didn't. Was I supposed to stand next to her? Was I supposed to stand behind her? When am I supposed to sit down? I didn't know what to do.' It must have just been hell—you can tell that when you look at all those early pictures. She was obviously in her early stages of pregnancy, unbeknownst to us at that stage. She looked awful; absolutely sick as a dog, painfully thin and absolutely worn out. And all the time she was, 'What am I supposed to do?' And it must have been really quite traumatic in a way, because everyone was watching every move she made. And I was stunned because she said, 'I never want that to happen to my boys, I don't want that to happen to my boys, I want to be around to show them exactly what they should do.'"

In the last year of her life, traveling in Bosnia with Jerry White, co-founder and executive director of the Landmine Survivors' Network, Diana had a telling exchange with Jerry that revealed a great deal about what was really going on for her in the early years of her marriage. "We went into a home in Bosnia and I said to Diana, 'Why don't you go in and I'll just stay out here and wait.' I felt that the fewer people the better, and if Diana can just be with this woman, that's the gift. I waited outside; she went in. I already knew the woman's story. She had recently lost her husband. He had survived battles in the war, but afterwards had gone fishing and reeled in a landmine. So, his fishing tackle is in the living room when they're meeting, and the stained clothing, and his two children, his widow, and his mother. Victims are not just people who step on landmines and die. It's the families, it's the community, it's a lot of things. This was early August of 1997, the death had only happened in May. The mother of the dead man was crying. It was awful. There wasn't a dry eye in the room, and the mother said, 'I saw my son, and he told me he was OK. He appeared to me in a dream and he said, "Mum, I'm OK."' She was telling this about her son and his widow is crying and the whole thing is very emotional. Diana comes out into the car, silent. After some time, as we start to drive, she said, 'That was really tough. I didn't realize how raw the family would be, and the loss was so recent. And then silence. Driving on for another five minutes, and she's still thinking about it, you can tell. She said, 'You know, every survivor we meet has a date, and they tell you their date.'

"And I said, 'I'm April 12th, 1984,' and Ken [Rutherford, co-founder] said, 'December 16th, 1993.' The dates we stepped on landmines. It's a day when your life changes forever, before and after. It's the definition of trauma that you have a date, I believe. She was quiet for a while. Then she said, 'Mine's July 29th, 1981.' And then she burst out laughing. She was being irreverent but what I'm telling you is probably the most telling, important reason why she had certain compassion, why she identified with survivors. Why was it she felt so comfortable with Ken and myself? . . . with all these survivors? It is not an easy thing to look this kind of trauma in the face and hear these stories. People would pour out their heart in gut-wrenching detail . . . and she absorbed it, took it away with her, and by doing that, transacted some healing in that process.

I think it's because a) she's a survivor, so she understands survivors, and b) she understood traumatic events. Things happen in your life that make you different: A date after which life will never be the same. It could be your cancer diagnosis, it could be your landmine explosion, it could be your marriage. It could be the loss of a child, a loved one. But those people who've experienced 'a date' understand before and after, and that life will never be the same. Inspired by this conversation, too, I thought, that is actually one of the most important things that people can express. At one testimony on Capitol Hill, I had survivors from around the United States, and internationally, and all they did was say their name, the country or the war in which they were injured, and the date.

"But that was also Diana. She threw her head back and laughed, because she was saying something profound, but she defused the situation with humor again and again. People who have a great sense of humor, very often are some of the saddest folk. They are people with deep emotional

capacity, but they also understand that with diffusion comes release. It's a survival technique."

❋ ❋ ❋ ❋

EARLY CHARITIES ~ "The first year of the marriage really was taken up with the pregnancy," says Jayne Fincher, "but after she got back from Australia she started getting into a pattern of charity events and traveling around the country quite a lot." Her own family was not surprised. Her mother, Frances Shand Kydd, believes that caring was absolutely at the core of Diana's character. "She was very much, 'you can do what you like with your spare time' so long as there's some input of caring for others. She was like that long before she was married. The fact that she was married to Prince Charles obviously made it easier in some ways to push forward the things she believed in. But she didn't have favorite charities. It's usually a writer of some description who says which her favorite charities were—I wonder if they were. She didn't have those sorts of favorites. She was a humanitarian. She would examine people and she would see who was unhappy and be there.

Robert Spencer, Diana's father's cousin, also thinks it was all part and parcel of her later work on global issues, which made him feel so "very proud and delighted." But, "I wasn't really that surprised because she had it in her. One had seen it slowly emerge, particularly starting with that visit to Australia 20 years ago and then coming back and starting to do events on her own I believe, after her marriage and particularly after Harry was born."

However she came to be involved, the charities that received her early involvement were thrilled and surprised by the amount of attention they received. Diana was introduced to Birthright by George Pinker the Royal Gynecologist who was, "extremely fond of Diana," according to Professor Sir Malcolm Macnaughton. "George Pinker looked after her when she had the babies. She was obviously a very charismatic person and he was trying to build up Birthright from the fund-raising point of view, so he managed to persuade Diana to become the patron. When I was president of the Royal College of Gynaecologists from 1984-87 she was very much involved. People said it was her favorite charity at the time. She did all sorts of fund-raising galas for us, like *The Mission* and *Starlight Express* when Andrew Lloyd Webber composed a special fanfare for her. She used to come in to the college and have lunch with us. She kept in touch and she knew exactly what was happening. In 1987 we made her an honorary president of the college. We had a lunch in this big room and she met all the others who had got fellowships. She had a really rough time because there were these people from all over the world and they all wanted to be photographed with her. They'd come up and stand beside her and their friend would take a photo, which of course was strictly taboo. But she just took it all in her stride. She didn't make any fuss."

Another early charity for Diana also reflected her interest in young children. "She became our patron in 1983," says Rachel Thomson of the Pre-School Learning Alliance. "We were probably one of the very first organizations to recruit her. Because she had been a nursery nurse this was a way of maintaining a link with her more ordinary past and also a way of showing her commitment to children and their families. I'm sure this was one of the reasons that she said yes. She did an awful lot for us, visiting individual pre-schools and playgroups across the country and helping us raising money. She even invited one group back for tea at Kensington Palace, which was lovely. But mostly she gave us a real sense of recognition. In the '80s, these parent-managed pre-schools were something of a Cinderella, but by having her name and her support, we achieved a kind of respectability that perhaps hadn't been there before. She once wrote that she supported 'the playgroup's crucial role in providing young children with the advantage of an educational start in life. We are often told that children are our future, and this simple truth surely deserves an appropriate commitment in time, energy and money, from us all.' I think her involvement with us was a pretty personal thing for her. We hadn't had a patron before her and we haven't had one since. Who could we have who would mean so much to so many people?"

The British Deaf Association (BDA) also couldn't believe their luck when Diana agreed to become their patron in 1983 and took it upon herself to learn sign language. To their delight Diana managed to master sign language and use it publicly. It was unusual for a public figure to take the trouble to learn and exceptional that one used it publicly. Mike Whitlam, who later became a friend and was closely associated with Diana's campaigning on land-mines for the Red Cross, first met her when they were both learning sign language. "We were both learning signing from different teachers so we used to compare notes and see how we were getting on. We used to joke about who was cheating and tried to communicate a bit with sign language. My friendship grew out of that time really. Later she actually did a public lecture, using sign language, something I never did. I'm still patron of the Cotswold Deaf Association, and I still don't have the confidence to do that, but she did. I thought that was pretty impressive."

Clark Denmark met her when she attended a British Sign Language (BSL) Tutors' Training Course in 1987. "When the time came for me to beckon her to the floor, she displayed her trademark, a bashful smile. I started by giving greetings and introduced myself, then I asked for her name—all in BSL. After a momentary hesitation, she greeted me and gave me her sign name in BSL. We then went on for two to three minutes conversing in BSL. She did it brilliantly. We were so proud to have witnessed that a princess could communicate in BSL reasonably well for a beginner. She laughed at the end, as if she was relieved that she survived the 'test.' It was no easy task."

"During her 13 years as a patron of the British Deaf Association," says Jeff McWhinney, chief executive of the BDA, "she was an enthusiastic supporter of sign language. In 1992 Diana captured the headlines and our hearts by launching the Sign Language dictionary with a presentation in BSL. She used her position to boost the status of sign language and deaf people in Britain." Few automatically think of her involvement with deaf people but certainly in her early years it was a charity that she gave a good deal of her time to. Later as she made trips abroad, visits to deaf schools were often included. She remained a competent signer for the rest of her life. The issues that came to the forefront in later life were present already: challenging the discrimination and stigma of disability and using her profile to win acceptance for difficult issues. "The number of people taking up sign language in 1995 was over 15,000, which bears testimony to the effect the princess's own usage of sign language has had."[6]

Elaine Phillips, a catering worker at Walsall Hospital says, "She made quite an impact on my two deaf daughters, because she learned first level sign language, which they were most impressed about. She's the only one out of the royal family that's really taken an interest in them. And they were really pleased about that."

In 1985 David Ireland, currently a director of SeeAbility, whose path was to cross with Diana several times more during her life, had just left the Anglican priesthood. One of his own children was diagnosed autistic, and he found himself fund-raising for a community center on the Broadwater Farm estate which sought to integrate disadvantaged and disabled children into the wider community through a community play group. "I had come out of parish life, in the Anglican Church, on a whim, just because I thought I'd like to do something that would impact youngsters with disability, in the light of my own experience at home. In those days, I was full of blarney, and I simply wrote to her, very early on after she had got married and said would she consider coming? I think what actually swung the deal our way was that the Broadwater Farm riots had just happened. So, there was probably a desire to be seen to be involved in that community.

"It was the mid 1980s, a political time just after the riots. Lots of my left-wing colleagues on Haringey Council didn't think we should invite royalty. In fact one colleague protested by turning up in his shirtsleeves! But his criticisms mysteriously melted away. He thought a royal visit would be all fluff and nonsense, but clearly she'd remembered her briefing incredibly well. What she did, intriguingly, was to show a level of informed knowledge of what we were about. But what I suspect had the greatest impact was that, far from being patronizing or condescending with the young people, she met them at their level. She knelt down and looked them in the eyes and she was very good with them.

"I had spent quite a lot of time working with these young people and had begun to understand their needs and the dos and don'ts with them. But she walked into it without any real warning, and somehow got alongside them, totally and utterly, and did so in the gentlest and most natural of ways. Whatever anybody may subsequently say, there was something about her that gave her a level of empathy, if you like, which, as a clergyman, let alone as a director of a project, I was really quite startled by. She was extraordinarily good with parents too, and we are talking about parents in this context, from very deprived backgrounds, quite unused to these sorts of occasions, quite unused to ever meeting anybody of any kind of fame whatsoever. Some of them were incredibly nervous at our meeting; they were in such a state. But within minutes she had put them at their ease. It was a huge success."

David Ireland's colleague wasn't the only critic to be disarmed by the visit. "At that stage Bernie Grant was the chairman of Haringey Council and Princess Diana's visit must have been a matter of weeks, I guess, after another one of his republican press attacks on the royal family. From the point of view of etiquette, obviously, he should be invited. So I simply wrote to him and said that I was informing him, as I was required to do, about the visit but in the light of the views he'd expressed, I was assuming he would not wish to be embarrassed by being asked to attend. And he wrote back to say that despite his own personal views, he felt he should be there. So I contacted his office and said, 'That's fine, I won't put him in the line-up, because I wouldn't want to embarrass him.' So they said, 'That's absolutely fine. But make sure he has a good place for the official presentation and opening speech.' So he sat at the front, but wasn't introduced and didn't join the tour of the building. Then I went with Diana for the tour and we went up onto that mezzanine floor. And as we went down the stairs, for the last lap of our tour of the building, there he was, suddenly. They were all supposed to have been kept in the hall, but somehow he had broken away from the crowd and found himself, miraculously, at the bottom of the stairs as she came down. And as we turned the top of the stairs, I saw him there and said to Diana, "I think you probably recognize the face down there." And she looked at me and smiled and just carried on walking down the stairs. And when we came to him she put out her hand and said, 'Mr. Grant, I've heard so much about you,' just like that. And he literally went gooey. It was wonderful, one of those moments I will treasure forever. We didn't give him a chance to say anything more and in the gentlest of ways, she swept on past him, and continued her tour.

"From that experience, and from subsequent meetings with her, I would have said that she was a naturally caring and very sensitive individual, who probably suffered as much from a kind of over-sensitivity as anything else. I can imagine that because she was so sensitive, she was, as most sensitive people are, vulnerable. If you are like this you either wrap yourself round with a kind of artificial shell which says, 'no one's going to come near me,' or you just become increasingly sensitive and increasingly hurt."

❅ ❅ ❅ ❅

BECOMING A FASHION ICON ~ "There are many beautiful and stylish people in the world who are icons and movie stars and pop singers, but they don't always draw people from all walks of life to them in the way she did, and I think that was definitely, without a doubt, her very inner self. The fact was that she had a very sweet and generous heart and was very tactile. She wouldn't be loathe to touch or put her arms around somebody, especially children, and she would not have worried if her dress got greasy or crushed or crumpled. It would have been the last thing on her mind," comments style expert Barbara Daly.

For the press who now followed Diana everywhere she went, the charities were at that point secondary to their main interest: what she looked like and what she wore. Everyone was watching the evolution of the shy girl in the paisley shirt into the most scrutinized woman in the world including her friends. Kay King remembers being amazed to see her nursery helper blossom in confidence and style. "At first she was painfully shy. She was always looking down, and she blushed terribly easily. I remember when she went down to West Heath [Diana's old school] to open a new hall. I watched her making a speech, which I'd never seen her doing. She was in a much less threatening environment than many in which she had to make speeches, but even so you could see that it was quite an effort to do it. It didn't come naturally and easy, but she became so much better at it. And it was amazing to see how she changed from the shy teenager when she was working at the nursery into this beautiful woman as the years went by. Every day I picked up a paper I could read about what she was doing and see what she was wearing. I probably knew what Diana was doing rather better than my own family. Her dress style and presentation changed dramatically. And she also increased in confidence."

"On that wedding day," says family friend Lucinda Hall, "it was unbelievable that somebody one had known was sitting there with 30 million or whatever it was, 500 million people watching her, and suddenly there she was, on every magazine cover, and it was extraordinary. Then the transformation of her look was so extraordinary, too. I've got a small enough brain to be interested in what people look like, and it was a fantastic transformation. From that shy Di with the see-through skirt, and then suddenly there she was—and we all wanted to dress like her. We looked at what she wore and we looked at what she did and how she presented herself, and she was the most famous person in the world."

No one had a closer seat at the ringside of this transformation than Anna Harvey, then editor of *Vogue*. She had been asked by Diana's mother to help her get together a wardrobe during the engagement. She continued to offer her advice through the years and was a lasting friend. "The first time I met Lady Diana Spencer was in 1980 in the editor's office. The engagement had been announced and she couldn't go anywhere without being mobbed. Her sisters had worked at *Vogue* and thought we might be able to help with her image. I'd called in far too many clothes because I had absolutely no idea of the kind of thing she liked. By the time she arrived I was shaking like a leaf but I took one look at her and thought this isn't going to be too difficult at all. She was about five feet ten and completely in proportion. Her eyes lit up when she saw all the racks—I don't think she had any idea how many lovely things there were out there—and her enthusiasm was contagious. After that I'd trundle over to Kensington Palace with a rail of clothes for her to go through and we'd sit on the floor in her drawing room, looking at sketches and swatches of fabric, while the butler brought endless cups of coffee.

"Diana has been called a fashion icon but at the start she was incredibly unsophisticated about it. Her taste was typical of her background: Upper class English girls weren't as knowing about clothes as they are now—there were no 'It' girls then. But she was very open to ideas . . . fashion might not have been a priority but she loved to experiment. In the early days we didn't know what was expected. There were so many functions and we also had to get a trousseau together. It's hard to imagine now but she really had nothing in her own wardrobe—a few Laura Ashley blouses and skirts and some bobbly jumpers. She wanted to wear British because she felt it was something positive she could do for the fashion industry. She was a very English girl and the romantic style suited her. Everyone was thrilled to do things for her; there was such a feeling of euphoria that here was this young, glamorous girl who loved clothes. Stephen Jones even sat up all night embroidering the Prince of Wales's feathers into the tam o'shanter she wore to the Braemar Games.

"She made a conscious decision to dispense with formality very early on. I ordered dozens and dozens of suede gloves in every shade for her because the royal family always wore gloves. Heaven knows where they all went because she never wore any of them. She wanted flesh-to-flesh contact. She was amazed at her approval rating and this newfound confidence made her blossom. We got braver and there were mistakes."[7]

Catherine Walker was one designer whose burgeoning career was closely associated with the emergence of the fashion icon. "In the autumn of 1981 I had only just started my career as a fashion designer and I was quite astonished when the Princess of Wales arrived on my doorstep. Diana, too, was starting a career, a little of which I was to witness at first hand over the next 16 years.

"I recall a visit in the spring of 1982 from a senior journalist who asked me why I was reluctant to talk about, or even publicly acknowledge this client whose patronage was every other designer's dream come true. I had my own reasons as a young widow to protect myself as I started a new life, and my answer was simply that I saw my role as a designer to provide Diana with the tools of her trade. The "trade" was one that Diana threw herself into with youthful commitment. For the many years that followed I was struck by her desire to "make a difference" and how much she wanted to give people pleasure."

There is little doubt that Diana put a lot of thought into her effect and Catherine Walker was crucial in helping Diana achieve it. "England and the world were warming to the young princess's innate poise and charm," says Catherine. "People wanted her to be something very special, something in their own dreams. The princess wanted to reciprocate their love by wearing the right designs. The look had to suit the occasion and always needed to suggest that the princess had made a real effort to look appropriate. For Scotland it was tartan, for the country. If it were, say, a visit to a hospice, we would design a more friendly or colorful and informal suit. For London, it would be something sharper for the day and for the evening there was the demanding task of designing something that matched her multifaceted stature as a beautiful princess, young mother and future queen. I had a sort of private brief to design a dignified show stopper. It was almost a contradiction."[8]

To the watching world, Diana's transformation was dramatic and in a matter of years, her style had become very big news indeed. "If you look," says Barbara Daly, "you can see her style evolving quite rapidly as she grew older and she found the way she liked to dress and of course it was the '80s and there were terrific changes. Fashion went quite rapidly from Laura Ashley to power dressing."

"At first she was quite mumsy in her style," says Louise Chunn, fashion commentator and editor of *InStyle* magazine. "But throughout the '80s she became very sophisticated glamorous fodder for magazines. It's hard to imagine who, if she hadn't been there, would have been the next one down from her because there wasn't any one else in the picture. It was the '80s, and a lot of that time was shoulder pads and earrings as big as teacups and fairly spectacular hairdos and really dramatic clothing. She was in the middle of all of that and she seemed like the most glamorous thing that Britain had ever produced. If you look at someone like Catherine Zeta Jones now, you see someone who is very high glamour and you may be impressed at how the girl who used to be on *Darling Buds of May* has turned into a glamorous Hollywood star. But even more glamorous than a movie star is a real live princess. And unlike most of the princesses that had gone before her she was incredibly tall and really beautiful and in general dressed really well. There wasn't anyone else like her: Diana first—the rest nowhere. I don't think there had ever been other royals used on the covers of magazines like *Vogue*. Diana also got a kick out of it. That's nothing to be ashamed of and maybe nowadays we're more used to it. Lots of things when you look back on them seemed extreme but now we've got used to them.

"She was enormously important for British fashion, a shot in the arm of an industry that, before she came into it, was very small. The designers working in Britain were small businesses; they weren't internationally known. All the shows, the status, and the prestige were only starting then and it was very important for people like Catherine Walker, Bruce Oldfield, and Caroline Charles. What Diana was wearing got people talking about London much more. Obviously she was trying to buy British because that was the right thing to do, but because she was really tall, really slim, she just looked great. In some ways the current situation in British fashion is attributable to what Diana started in the '80s. In the '90s, many of those little British designers went off to join French houses. Designers like John Galliano and Alexander McQueen and Stella McCartney all happened after her really. But I think that nobody would have been looking at London without Diana having given British fashion a huge boost." "A lot of international press and buyers," says designer Caroline Charles, "came to London in the '80s because of her, just as they'd come in the '60s because of the Beatles. She brought some international glamour to British public life when we'd been loathe to show it before."[9]

"I met her at the beginning," says designer Valentino, "when she was married to Prince Charles and of course I immediately realized she was really one of the most beautiful girls in the world. Year by year, she became more sophisticated and more sure of herself. . . . Every designer was inspired by her. To me she will remain one of the most beautiful darling ladies in the world."[10]

David Emanuel says, "Nobody, but nobody—has ever been scrutinized like she was. Scrutinized from 18 to 19 years old right through her life. This woman, whether she liked it or not, was on the front of the national newspaper every day of her life. If she wore pop socks, pop socks sold out in every store in the world, let alone London. If she wore polka dots, suddenly polka dots were big news. On the scale of people say like Marilyn Monroe, like Jacqueline Onassis, forget it. There was nothing like her. And we were hungry—we, I'm talking about Britain. We were so desperate that we had not

only a fabulous . . . we had this amazing—they saw her as a model girl. She was a model girl but she was far beyond that. Oh, we've got this supermodel representing Britain. Little did they know she was far bigger and greater than that. She had another agenda."

Whether the press praised or criticized, it made great copy and the photos were invariably fantastic even when she made mistakes. Never had fashion disasters looked so glamorous. "She had this cheekiness," says Jayne Fincher. "She would devise an outfit to wear to match the occasion, like a majorette outfit to meet the troops or integrating a country's flag into her dresses. When she got off the plane she'd have an outfit on that would sort of honor the country she's visiting. So, when she got to Japan, a red and white dress that looked like the rising sun. When she got to Saudi, she had the Saudi national colors. All those sorts of things."

❋ ❋ ❋ ❋

CHARITY WORK ~ While Diana's star was continuing to climb, the charities with which she was involved were getting to see another side. Not long after Harry's birth she took on several of the charities that were to remain central to her working life until she resigned the patronages in 1995-96. Roger Singleton, the chief executive of Barnardo's, now a trustee of The Diana, Princess of Wales Memorial Fund recalls: "In 1984, the then Chair of Barnardo's, Dame Gillian Wagner, was with Princess Margaret on a visit and Princess Margaret said, 'Well, I've been president of Barnardo's for 40 years. I do sometimes wonder whether it's about time I gave way to a younger member of the royal family.' So Gillian wrote to her that evening and said if those were her wishes, we wouldn't dream of standing in her way and would she use her good offices to help us to encourage the Princess of Wales to accept and she wrote to the Princess of Wales and it was accepted." The association with Barnardo's was to be one of Diana's most significant and long lasting. "Her first engagement after Prince Harry had been born was with Barnardo's, so she'd have been about 22 at that point, probably a little older, but really she was very young. It was a very early stage in her public life, but her involvement continued until she did the major withdrawal from 100 of her charitable organizations. So it was a long involvement and during that time she must have done about 120-130 engagements for us."

Right from the word go Roger Singleton recognized that, along with the enormous help a patron like Diana would give to income and profile by fund-raising galas, speaking on their behalf, and launching initiatives, she also made an "exceptional contribution" on her numerous visits to Barnardo's projects throughout the country. "Her visits, even among the most cynical people, the most anti-royalist, were an enormously successful experience. Her capacity to make people feel good was really quite exceptional and I've seen her sit in a group of young mums struggling to bring up a handful of children very often on their own, almost choking with cigarette smoke. Perhaps some of them themselves were in the care of public authorities when they were children. She would just sit and listen to what their everyday lives were like. Very often she didn't say a great deal in response although she would always answer questions about herself and her own children. But after she'd gone and everyone relaxed, that group of people would feel sheer exhilaration about the fact that they'd been able to talk to a senior person in public life, a world figure. She left them with the very full impression she understood what they were talking about and she knew what it was like and if perhaps not quite having been there herself, because that would have been pushing it too far, nevertheless that whole experience made them feel good. That was a particular skill and I would say that her biggest single benefit to Barnardo's was the difference that she was able to make by dint of those visits to people's lives. I can visit those same projects five or ten years later and if some of the same people are involved they will almost invariably bring out the photographs and say, 'Do you remember?' That quality is very difficult to bottle, very difficult to replicate, very difficult to purchase.

"Her great strength was that although many of her visits were staged and timed events she managed to make them meaningful for the people she met. I remember she visited a project in Salford that was particularly heavy in the number of civics who accompanied us. There was one room with a settee and two parents who had a profoundly disabled child who was on the floor in front of her and they were going to meet the princess. There was going to be a photo opportunity too so we had the press rotation with about 12 people in it, the hangers-on like me, the mayor in his chains, and the lord lieutenant in spurs and swords and so on. And she knelt down on the floor with those two parents and they just sort of unburdened themselves of what their life had been like with a disabled child. Quite personal stuff about how it had left them feeling, about their inhibitions about having further children, what the impact had been to their personal and their marital lives and so on. And this circus is going on literally no more than ten feet away. That ability is absolutely amazing. Obviously a professional in very different circumstances can encourage people to talk in ways that make them feel better and supported, but her unique quality was being able to create that situation with such immediacy. These were the intrinsic skills and style that she had. She could look very intently and those big eyes were quite an asset. People felt that she listened. She had an approachability that was a real surprise because we were so used to seeing a certain stylized form of royal behavior keeping its discreet distance."

Singleton was impressed by her thoughtfulness and professionalism. "Diana had an excellent memory. She could recall things very effectively from one event to another. And she was very good at sending little personal notes." He was also amazed by her ability to relate to the individuals helped by Barnardo's. On one occasion he took three young people from various projects to help publicize a new initiative with a launch at Kensington Palace. "Two were in wheelchairs and there was Gerald who had rather complicated learning difficulties. Certainly his social skills needed brushing up. He could read, but he was clearly a needy young man. We'd all met up the night before—the young people, their carers and myself—for dinner. The next morning we all got in a minibus and trooped off to Kensington Palace and sort of all got in and the princess had got drinks organized and doled those out. And the first thing that happened was that I was trying to encourage Gerald to talk to Diana and I said to Gerald, 'Tell the princess a bit about some of the things we did yesterday, Gerald.' Because it was the first time he'd been on a plane and the first time out of Northern Ireland. So we coaxed him on to say he'd been on the plane and so on and then he said, 'Supper.' I said, 'Oh yes, we had supper.' So she tuned in and said, 'Well, what did you have for supper?' And one of the things we had been working on with Gerald was to try and teach him that it's not appropriate to get too close to people facially and to try and teach him that we all need a bit of personal space around us. Once or twice either his caregiver or I had just to whisper, Gerald, personal space.' But anyway, he got so excited he lunged forward. Yes, he'd been to supper. And she said, 'And what did you have?' And he said what he'd had and then suddenly he said, 'Oh—and garlic!' And he came right up within inches of the front of her face and breathed it at her and she did not blink an inch. 'Mushrooms and garlic!' Personal space was totally forgotten.

"And then Gerald got a little bit bored with all this standing around talking and started to wander around and went in one or two of the rooms off the sitting room, including the back stairs room. I went to get hold of Gerald and Diana said, 'It's all right, let him go.' So he did and he was roaming around while we launched this initiative. But then he started to get a bit bored again and he went up to her in the middle of the proceedings and said, 'Thank you very much, but I've got to go now.' And she said, 'Well, that's fine, Gerald, if you've got to.' Now, I was wondering, 'What's all this about?' And his caregiver whispered to me, 'He wants to be first in the van to sit in the front.' Wonderful.

"Now those were the sorts of things that she was really so expert at, running at the pace of things. There was a natural pace about Gerald and about how he worked and operated and how he coped and she got into the stream of that and that too was a technique that I mean frankly you don't get from other members of the royal family. That was really quite wonderful."

Help the Aged was another charity that couldn't believe its luck in getting in Diana so much more than the attractive young figurehead they had imagined. Peter Bowring, currently president of Help the Aged, wrote asking for her involvement in 1982 almost as soon as she was married. "We thought that this charming new princess would be just the person for us. The answer was that, possibly in the future, but not just yet. In due course, she agreed, in April 1986, to become patron. We knew that she would be an ideal person to, as it were, show off Help the Aged, but at the same time we didn't realize how immensely conscientious she was going to be.

"That became apparent when we went to visit one of our sheltered housing projects in Slough. It was absolutely typical. We went in and there was a semi-circle of elderly people sitting round a television set. She went straight for the most distressed looking old lady, who was in a wheelchair, sat on the floor beside her, held her hand, and talked to her for several minutes. There were no cameras, nothing. It was not a publicity stunt; it was absolutely straight from the heart. And I realized then, and I think everybody else did, too, that we'd got an absolute winner as a patron."

Colonel John Mayo, ex-director general of Help the Aged, who later accompanied Diana on a number of important trips abroad and came to know her well, also remembers the occasion. "Now, she was 24, and it was quite a thing to be chucked into a lot of octo- and nonagenarians. I'm not sure who was more nervous, she or the old people. But she did it superbly. She walked into the room, and she sat down on the floor, caught hold of a hand of one old person on either side and said, 'My name's Diana, what's yours?' And, of course, they were tickled pink, and that broke the ice. That was the very first visit she did for us."

"She had the immense ability to be able to communicate very simply," says Peter Bowring, "whether it was people in this country or people abroad. She had the ability to give the impression that the person she was talking to was really the only person that really mattered in the whole world, and that, I think, is what endeared people to her."

Her sister, Sarah, remembers noticing that "she was particularly brilliant with old people. She did a lot for Help the Aged. She would go into the room of a nursing home and two of them would be playing Beggar My Neighbor, or something, and she would go across and say, 'Who's cheating?' you know, just the sort of wonderful entrée. And these people lit up in her presence. Sometimes people died very shortly after she had been to see them, who should have died way before. But because they knew she was coming, for some reason—I don't know how they did it—they hung on. Once she had gone, they had achieved that ambition, so they went. It was extraordinary the number of times she would say, 'Do you remember that man, that woman?' whatever, 'they died two days within my seeing them.' It was very strange."

Over the following years, Peter Bowring and John Mayo were amazed and delighted at just how much work Diana put in. She turned up for numerous glitzy occasions and receptions where people came to meet her. "At one of them, Norman Wisdom managed to be photographed at both ends of the line of stars being presented to her. He met her once and then ran round to the other end. He said to John Mayo, 'I'm going up again, I'll tell them it was my twin brother.' She visited day centers up and down the country, she attended special functions, fund-raising events, film premieres, a polo day at Smith's Lawn, a number of visits to Help the Aged and Help the Aged International overseas. On average each year she'd do seven or eight little functions of one kind of another, some were quite big ones, for the charity. Often a charity counts itself lucky if they get one royal appearance a year but she was marvelous." "There was a total mixture, really, in that personality," says John Mayo. "A depth of compassion which was very real, sympathy, and the ability to converse with people and make them feel terribly, terribly important, but also the ability to be the star at some pompous event."

"The media annoy me," says Peter Bowring, "because they made presumptions. Just because you don't pass exams doesn't mean to say you are not an intelligent person. I found her to be extremely intelligent. I felt terribly sorry for her. She had a very rough time at the hands of the press. It was down to their efforts that she was seen as frivolous and they didn't recognize that here was a very serious-minded girl who was doing her very, very best, and her best was jolly good.

"When she joined us, the public awareness of Help the Aged was pretty slim. When she came to us we were pulling in about eight million pounds a year, and by the time she'd given up being our patron, it was over 40 million. Her being our patron meant that when the press came to our functions, they were great. I've no doubt whatever that she put us on the map.

"You know, the crowds used to turn out in their thousands. Before that, no crowd ever turned up for Help the Aged, they didn't know who the heck we were. But because she was our patron, if there were people to talk to outside the place she was visiting, she'd spend a long time talking to them, chatting up the children, leaving posies. I used to enjoy every second of it because it was so heartening. What I saw was this extremely attractive princess mixing with ordinary folk who came along to see her. I don't know, you just felt here is somebody who almost works miracles when it comes to getting people interested in what she's up to. That, of course, is a two-edged sword, because when her life went a bit awry, people were interested in that, too. Then I think life became uncomfortable, very uncomfortable indeed."

Christopher Spence who met Diana later through her work with The London Lighthouse and who is now chair of The Diana, Princess of Wales Memorial Fund has said, "One of the wonderful things about Diana was she dared to do her charity work intimately. She brought her whole self." Diana's first charities were just beginning to find this out. She connected in a personal way with many of the people she came into contact with. It is clear too, that she also greatly valued the relationships she built here. Many were surprised by the level of friendliness and consideration she showed to them, a pattern which continued unfailingly throughout her life and which was rewarded by their devotion to her. Neither Roger Singleton, John Mayo nor Peter Bowring (nor later others like the late Reverend Tony Lloyd of The Leprosy Mission, Mike Whitlam of the Red Cross, or Ted Unsworth of Turning Point) would describe themselves as close friends yet all developed relationships with the princess that they treasured. In return she viewed them as informal advisors.

They helped on speeches and planning tours. She rarely forgot to acknowledge their significant life events. "She was always very appreciative of the background stuff that I did," says Roger Singleton, "and said I wouldn't have been able to do it without you and thanks very much and she made nice little gestures like sending tickets for my wife and me to go to the ballet or the opera or something. Our relationship wasn't purely professional if you like, nor was it sort of wholly personal either, but we did talk." "It was just a charming relationship, for my wife and me," says Peter Bowring. "We just got on very well with her. We met up with her many times at galas . . . and over lunch."

John Mayo, who later made many foreign trips with her, felt supported when his wife died. 'My wife died in 1993 from cancer, and she'd obviously met Diana a number of times. And she was jolly good; she wrote to her in hospital and sent her flowers and things. And the very first letter that I received at home after my wife died was from Diana. Now, I thought that was remarkable. She took the trouble to write the letter, but she also took the trouble to make sure it got there straight away. That's the sort of personal side. My son is in the army and she was colonel of his regiment and about three days after my wife died, Diana asked us both over to Kensington Palace. Charles, I suppose, was about 27 at that time, and she obviously had met him once or twice. She came running down the stairs, when we got there, flung her arms around Charles and said, 'My dear Charlie, I'm so desperately sorry for you.'"

John Young, chairman of Young's Brewery was also chair of the Development Foundation of the National Hospital for Nervous Diseases where Diana's father had been treated after his stroke. On the basis of this connection, he quickly recruited her to being patron of the hospital and equally quickly formed an affectionate friendship. "My wife absolutely loved her. I loved her. I fell in love with her in a way, oh, yes. There were lots of lovely things that she did. I always wrote to her by hand and my handwriting is rather bad. Once she sent me a pen, and wrote, 'Why do you write with a spade? I'm sending you a pen.' On one gala night with a Spanish theme we sat with her in the front row of the dress circle. It was decorated with real lemons, and she picked one off and gave that to Yvonne and said, 'Put that in your bag, nice and fresh for your gin and tonic when you get home this evening.' She knew that was Yvonne's favorite."

But the intimacy that Christopher Spence describes extended far beyond this sort of friendliness. He is referring to the qualities that she brought to bear in her meetings with people through the charities she was involved with. Working with her was "a wonderful experience," says Peter Bowring, "Just to observe her in action. There was no sort of strutting about, she just made her way gently into crowds—she went up to everybody and was happy to spend time talking to them. I don't know of anyone else who can work that kind of magic whether a member of the royal family or anybody else. Charisma's not a word I'm terribly fond of, but she had this extraordinary, enchanting character."

Phyllis Cunningham was chief executive of the Royal Marsden Hospital which enjoyed continuous support from Diana. She was amazed at how much rapport Diana had with the patients. "She was very young. After she had left, I said to my colleagues, 'I have never seen anyone so young and in the public gaze, who had such empathy with people—patients and staff, particularly with the patients.' She was oblivious to everybody around her when she was actually talking to the patients. She was so natural, kneeling on the floor beside the bed. To me, who had been in public life and the health service so long, I was just really quite bowled over by someone that young having that sort of relationship."

Tim Graham who followed her on so many of her charity engagements never failed to be impressed by her ability to talk to anyone she met and to bring such delight. "In one hospice she was able to sit down with an old lady, to be able to ask her, 'How's your treatment going?' And not be in any way embarrassed about that or feel reserved about it. Then she spoke to a man at one of the other beds, and he'd got the racing card open for the day's racing, so she had a good chat with him about racing and jokingly asked if he was wasting all his money on the horses."

Anthony Duckworth-Chad, who had known Diana since she was a child, was astonished at her effect on ordinary people. In 1988 she agreed to come and open the Splash, a fun pool for families in the north Norfolk town of Sherringham. "The local populace turned out in force when Diana arrived. And this is where the natural touch came in. She did all the correct things, but she was terribly good at darting off to see a little child in the crowd. She was very clever at seeking out the rather shyer, quieter ones. Because I'm a deputy lieutenant, I go to a few official functions, and you see members of the royal family, and they are brilliant at it, absolutely superb. But here was somebody who had married into the family, hadn't had vast experience, but, my goodness me, she picked it up jolly quickly. We'd stayed with them several times, so one had seen her in private, not on official duty. But this was the first time I'd ever actually seen her doing something other than watching her on television. And she was an absolute role model of how it should be done. She had this affinity and this charisma and this way of being able to talk to people in a very touching manner—and a quick wit too, never a put-down wit, a very nice quick wit. In my speech at the opening of the Splash, I said, 'It's a lovely place to bring all the family. You could even bring your mother-in-law.' Afterwards, Diana said to me, 'Good speech. But I don't think I'd bring my mother-in-law along.' She was funny, terribly funny."

Even her family was amazed at how well Diana adapted to her new role with the charities. "I think she probably did know the way people felt about her," her sister, Sarah, says. "I don't remember discussing it with her but I certainly knew it about her. I mean you would hear people talking about it afterwards. When she visited nursing homes or hospitals or hospices, you know, she always went in with a smile and always seemed to find the appropriate word. She had the capacity to say the right thing to people. If they had a sense of humor she would make them laugh, if they were incredibly shy they would lose the shyness. It was an amazing quality—this ability to choose the opening remarks or questions, the conversation, every time a coconut. Never failed.

"She'd go in to a 14-year-old boy who was terminally ill, life-threateningly ill and say, 'So how many Valentines have you sent?'—not got—'sent.' See the difference? One would have made him feel anxious and one would have made him feel good. And she said the right thing. It's just that ability. It was quite extraordinary to watch.

"But it wasn't because she said predictable things. She often said the unexpected to the people she was meeting. I don't know what they thought she was going to say, but they wouldn't usually expect something practical from someone in that situation. But if it was someone homeless she'd ask, 'Are your feet warm?' And those practical things are the right thing to ask people who are cold or in difficult situations. As I say, common sense."

How much was this just her style and how much a conscious way of doing things differently? Or did she come to realize her instinctive style was what people wanted from their royal family? "I think she looked at the traditional way the royal family go about these things, which is opening hospitals and being head of various charities, and just felt perhaps the link wasn't strong enough in terms of how the public perceived it," says Tim Graham. "Or this was her style, she liked to meet the people and be very hands on. There aren't any other members of the royal family who would walk into a hospital and plump down on the bed and, within a moment, be laughing with the patient. But she had the ability to do that. She was a huge breath of fresh air, there's no question."

※ ※ ※ ※

MOTHERHOOD ~ It wasn't just in her approach to charity and the kind of interaction she expected and enjoyed with ordinary people where Diana was beginning to break with previous royal behavior. Her approach towards her children was instinctively modern both in terms of refusing a traditional royal upbringing for them and in terms of integrating them into her public life, which later went as far as involving them in difficult charity work. Although her position was unique and extreme, Diana's situation and her hopes put her in touch with what many women were going through in that era; trying to combine motherhood with a public role. She too was a woman trying to break out of expectations and meet a number of different complex obligations. Her own father worried about the complexity of her life: "In my day, the royals only had one job a day. My Diana sometimes does two or three. She loves it, but I am worried she is working too hard."

Although the public saw she was close to her children and informal in her approach—as evidenced from the way she took William to Australia, the way she interacted with them in public—they were perhaps less aware of just how differently she was bringing them up and how much it mattered to her. Diana's public role was being forged in the context of an absolute preoccupation and protectiveness toward her children. "The children were her absolute priority," says Sam McKnight, her hairdresser. "The thing that mattered most to her was her sons. They were at the heart of her life and her absolute preoccupation was to give them as normal a life as possible. She saw her whole mission as being to prepare them for their future roles but she wanted that to be based on as normal a life as possible."

"Right from the start," says Jayne Fincher, "she seemed an extremely maternal person to me. She was a real mother hen with her own children. When she was with them, she couldn't stop touching them, cuddling them, and fluffing them about. You could always see the bond with the boys." What was also obvious to the royal press was that here was a person who had no intention to bring up her children in the traditional ways of the British royal family.

"'Normal' relationships for the royals are so formal," says Fincher. "It was obvious she wasn't going to have any of that. At the earliest photo calls with William—there was one at Kensington Palace and one in Australia a bit later when he was crawling—it was very hands-on. She was the one that was going to carry him out, on her hip; he wasn't going to be carried out by the nanny. As a photographer you noticed these things, just the way she couldn't take her eyes off them when she was with them.

"She was absolutely obsessed with protecting the boys from the press. In the early days, it was quite easy because they were too little to go to state occasions, like Trooping the Colour. They would give the odd photo call to take the pressure off and to stop paparazzi hanging around down at Highgrove and whatever. That worked quite well. It was when the boys started to go to school that things began to change a bit then, because she did not want the photographers hanging around. She wanted to be able to take them to school in the mornings without being photographed every day.

"Diana wanted them to go to schools in London with ordinary kids. Even the school—it was just a normal little school, nothing particularly grand—was just so different from what had gone for royalty before. She would drive them to school herself in the mornings in her jeans and her canvasses. It was a miracle that the press laid off but she had a very good press secretary at that point, Vic Chapman, whom all the photographers respected. He was very clever because he instilled this thing where if you break the rule, if you go down to that school and you take a picture, you will not be getting what I'm planning in three months' time. He did that sort of dangling the carrot the whole time.

"I do remember one day at school, when William was in the school play. He was very little, probably three and a half—and he came out with his school friends, all dressed up in their little nativity outfits. And there was this huge bank of photographers all on ladders. They've even got big coats and woolly hats. They look like a rabble and they've all got these big cameras. It's terrifying, anyway, let alone if you're a little tiny boy. And, of course, everyone was shouting out, 'William, William!' It must have been incredibly difficult for a child of that age to understand why they were all calling for him. I asked her once, 'What do you do about that?' 'Because she was very, very aware of this and was very worried about this with him. And she said she had had to say to him, 'You're going to go to school today, there's going to be all of these people who want to take your picture, and if you're a good boy and you let them take your picture, then I'll take you to Thorpe Park next week.'"

When the children were young, Diana often took them to polo on the weekend. "It was quite a laidback place and she just wanted them to go and play like normal little boys and run around and go and see the horses. She didn't want them with people running up and down after them. Vic Chapman managed to control it. Whenever the press did turn up it was very controlled, that's why you see it from very long lenses. . . . On the days when the children were there, we weren't allowed to go to the toilet, use the phone, go to the club house. You would be kept back at a distance so the boys didn't feel they were enclosed."

"I've been asked many times," says Ken Wharfe, who was initially a personal protection officer for the boys, before becoming Diana's bodyguard, "what I would choose if there was one thing I had to remember about the princess. And I always say it would be my memory of her influence over the children as a mother and her care of them, because it was one arena that she felt totally confident in. I suspect, right from the day they were born she knew 'this is the way I want these children to grow up.' They were still in a very privileged, fortunate position, they were not going to be re-housed in any local funded program, but given that, she did everything she could to give them a normal upbringing.

"The days were always set around taking William and Harry to school and, wherever possible, being home to pick them up. Or at least be in the house when they got back. Her day was exactly like many mothers of that social class. She'd arrive at school in the morning in a tracksuit, no make-up, drop the kid off, say, 'hello' to the other children. It was so relaxed. One of the other parents would say, 'Oh, William's coming 'round to us tomorrow night.' 'Oh, that's fine,' she'd say. So they would go off to his friend's. 'Oh, well, you must come back to us,' and they'd all come back to the nursery at some point, throw jelly at each other and have a fight behind the garden or go to High-grove. So there was this natural interchange of friends that was approved in its entirety by the princess because the prince chose to be elsewhere. Presumably he thought, 'Let the princess go and organize this side of their life, their schooling and so on.' And I think that the success of that is what we see in

William and Harry as young adults. I'm absolutely certain that that is why a lot of their friends now are the friends they met at prep school, through Eton and so forth.

"The reality of her life was so much more than this image of somebody performing on the royal circuit, shaking hands, and taking bunches of flowers. Here was somebody with this incredibly complex life, able to find time, with all these pressures, to take her children to school and be there for them. But also educate them in a way that was going to be of value to them in later life. For example there weren't any grand teas, there weren't these images of decorated butlers laying tables and high teas and neatly cut fingers of tomato sandwiches. They'd sit with their mother in front of the television with a bowl of beans on toast, or cheese on toast, or we'd go to the kitchen and just sit there and knock up something together. So the children would have this interaction with normal people. And so it was a great education to them, frowned upon, I might add, by the prince, I think, in those early stages. I don't think he'd like what he would deem as a familiarity. I think it was crucial to William and Harry for where they now find themselves.

"The whole William and Harry issue was crucial to her life in that she knew, through reputation and through hearing from Charles, I suppose, how he had been educated. And she was quite adamant that this wasn't going to be the case with William and Harry. They were going to have as near as normal schooling as possible. OK, they went to a pre-prep school and Wetherby and they went to Ludgrove and subsequently Eton, but so do many thousands of young men in that social class. And in my view her thinking is crucial to the survival of the monarchy that we see. She saw the success of her own brother in that style of education. I remember her mentioning that she always wanted William to go to Eton because her brother Charles went there. It was totally different from my education, but then I wasn't in that social niche. But it didn't stop me from thinking, well, actually it's quite right for them. Because, you know, whether we like it or not, the monarchy now has to appeal to the younger people of this country and it's William who will have to take that forward if it is to survive. The influence that Diana had is crucial to that. William is the first royal who has had as normal an education as possible, outside the old-fashioned system of, you know, private education, governors, governesses, or whatever. And that was strictly of her doing."

Diana's approach to mothering and integrating her children into her life was something that was noticed by most of the people she came in touch with. John Mayo from Help the Aged also noticed how, in spite of beginning to develop her role for the charity, in so many respects Diana's life was like that of any young mom. "The winter of 1987 was a very, very cold winter. And I was rung about seven o'clock one evening by her lady-in-waiting, to say, 'The princess would like to go and visit a day center to see how the old people are managing in this weather.' Anyway, she arrived at the Help the Aged offices about quarter past nine, in boots and jeans and a sweater and said, 'I've just taken the children to school,' and sat down on a desk swinging her legs up as she was briefed. And then we took her off to visit these day centers, and I think we went to three, and she chatted to all the old people, who were pretty miserable because it was so bitterly cold. And that evening we had a First Night in Leicester Square. I think the film was *Short Circuit*. And after the visit to the day centers, she went back to Kensington Palace, but LBC, the London Broadcasting Company, said to me, 'Do you think she'll do a broadcast about the visit she's made?' At half past three they rang and said she had done a recording, which was going out at five o'clock. So I listened at five o'clock, and the theme of her little interview was that old people need a bit of love, and the best thing you can do for old people at the moment is to give them a hug and warmth and make them feel they're wanted. It was brilliant, absolutely brilliant. But when she arrived at the Leicester Square thing, she said to me, 'Did you hear my broadcast?' And I said, 'Yes, it was absolutely brilliant.' She said, 'Are you being serious?' I said, 'Yes, it couldn't have been better, Ma'am.' And she said, 'Well, I couldn't hear it because I was bathing the boys.'"

Jean-Paul Claverie, advisor to the president of LVMH, the Moët Hennessy/Louis Vuitton group in Paris, who knew Diana well, says, "The main thing for her was that she wanted to protect the children against the weight of the system and the monarchy. She was very involved in preparing them to be princes. But she wanted to open them to the modern world, and to make them sensitive, to make them light with their life, familiar with life, and open to the problems of the other. Because she had a sad childhood, with the separation of her parents, and she suffered a lot with that. And it's the reason why she refused to divorce. In fact, she didn't want to divorce."

"One of the nice things about going to Kensington Palace if we had a meeting with her," says Roger Singleton, "was the general racing around of the kids and the normality of that. When you see these rather stylized photographs through films made about the royal family in the 1960s about how Prince Charles and Princess Anne were brought up, to have them racing around and taking a normal interest and hurtling sort of headlong into the door I always found very refreshing." Kay King describes how Diana occasionally dropped by to the Young England Kindergarten with her own boys, casually and unannounced, just as any other ex-nursery helper might do with her own young family. The only difference was that in Diana's case the visit was often even more casual than most. "Even when she came to see us, years later, I always remember her going in the kitchen and putting on the rubber gloves, she never minded that side of things at all."

❋ ❋ ❋ ❋

INTIMACY ~ Even at this demanding time of her life it was becoming obvious that Diana had a rare gift of friendship and concern for people she met from all backgrounds. "One of the most moving things that happened was we used to put on an annual event at the Savoy Hotel called 'Champion Children' which was a sort of competition for children who'd exceeded in the arts and ballet and we had a couple of categories, triumph over adversity and public service and so on," says Roger Singleton. "One of the young people who had triumphed over adversity was a young woman who was dying and in a wheelchair. When the time came for her to receive her award she wanted desperately to be able to walk on the platform and she did, at great cost. It was probably the last time she ever walked. As the princess left she took over her bouquet and gave it to this young woman. I was with the princess down in Wales about a fortnight later and I got a message to say that this young woman had died. I knew the princess had written to her in-between time and I muttered to a police officer who happened also to have been at the Savoy lunch that the young woman had died, and asked when we should tell the princess. He said, 'Let me tell her in the car between the two events because I think she'll be quite moved,' and apparently she was. She wrote to the girl's parents again personally afterward. One can speculate on what her motives might have been but the outcomes of those actions were wonderful for the people on the receiving end."

In 1986 Diana met Simon Barnes who, following an accident two years previously, was paraplegic. They became friends and remained in touch until she died. It was a friendship which said a lot both about Diana's capacity to transform acquaintances through her charity work into friendships and also

about how she was bringing up her own children. "Sir Jimmy Savile (who does a lot to support those with spinal injuries) was aware of a fund-raising event I was doing with a couple of friends, all of us in wheelchairs. We were going to push ourselves from John O'Groats to Land's End, to raise money for spinal research. Jimmy, having done it himself to raise funds, knew how great the challenge was and I think he was quite impressed by our determination and courage. So on our completion at Land's End we got a message: 'You have a special appointment in London in two days' time, so could you get on a train and get back to London as soon as possible.' We didn't know what it was at that stage; there were lots of things happening, media interviews and celebrations. It was an amazing time. We were told, 'Get your best kit on and get ready. Then we were driven in through the gates to Kensington Palace. We couldn't believe where we were going. We were taken into the garden and given Pimms, and then the princess and Prince Harry came out.

"Harry was only a toddler, and, of course, I don't think he'd ever seen wheelchairs before, so he was really intrigued by these three chaps and these wheelchairs. He wanted to get on my lap, so I gave him a kind of wheelie up and down the grass. Obviously, at that stage, we'd never met Diana before, and she was very much in the public eye. It was early days in her married life but she was as popular then as she'd ever been and, for us to suddenly find ourselves in this place, in such a relaxed atmosphere, was the icing on the cake, more than we could ever have wished for.

"When we were first introducing ourselves, three of us sat round in a semi-circle in front of her, and she said, 'My God, look at all these muscles, I'm surrounded by men with great big muscles.' Well, we were looking fit, and totally not what people normally expect when they get introduced to three wheelchair users. But it was a charming comment to go straight into something totally not related to our injuries. She was very much like that. She was aware of the differences but it wasn't something that she was scared of or avoided on purpose. She had a way of including it but not necessarily focusing on it. She asked questions about the logistics of our trip: How did you manage it, what were the good points, what were the low points. And, of course, some of our high points were the parties that were organized for us on the way down. There was one Young Farmers' group in Oxford that had been fund-raising for us and they had organized a disco for us one night. And we were presented with a check, but, the young farmers wanted to party. And we were meeting all these lovely people and loads of lovely girls, and there were all kinds of shenanigans there. So she really understood the kind of the characters we were. OK, a nasty accident happened to us, but we were really living life to the fullest."

A friendship developed between Simon and Diana. They kept in touch with letters and cards and he was invited many more times to lunch at Kensington Palace. He found her someone prepared to hear and understand about all aspects of spinal injury. "I was quite honest and frank with Diana about the detailed aspects of spinal injury; it's not just a question of being unable to walk. She was quite intrigued and said, 'What do you mean?' There's things like bowel, bladder, and sexual function which are lost, as well, and you're susceptible to pressure sores, the whole range of problems that come with being in a wheelchair, and not being able to feel or move the paralyzed parts of your body. And when I went into this explanation, she was quite inquisitive about, 'Well, can you still have children?' And she asked me a lot about relationships. We were quite frank with one another. But she was a consummate diplomat; she would always ask in a very polite way and could defuse the intensity of a question that might be upsetting or tricky for someone to deal with. It was always done in a very sensitive manner. But, nevertheless, it deserved an honest and forthright answer, because it was important to her to understand fully what paraplegia meant, all those kinds of things that were never really discussed anywhere or never really publicized in any literature, because it was always too difficult a situation to explain. So Diana had a natural interest in realizing the full extent of spinal cord injury, and I think that's why she became patron of the charity Spinal Research in 1990."

Simon was especially impressed by the way in which Diana was bringing up her sons both in how she integrated them into her life and the way in which she encouraged them to relate to disabilities. At one lunch Simon wanted to show her how he could stand up with the use of crutches. "I can stand up, using leg callipers, which stop my knee from flexing. They lock my legs out, so both legs are stiff and I can walk with crutches. I put the crutches down and lift those legs up and then swing them through, moving along like that. It's a bit precarious but it's nice to get up on your feet now and again. And she said, 'Oh, come on, Harry, William, you must meet the boys.' I think she was very keen for the lads to be exposed to different types of people, and they were really intrigued by the wheelchairs, but also how these callipers worked. So I went down the main stairs at Kensington Palace, which was a massive great big flight of stairs. And it was very slow, it's a very slow process, but they were quite fascinated as we were going down especially as the crutches have gas shock absorbers in them so they were kind of making all these funny noises. But, I remember thinking she wasn't saying, 'Come and look at these freaks.' It was more, 'Hey, I want you to meet some of my friends, and they're challenged in a different way than you and I are. Just look at how they cope and absorb some of the difficulties they're overcoming.' It seemed a very positive way of putting it. And, of course, putting Harry on my lap at three or whatever he was, just got him used to the idea that wheelchair people are fine, aren't they."

There can be little doubt that the complexities of Diana's life when she first met Simon were pretty formidable. Just the bare facts of trying to combine mothering with such demands for her to be in public might have been enough. But the particularities of her situation were extreme. Her natural instinct was towards informality and intimacy in both her charity work and her home life and this brought criticism of her from more traditional quarters, but at the time, Diana was struggling to come to terms and cope with these multiple demands and problems.

Diana had been plunged into the most extreme situation imaginable. "You've got to remember," says Tim Graham, "she was 19 at that stage, 19 or 20. It's not easy suddenly to go from someone who's not really known about at all, even though she was an aristocrat from one of the most famous families in the land." The intense scrutiny she was under from the press was taking its toll. Louise Chunn remembers the speculation about Diana's weight and also the ignorance of the speculation. "There was a lot of speculation at this time about why Diana was so thin and whether she was anorexic. Undoubtedly she was under great strain with the disillusionment in her marriage and the difficulties of adjusting to a new role, but her eating disorder was also a recognizable response to that terrible scrutiny which female celebrities are put under. We understand that process more clearly now and I think we'd be more sympathetic than people were then. Then there was a lot of prurient and ill-informed speculation. Nowadays we know much more that eating disorders can be the effect of being constantly photographed and shown in magazines. There you are driving along and you go past a magazine shop showing covers with pictures of you on it and you think—oh, God, look at my legs. Nowadays we see it with pop stars like Geri Halliwell. The effect of stardom—and all the scrutiny that goes with it—is to make you very thin. Because according to the

newspapers and celebrity magazines, the worst thing is to be fat. They say they are worried if someone is too thin, but what they show if they think someone is fat, is horror and disgust. The newspapers treat cellulite or flab as the ultimate crime and are very punitive towards anyone in the center of attention at all, plump or fat. I think we understand this process so much better now than we did when Diana was a young bride and thrust into all that attention."

Sam McKnight says: "She was a baby in this weird situation. I think what happened to her was something like what happened to the supermodels. They were all babies when I first met them, like confused little rabbits caught in the headlights, but having to deal with all this fame by themselves because it was a new phenomenon and there was no one there to guide them. It was a bit the same with Diana and that's why later I wanted her to meet them. I'm not in any way wanting to belittle her with that comparison but they all have had to struggle with controlling the power of their image you know. Actresses are different; they have to work for it. But models have it thrust upon them, it just happens to them and the camera loves them. Diana had it thrust on her because of the position she was in. But in spite of all that she was one of the most normal people I ever met in my life. She wore her heart on her sleeve a lot and she was very vulnerable. She was so open and because she was so open you could tell her anything. But it was great she talked about things. It must have helped a lot of people."

Looking back, Simon Barnes thinks one reason why they connected was because it was early days for both of them in struggling to come to terms with such life altering events. "My accident was on an army assault course. A lot of safety netting wasn't secured properly, but I didn't realize that at the time. I went through a motion and as a consequence came off and fell awkwardly, about 20 feet. That was in '84, so I'd had a couple of years of adjustment before meeting Diana but, even so, it was early days for me too.

"When we first met, obviously she was this very young and frightened mother of two. She was Princess of Wales. There was all the stuff going on in the background, and she was very thin at that time, as well. Now I look back, I realize that she alluded to her problems. She said to me once, over lunch, 'Oh, Simon, we're all brought up on fairy tales, and then one day, we come to realize that, painful as it is, these fairy tales aren't true.' She was very ambiguous with some of these things; she wouldn't come right out and say it. I think she was protecting me from it as well as being a bit circumspect. But again looking back over all these things, I think, 'Oh, my God, of course, your fairy tale was you met Prince Charming, where he's going to whisk you off your feet, and all of a sudden that turned into a rather bitter pill to swallow.'

"But she was quite philosophical about life because she mentioned things like: 'People think it might be really easy being the Princess of Wales but, in fact, it's quite hard, and being a mom, too.' It was almost like we were sharing our strengths, or gaining strength from one another, because she kind of explained the problems and pressures she faced and how she had to keep going because it was her duty. And I related to that and said things like, 'Well, you can either play the cards that are being handed out or you can chuck them in and quit and do nothing.' And we both agreed that you've got to keep just putting your best foot forward. She had a similar approach to life. Her attitude was: 'Yeah, the ship's gone down, but we've got to hold our heads up and enjoy the moment, live for the moment.' I think there was a bit of reciprocal encouragement and inspiration going on."

But Simon also noticed something else important. As time went by, Diana was growing in stature and significance, something that he most definitely attributes to her beginning to feel empowered by the effect she had on the people beyond the confines of her unhappy marriage and the court.

"Our relationship became much more friendly and relaxed as we went on and it was great to see this character, this friendly character I knew on the world stage, doing all of her things, and really starting to move forward. And then, of course, all her own battles started to become more public. But the strength that she demonstrated there was really quite something. Obviously, inside she was hurting, and it was very, very difficult for her. But she involved herself with people who had other difficulties in life, physical or mental disabilities, and I think her compassion grew through that kind of understanding of what suffering is. They say you reap what you sow and she gave a whole amount, just by taking time and being open-hearted with people. Her compassion flowed in situations that most other people didn't want to bother with or felt uncomfortable about. And I think she got a whole load of strength back and I think that helped her to move on. She was always a great inspiration to me because of her attitude to life and her compassion. She was just one of those people who are exciting and lift you up. She also had this wonderful energy that meant you came away feeling energized by spending time with her."

This perception of a confidence growing from her interactions with the wider public is something shared by other friends and colleagues. Friend Lucinda Hall says, "She was 'touchy-feely.' She was the first royal, wasn't she, to have that kind of physical contact with people. Diana's was a new way of doing things, and it worked incredibly well. I don't think she worked it out. I think she realized that's what people wanted and the good that she was doing must have given her huge confidence, early on."

Diana with a new touch, a new style, was bigger and massively more popular than anyone else: It ought to have been a cause of joy to the royal family, but it wasn't, either on a personal level or a public relations level. Roger Singleton noticed the complexity of what Diana was being confronted with and was relieved that she had the good advice and support of Anne Beckwith-Smith (her lady-in-waiting) to face this maze. "Anne would be the last person to say it, but she was an excellent source of support and guidance to someone who was new to the royal family, very much in the public gaze and having to cope with public embarrassments especially around the patently obvious fact that she was more popular than her husband. That would be hard enough in the mundane suburban life that most of us lead, but in the full glare of publicity with people drawing attention to it couldn't have been easy."

Later Diana described the dismay she felt when she realized her husband was jealous about the attention she was receiving. She felt "very uncomfortable" with the preference crowds expressed. "I felt it was unfair because I wanted to share." Nor was she flattered by the media attention. "Because with the media attention came a lot of jealousy. A great deal of complicated situations arose because of that." Whatever her husband felt, the genie was out of the bottle. Richard Stott, then editor of the *Daily Mail*, said, "They couldn't have bought the publicity they were getting and they loved that. But the problem with them was that they thought she was just going to be an adjunct to the royal family when in fact she was going to become it, and that was a problem for them."[11]

"When Diana first appeared on the scene," says Tim Graham who had photographed royalty for ten years before the royal wedding, "we didn't think of her appearance as a 'bonanza' or anything like that. We just thought, here's the girl that's going to marry the Prince of Wales and we'll be doing tours with the two of them. Nobody ever thought that she would turn into this massive worldwide, famous, iconic figure.

I don't think anybody really knew what she was supposed to do when she got married . . . She had to work out her own role, in relation to Prince Charles, too.

Lucinda Hall

The things that struck you about her were her youth—she was a very young lady—and her beauty, her vivacity, her joy of life.

Bob Hawke

There are many beautiful and stylish people in the world who are icons and movie stars and pop singers, but they don't always draw people from all walks of life to them in the way she did . . . she had a very sweet and generous heart and was very tactile. She wouldn't be loathe to touch or put her arms around somebody, especially children, and she would not have worried if her dress got greasy or crushed or crumpled. It would have been the last thing on her mind.   *Barbara Daly*

I started by giving greetings and introduced myself, then I asked for her name—all in British Sign Language. After a momentary hesitation, she greeted me and gave me her sign name in BSL. We then went on for two to three minutes conversing in BSL. She did it brilliantly. We were so proud to have witnessed that a princess could communicate in BSL . . .

Clark Denmark

The reality of her life was so much more than this image of somebody performing on the royal circuit, shaking hands and taking bunches of flowers. Here was somebody with this incredibly complex life, able to find time, with all these pressures, to take her children to school and be there for them. But also educate them in a way that was going to be of value to them in later life.

Ken Wharfe

I loved the fact that she was hard working and she gave me some great pictures, she gave me some great laughs. . . . I was in Tokyo with her once and we were looking at a car—a Honda-McLaren racing car. . . . I remember that she'd just been stopped for speeding before we left and I said to her, 'I'll never catch you in that, Ma'am, on the M4.' And she said, 'I'll tell the jokes, Arthur.' . . . She was like that, full of quips.   *Arthur Edwards*

The children were her absolute priority. The thing that mattered most to her was her sons. They were at the heart of her life and her absolute preoccupation was to give them as normal a life as possible. She saw her whole mission as being to prepare them for their future roles but she wanted that to be based on as normal a life as possible.

Sam McKnight

She had the capacity to say the right thing to people. If they had a sense of humor she would make them laugh, if they were incredibly shy they would lose the shyness.

Lady Sarah McCorquodale

D

9.9.90.

Dear Simon,

It was lovely to
get your letter & hear all your
news!
I'd so love it if there was a
chance of you, Danny & Chris

coming here to lunch & I
wondered if you could suggest
some dates which might find
the three of you in the big
city?
I look forward to hearing from
you & a big thank you for your
letter. ☺
Yours sincerely, Diana.

D

June: 16th
1992.

Dear Simon & Chris,

Thank you both
so much for writing to
me - the contents of
your letter brought a
great deal of comfort
& I did want you both

to know that . . . .
I value your support
enormously & thank you
from the bottom of my
heart for your concern.
With my best wishes
as always.

From.
Diana.

86

CHAPTER THREE – THE EXTRAORDINARY

"It is not easy being forever in the public eye," Diana, Princess of Wales once said to me. "But it does help you do things," and here she smiled, "or get others to do them for you!"

These sentiments were true and the princess was prepared always to use her public persona to throw a spotlight on hardship and help alleviate it. She had that rare gift of instant rapport with those in need or in pain and her sympathy for them never failed to warm their hearts nor, I suspect, to comfort her own. Frequently, when we spoke, our conversation turned to Princes William and Harry: "I am joined to them at the hip," she would say. She spoke of her charities too: "It is what I am for." This compassion is also, for untold millions, how she will be remembered.

John Major, former UK Prime Minister

In November 1985, on her first official visit to the United States, Diana danced with John Travolta at a White House dinner. As commentators at the time remarked, 'Saturday Night Fever' broke out. The occasion highlighted just how big an international figure Diana had become. In an era when the notion of celebrity took off, Diana was more glamorous than the stars of *Dynasty* or *Dallas*, better dressed than the most fashion obsessed, as beautiful as the super-models and with the added glamour of an incomparable status: She was a princess. No other face on the front page sold papers like Diana's.

This public profile was clear to see on the foreign trips Diana under-took, mainly in the company of her husband, in the years after Harry's birth. Together they visited numerous countries including Nigeria, Thailand, the Gulf States, Italy, France, Spain, Japan, and Hungary. The media followed her everywhere. Wherever Diana went, officials, government ministers, royalty, and the public fell under her spell. Back home, many people recognized that Diana's appeal was the best thing that had happened to the UK in years. At the time most people believed she was an asset as part of a royal couple. Unknown to the vast majority, however, Diana was painfully coming to terms with her unhappy marriage. "She was our greatest royal personality since Queen Victoria. She could have been the most valuable," said the columnist Paul Johnson. "Properly helped and guided, Diana's extraordinary combination of gifts could have transformed the relationship between royalty and the public, deepening and strengthening it and making it almost invulnerable."[1]

At the very moment Diana was growing into this public persona, her marriage was disintegrating. It was becoming clear that it could not be saved. Hints at this only increased the public's fascination, although the idea of a royal divorce was then so utterly shocking that it took even the most atten-tive royal watchers a long time to admit that the unthinkable was happening. Only when Diana herself used the conduit of author Andrew Morton to tell the world what was really happening within her marriage in 1992, in his book *Diana: Her True Story*, did the public finally realize what was going on.

It was during this personally painful time that the foundations were laid for the subsequent emergence of Diana, the humanitarian. By the time of her death Diana had undergone a remarkable transformation. But the woman who walked out onto the minefields of Angola forcing the world to pay attention didn't take up this cause on a whim, casually advised by her latest guru as some versions of her story like to suggest. It was the end of a process of evolution.

The story of this evolution is not well known, still less understood. In fact while the royal marriage was unraveling, Diana's involvement with charity work and various organizations, her "job" as she called it, was intensi-fying. Most of the charities noticed a change from the shy and dutiful young woman to a more confident person, who was overcoming her inhibitions about public speaking and taking on some surprisingly radical causes. Many also noticed extraordinary qualities in her interactions with the people she met through the charities. They saw a connection with the public that bypassed the establishment and, to some extent, the media, and which would underlay the extraordinary outpouring of grief when she died.

However lacking in formal education, Diana, alone of the royal family, seemed to understand that this rapport with the public was something to which a modern monarchy should aspire. According to former editor of *The Times* William Rees-Mogg, the period between the mid-1980s and the publication of Andrew Morton's book in 1992 was "one in which Diana was becoming increasingly effective with the public and increasingly aware of issues about the future of the monarchy, but the cooling of the marriage and the eventual divorce were undermining her position. Some conservative

courtiers were relieved when the divorce actually occurred; they regarded her as an uncontrollable 'loose cannon.' They would not accept that their attitude was already out of date, and that she had a better instinct for public opinion, on which all monarchs ultimately depend."[2]

❋ ❋ ❋ ❋

WORLD'S MOST GLAMOROUS WOMAN ~ By the mid-1980s the journalists and photographers who now followed Diana everywhere had woken up to just how big a phenomenon she was. It wasn't just her looks, but her personality, too. However she was feeling, she dressed impeccably, delivered dazzling smiles, and was often warm and witty. "There was never any question of whether or not we would cover the trips," says royal photographer Tim Graham. "She was the one; there was no question. I don't think I will ever, in the rest of my career, photograph someone who became such a massive personality. She was very lively. Whether she met a president, another royal, or a kid in the street, she always had a giggle or a little aside that made her very easy to get on with, and that was part of her success."

"For 17 years," says royal photographer Arthur Edwards, "she was the only member of the royal family that mattered. Even in jeans and an old shirt or a jumper she looked great. She had the figure of a supermodel and she made any dress look fantastic."

"I would go on any engagement that she did, anywhere, frankly, because it made copy," says Richard Kay, royal correspondent for the *Daily Mail*. "All the papers loved it. She always had the knack of saying something interesting that was revealing about herself or her position on these engage-ments. In terms of Charles and Diana it was always Diana, not Charles, that we wrote about." Prophetically, *Time* magazine reported one member of the press saying to Diana, "You didn't realize you were married to us too, did you?"

"Diana was huge news," says the former BBC royal correspondent Jennie Bond. "We'd go on a tour with Prince Charles; there might be 20 journalists. You go with Diana, there'd be double because she was beautiful, she was controversial and she'd provide a brilliant picture opportunity. She wouldn't just walk past a row of disabled kids; she'd probably crouch down on the ground and touch their knees, their faces. You'd get glamour, a great pic-ture and often a bit of controversy as well. Parallel to everything she did was the question: what was the state of the marriage? There was always another reason for the press being there. Charles will joke and, in his own way, he's quite fun too. But Diana was a star, because of her looks, her glamour and people's reaction to her. They would be gasping and saying: 'Diana!' They would be in a state of hysteria."

Even other celebrities were bowled over. "If Diana walked into the room," says Sir Cliff Richard, "you wanted to sidle alongside and talk to her, you were drawn to her, she didn't have to do anything. There are various people who have charisma; some of it only comes to life when they're in performance mode, some of it is just there. But Diana was one of these people that quietly just had a way about her that attracted people. It attracted every-body, the camera included. And it wasn't just the fact that she was beautiful, though that does help, of course. As we all know, beauty is only really skin-deep unless there is something else that is also exuding"

"I was awe-struck by Princess Diana, like everybody else," says singer Chris de Burgh, who met her first in the early 1980s. "She had a gift. It's a rare thing, but I have seen it occasionally among very famous people. They carry an aura about them. When they have left the room everybody just looks at each other and goes, 'Wow.' It is very rare. Nelson Mandela would obviously be such a person. It's an aura that creates warmth, a love, and affection and it's a really extraordinary thing to encounter. She had this innate understanding of what it meant to be a star and she used it in a generous way. There were people who—you saw when she died—really believed in this woman. She had the ability to walk in and make them feel that they were special in her life, not just the other way around."

In France it was Diana who was the big attraction. On her first official visit there in November 1988, the crowds were adulatory and the then mayor of Paris, Jacques Chirac, raved about her blue eyes. On a later visit, President Mitterand also fell under her spell. "It was remarkable that at this moment, she was more in the forefront of the media than Charles," says Jean-Paul Claverie, then in culture minister Jacques Lang's office. "We had many photographers from *Paris Match*, and from international agencies, but it was Diana who interested the media. We felt it strongly at the Elysée Palace with President Mitterrand, because she was so beautiful." The royal couple also visited Hungary. "Prince Charles did a little speech in the University of Economics," said Arpad Gonz, Hungary's president. "In the hall was the statue of Karl Marx. Lady Di was seated at the feet of Karl Marx. Karl Marx was looking down on her, which was very nice, because I'm absolutely sure that in his life Karl Marx had never seen such a nice lady, as pretty a lady as Lady Di was."[3]

On the trips to Pakistan and India, witnesses said the whole country seemed to be on the streets. "She was extremely glamorous by any standards and therefore people wanted to see her," says Sandy Gall, whose charity, Sandy Gall's Afghanistan Appeal, runs a project on the borders of Afghanistan, visited by Diana in 1991. "The visit to Pakistan in 1991 proved an outstanding success," says Sir Nicholas Barrington, then British ambassador there. "The princess shook hundreds of hands and looked like everyone's ideal of a fairy-book princess, but she made a special impact when she showed her caring side. I remember in particular visits to two schools, one for deaf children, to a family planning clinic and a college for girls, and to a hospital ward with people debilitated by drugs. Also the visit the princess made to the Sandy Gall prosthetics clinic in Peshawar. In each case the princess created an immediate rapport with the children, or those suffering. She squatted down beside small children in the classroom—astonishing their teachers!—and sat on the beds of the invalids.

"With the press following her every move in an unfamiliar Islamic environment, it must all have been quite a strain. She did her duty in making speeches, talking to politicians, and businessmen and visiting local antiquities and fine scenery, but she showed most interest in people, and this was appreciated. The Pakistan public was attracted by her glamour and her royal connection, but also by her reputation as someone who genuinely cared about people. Thousands stood in the streets to watch her drive by. The visit was a great boost to British relations with Pakistan."

In Japan too, she was adored. "You know, I have traveled and seen many people who are important and great campaigners," says Tokuo Kassai, president of the Japanese company Aprica. "However, she was when I met her absolutely beyond my imagination, charming to the ultimate. I don't think there will be anybody in this 21st century that will come equal or close to her level of charisma. She was well above everybody else."

✳ ✳ ✳ ✳

BEHIND THE SCENES ~ In 1989, Diana's sister, Lady Sarah McCorquodale, started acting as a lady-in-waiting and began to see first hand the roller-coaster existence of Diana's public life. The first occasion was a baptism by fire. "My first unofficial lady-in-waiting duty was September 1989 when she came to present the prizes at the European Championships at Burghley near Stamford. Unfortunately the plane broke down and she had to drive. So I was left at Burghley, first time ever as a lady-in-waiting, six months pregnant, pretending not to be pregnant, and she's somewhere in Gloucestershire. People were desperate to do things because they wanted to fill up their time while we were waiting for her, so I made them all chicken sandwiches and felt very pleased with myself. But nobody ate them except me. It was a shocking introduction to troubleshooting as a lady-in-waiting.

"Usually there were two or three ladies-in-waiting at a time. It wasn't a full-time job, those with children did it for two or three days a week; others, without children, might do longer stretches or the foreign trips. I was only an extra lady-in-waiting, which meant that I didn't have to do any office work. The private secretary would set it all up and then produce a printed schedule of what you were doing throughout the day. A lady-in-waiting is usually there to do all the little things, such as taking the bouquets, and making sure everything runs smoothly on public occasions. I always preferred the French term: 'dame d'honneur.' As a lady-in-waiting you're sort of second-guessing—do I need to be here? Do I need to be there? Does she want to get rid of those flowers now, or should I hang on to them? You have to think intensively all the time about organizing everything.

"The visits I obviously remember the best were the foreign trips: Hungary, Nepal, Zimbabwe, and dinner, bed and breakfast in New York—the Christian Dior show there was amazing. But we did quite a lot within England. We did Warrington, Bolton, Leicester—all the glamorous jobs! In England, the day would be made up of four or five visits, mainly charities. You would meet what Diana called the 'chain gang' first: the lord mayor, the dignitaries, the lord lieutenant, and the high sheriff, who were your hosts for the day, and I think they basically made the day up. They would write in and say these things and you would put them all together and make a day of it."

According to her sister, Diana "got a real high from visiting these places. These days used to be very complicated. You'd be in some civic center at 11 o'clock and you'd be in some AIDS drop-in center, or whatever, at three o'clock, and I think the contrast was amazing. It certainly was for a lady-in-waiting. And then by the end of the day, you were exhausted. Everything hurt. Your brain was pounding away. There's no doubt she found this work satisfying. She loved it. It's the same, in a way, as my father. She made a connection with people and got a real buzz from the days, although they wore her out.

"The day took from her. She was a giver. In a tactile way she gave. Emotionally she gave. She gave in every sense of the word. And people were like sponges. They soaked it up. So when she went out of the room, went out of a building, these people were left on a high. She dispensed hope, happiness, whatever you like to define it as. I was always two yards behind. And after she'd gone, people were just gob-smacked.

"The bulk of the work I did for her was when she separated from Prince Charles, and she couldn't go out in the evenings then—she couldn't do anything. So she often had a TV dinner. She always went to bed quite early anyway, and got up early, but her day had usually been full and she was tired.

"Often after a particularly harrowing visit, she would climb back into the helicopter and start joking. Some people have criticized her for this. But it's the only way to get through a day when you have held a baby in your arms that you knew wasn't going to be there in a week's time. The only way to cope with this is to make a bad joke. It's sort of a survival thing. If you've had a day of hospices how else do you cope? By doing something like getting in a helicopter and saying, 'Have you heard the one about . . . ?' It's a form of making sure you survive really, isn't it? If you've given so much, you've got to have a cut-off. When she got back into the helicopter or the car and made a bad joke, it was her way of saying, 'Right, normality starts again now. I don't want to talk about what I've just seen.'

"The trips I did with her made you either cry or laugh and there was very little in between. You either laughed with relief or happiness, or this lump in your throat sat there, and you just felt humble and lucky. I think the first overseas trip I did was Hungary in March 1992. I'd never been to Hungary before. It was a fantastic trip. We were in and around the city to start with and then we went out to the refugee camps on the border, and the number of people and the squalor in which they were living was incredible. But they were happier to be there together as a family unit than to be in their homes and liable to not make it."

Back home, Diana was patron of the National Institute for Conductive Education, which used some of the pioneering techniques of the Hungarian Peto Institute with children with cerebral palsy. At the time of her visit several families from Birmingham were staying there. Lady Sarah McCorquodale remembers: "We went straight to the Peto Institute from the airport. It was real lump-in-the-throat stuff; you wanted to help them. It seemed quite cruel because it's quite tough, but the parents of the children that were there were very supportive of what was going on. It was a joint trip, but I don't think Charles came to that. They flew out together, did different things."

As always, laughter was never very far away with Diana, especially together with her sister. "We were both very keen on a type of Hungarian porcelain and before we went someone told us that if you liked a piece you should look under it for the numbers and mark. Sure enough, we went to a formal meeting with all the top officials and they put out this lovely coffee set and we spent the whole meeting trying to get to look at the bottom of the cups. We tried to look under our own and under each other's and we just had a fit of the giggles. I also went with her to Nepal. That was an incredible trip too. On the first night in Kathmandu, the crown prince—the one who later murdered his family—turned up in a fast car and took her for a spin around the town. She didn't think he was mad; she said she felt sorry for him.

"We did have a wonderful role reversal once. She came to stay when I was presenting some prizes locally at a golf club for the Mental Health Foundation, which I had done every summer for 12 years. She asked if she could come; she'd like to see how the other half worked. So across we went, and they were absolutely stunned, but there was a big problem because a lot of clubs have this weird rule about not being allowed to wear jeans. She was wearing jeans, mind you they were wonderful jeans, and she had a very smart jacket on but they were jeans. They took the view that they wouldn't bother too much on this occasion, given who she was and she sat there and watched me presenting the prizes."

❈ ❈ ❈ ❈

FROM GLAMOUR TO REALITY ~ As Diana emerged from shy girl to superstar she seemed more than ready to lend this glamour to help charities raise money and their profile. "Just tell me how I can help you," was her most common request to her charities and many recognized the significant impact she could have on incomes. "If she was prepared to turn up to a lunch or a ball or an event, you could just about double the price of the tickets and be

guaranteed that it would be a sell out, and she knew that,'" says Barnardo's chief executive, Roger Singleton.

Diana took these responsibilities toward the public very seriously and always turned out looking immaculate. The effect as many of the charities noted was like having been at a show. Hereward Harrison, director of ChildLine, noticed: "She was very visual but it wasn't just visual. Her presence was enormous. The car, the arrival, I mean it was a royal event. Her physical presence was enormous and she was a very beautiful woman and tall. But along with the physical were the verbal and the intuitive. It was a combination effect." "She had a 'princess aura about her," says Professor Malcolm Green of the British Lung Foundation. "One of the things that amazed me is that despite the trauma that was clearly going on in her personal life, throughout all this time, she always looked absolutely stunning, completely wonderful." The public adored it when Diana turned up looking as dazzling as a fantasy princess. Elaine Phillips, a hospital worker in Walsall, saw Diana twice and was delighted by the new glamour. "When I first saw her she hadn't long been married. Her dress was red and white spotted and she looked rather old-fashioned for a young girl. Then when she came to our hospital she was completely different. She looked wonderful that day, she really did."

This glamour and performance took work and no one worked harder on it than Catherine Walker, who designed many of Diana's dresses through this period. She was a designer highly attuned to royal performance and the need for appropriate symbolism. "In the early '80s Diana's designs had to be more elaborate. It felt as though she needed a sort of royal uniform that was a legacy from 18th century court dressing. Her designs could not be simple. Later on this changed and I worked on a look that was more pared down and less elaborate, and one that was beautiful from all angles." When Walker designed for the trips abroad she says, "Always there had to be the formality that set the princess apart from the crowds and showed her respect for the country in question such as little emblems incorporated into the embroidery. The research was often an education in itself. I was learning all sorts of things about Japanese colors for mourning, Czech folk costume, Indian marquetry, Indonesian flowers, Nigerian batik prints, and even what braids represented which rank in foreign military uniform."[4]

"Diana was very clever," says Barbara Daly, the make-up artist who did Diana's make-up on her wedding day. "She was growing to find her own style and she also knew people were very interested in the way she was going to present herself and that would actually get people alert and looking at anything she was interested in. She wasn't about to turn up not looking at her professional best, because if you are out there doing your job you have to make sure you look right for the part."

But while the performance took work, it is clear that Diana never saw the dressing and performance as an end in itself. Her clothes both did and did not matter to her, says designer Jacques Azagury. "Her looks were important to her. She always liked to look good because she knew it would make people happy. People just used to wait to see the princess, whether she was opening a new charity or going to an old peoples' home, to see what she was going to wear, how she was going to look, what her hair was going to look like. That was all part of being a princess. Perhaps it sounds shallow, but behind it, her intentions were to do the best for the charity."

"She was a star," says Esther Rantzen of ChildLine, "and stars are different from the rest of us. She had that instinct for communication—not only with children, but also with the public. She came to ChildLine and did all the photographs that we asked her to do and then there were about 500 postmen all gathered to wave to her because we were in post office premises. She said to me, 'I'll get into awful trouble if I don't say hello,' and she went over to the post room and they threw their hats in the air and that was the picture that got on all the front pages. She was, in that sense, almost like the most consummate artist. Michael Grade [a businessman] once said to me the royal family was expecting the Duchess of Gloucester and they got Judy Garland. And there was something in it, because when you get a star, you get the temperament, the personality, the skills and the volatility. But from that whatever it is—nervous tension, adrenaline—you also get a consummate performance."

Many of the charities with which Diana was involved had not previously experienced this kind of fund-raising and were amazed at the effect. "Several events which Diana did for Turning Point (a charity working in the areas of drug and alcohol misuse, mental health and learning disability) raised £100,000 each, a considerable amount for us at that time," says Wendy Thomson, formerly of Turning Point. "She did lots of film previews for us like *Jurassic Park* and *Apollo 13* and we would get our clients to staff them because they were so much fun. Those glitzy things made us a lot of money."

The late Reverend Tony Lloyd, former executive director at The Leprosy Mission, was astonished and delighted at the way Diana used her charm to raise funds for them. As with many other causes she would often host occasions where she would bring together wealthy individuals to meet deserving causes. She could also be completely upfront in fund-raising. On one occasion The Leprosy Mission held a fund-raising dinner in Hong Kong, hosted by David Tang. "I gave a presentation and then we set the princess on these people. She was very straightforward and demanding. She didn't pussyfoot around," says Tony Lloyd. But he was impressed by the way Diana combined this financial acumen with fun. "After the meal, first one woman, then another, then everybody wanted their photos taken with her. I thought she might object but she was saying, 'Oh, let them all come in. We will have photographs all over the place.' So she turned the occasion into fun."

Some of the charities raised staggering amounts through Diana's presence. John Young, Chairman of Young's Brewery, recruited her as patron of the National Hospital for Nervous Diseases and immediately put her to work. "I was extremely lucky there, because she absolutely waded into it, and, in fact, in the first 18 months, we did 18 engagements, and raised between us nine million, then 12 million and then 15 million pounds, so it wasn't bad, was it?" Some charities of which she was patron mainly saw her as a source of fund-raising, something about which Diana had few illusions, and would gradually became more critical of. "The princess," says her former private secretary Patrick Jephson, "recognized that so much charity income depends on people who are maybe quite egocentric, so she recognized that part of her job was delivering those people to her patronages who were staffed without exception with people who knew how to spend a million pounds for the benefit of others but didn't always know how to make it." On one occasion Diana whispered to Patrick: "They would tip their money in the bin if I asked them to."

The charities Diana developed the closest working relationships with were those which delighted in a patron who moved effortlessly between earning them huge amounts of money on glamorous occasions, but also had immense private skills. Colonel John Mayo at Help the Aged loved the fact that the woman who dazzled at galas was just as happy in nursing homes chatting to the residents. "We did a number of glitzy things, like the preview of *Phantom of the Opera* when Pall Mall, Regent Street and St James's Street were totally closed for that evening, heaven only knows how we achieved it. We had buskers outside in Victorian costumes in the alleyway behind the theater, and it really was a great evening, which she absolutely loved. I think she saw *Phantom of the Opera* about another six times after that. So there were the two extremes,

visiting very poor day centers in different parts of the country, and the glitzy first night events that enabled us to raise immense amounts of money."

When Diana first became involved with Great Ormond Street Hospital for Children jointly launching the Wishing Well appeal with Prince Charles, the charity not only hit but also exceeded its targets well before the deadline. Afterward, however, the hospital rarely used her again for direct fund-raising. Instead she was seen as someone who could make an unparalleled contribution to the morale of people working with sick children. Former chief executive Sir Anthony Tippett is clear that this contribution was just as important as the millions. "She gave the hospital tremendous uplifts year on year. Great Ormond Street was a place of great contrasts—great joy and great sadness. Some of the treatments were difficult for the children and some of the children were not going to recover. There were fewer people in the country more expert in their field than the staff at Great Ormond Street was, and fewer people on whom more demand was being made. Against that background anybody who could lift morale made a huge contribution to the hospital, and she was ace among them. When the Queen comes she gives that sort of lift, but she isn't the bended knee that Diana always was. She always left the hospital in a better place than when she'd entered it, because of this lift she gave people."

In the mid-1980s much of the world's attention was on Diana's dresses. The addition of Sarah Ferguson to the royal family in 1986 with her eagerness to recruit Diana to her more frivolous lifestyle added to the impression of a lightweight. But those who met Diana through charity work noticed something different. After Harry's birth she was working very hard, doing three or four days a week with the charities. Her expectations were changing too. "What Diana wanted from her charities was increasingly something emotionally rewarding, something that she could deal with, something that tested her," says Patrick Jephson. "She went away from the fluffy end and more and more towards the gritty end. In 1987 when I first met her she would do what we used to call an away day, she'd do a short engagement and a long engagement. A few years later we were doing five or six engagements in a day, and she was really committing herself to it, making huge emotional and physical investments in her work which is one reason why it made it so exhausting for her and one reason in 1993 she took the option of saying she was going to step back from it."

Roger Singleton of Barnardo's says in the early years Diana was learning about life as a member of the royal family, as a young mother, and as a public celebrity. "Then she seemed to move on to a new life as a sort of fashion person. No doubt all that gave great satisfaction—I'm sure the princess loved clothes—but the fashion icon bit was only one side. She was increasingly prepared to speak out on issues that were important to the organizations she was involved with."

Peter Bowring, then chairman at Help the Aged, also saw a development: "She never lost her charm, ever, in fact it grew, but she also became more aware of the importance of what she was doing. There was no doubt that she was becoming more and more deeply involved. She was absolutely incredible. Once her lady-in-waiting said to me how extraordinary it was, the amount of work she had taken on and the conscientiousness with which she did it. She was definitely maturing in this particular role. I saw her taking more and more of a general interest in everything that was going on. She was thoroughly intelligent and interested in the things she was doing, and asked splendidly appropriate questions."

"When we first met her she appeared rather shy and retiring with not much to say," says Les Rudd ex-chief executive of Turning Point, which later became a favorite of Diana's. "Over time, she became very well informed about what we were dealing with. Obviously we'd give her briefings and she would have met various experts in the field, so she would have been able to test out some of the information we gave her. We introduced her to the head of the world AIDS program from the World Health Organization, for example, at Kensington Palace and that informed quite a lot of the things she did subsequently when she became a real standard-bearer, for the work on HIV and AIDS."

Some of those involved with the charities noticed Diana was beginning to ask questions about deeper causes and to make links between the different charities she was involved with. "Her understanding of homelessness evolved from a very sympathetic knee-jerk response of 'these kids are sleeping rough and need to be indoors' into understanding the complexity of what leads people to that point," says Mark McGreevy, chief executive of the home-less charity the Depaul Trust. "You start to think there should be provision for drugs and alcohol treatment and there should be other things and I wonder whether that chased her into thinking about other areas she needed to get involved in."

Ken Wharfe who, as her personal protection officer, saw all aspects of Diana's life, and accompanied her to women's hostels and high security prisons, also witnessed a progression. "Once she came to trust the charities and understand their issues she began to make a big contribution, far more than the royal handshake of old. She worked incredibly hard and if she could have slotted more charities in would have done so. People like David French of Relate, Roger Singleton of Barnardo's, and Mike Whitlam of the Red Cross were key players in her life, people that she trusted, people not fazed by her position. They didn't just see her as a figurehead. They valued her input. And once she felt trusted she actually had some very good suggestions and very good ideas."

❋ ❋ ❋ ❋

HIV/AIDS ~ It was in 1987 that the wider world woke up to the fact that Diana's approach to charity might have far greater reverberations. "At the beginning," says royal photographer Jayne Fincher, "the papers were more interested in what she had on than what she was doing. It wasn't really until we saw the start of the AIDS things that we really began to notice the issues." "She began to use the power of her image," says Tim Graham.

Diana was 26 when she was photographed shaking the hand of an AIDS patient. Hard though it may be to believe now, this simple gesture from a young woman was her answer to the question she had begun to ask herself: "How do I make a difference?" "HIV and AIDS have come such a long way in the past 20 years," says Derek Bodell, director of the National AIDS Trust. "It's hard to remember in the mid-1980s that people wouldn't touch anyone with HIV. People were frightened about being infected from toilet seats or sharing cutlery, or even being in the same room. The fact that Princess Diana actually touched someone with HIV, but more than that, touched him without gloves, was very, very significant. This social gesture made such a huge difference, and you couldn't buy publicity like that." David Harvey of the Washington-based AIDS Alliance for Children, Youth and Families agrees: "Here was the world's most famous woman embracing AIDS with one simple act . . . and with that handshake, she educated the world about compassion, love, and understanding."[5]

Diana's involvement with HIV/AIDS is always dated from that moment, but it came as no surprise to her family. Robert Spencer, her father's

cousin, suggests she was interested in the problem of AIDS as early as 1984. "When I saw her here [in the UK] just after Harry was born—and that was a couple of years before the famous handshake—she did discuss AIDS with me. I was involved with the Red Cross and other activities in Florida, and I can remember her asking interesting questions. From the beginning she realized this was something that needed concern because at the time people were pretty hostile." Diana almost certainly had some experience of the suffering caused by AIDS first hand. In 1986, Stephen Barry, who had served as a valet to Prince Charles, died of AIDS and Diana's involvement with the world of performers meant she came across other AIDS sufferers including her ballet friend, Adrian Ward Jackson.

Diana's brother, Charles Spencer, believes "she knew instinctively" that these difficult issues previously untouched by royalty were areas where she could make an impact. "She knew that by doing relatively little, like holding a man's hand who's dying of AIDS, you can change the perception of the west-ern world, as she was keen to do then. It was a very simple thing for her to do and she did it beautifully." Her mother says, "She inherited from her father a great in-depth knowledge of medicine so she knew her facts, she knew exactly what was infectious, what wasn't, what was true, and what was untrue. And she exposed it. That was bold. With things like AIDS and some of these other medical kind of areas, I guess like leprosy as well, she knew about touching, about whom she could touch safely. The papers called it manipulation, but, in fact, it's using your advantage to display something which she felt should be known. [Touching people with AIDS] came to her naturally, but when she read about the effect her actions were having, she realized the deeper signifi-cance. She knew what she was doing. We talked about it."

It was at Middlesex Hospital in 1987 at the opening of the first UK AIDS ward that Diana shook the hands of an AIDS patient, a simple gesture with remarkable consequences. Professor Mike Adler, the doctor in charge of the ward, says, "A letter was written to the palace asking whether a member of the royal family would be prepared to open the ward, and I think we actually expressed a preference for Prince Charles. We got a letter back saying no, but would we consider the Princess of Wales? We jumped at it. On the day she was very nervous and we were very nervous. We had been crawled over for weeks by the media and the palace. But the moment she started meeting the patients she did relax and then there was that very famous photo of her shaking hands with a patient who had AIDS and that was wired all over the world. It made a tremendous impact."

"There was the huge fuss about her not wearing gloves," says Baroness Jay, a founder director of the National AIDS Trust, "and the fact that she didn't and that the world's media took it up was incredibly important. [That handshake] was the moment when we realized the power she had to influence public perceptions and she wasn't even at the height of her power then. We recognized then that she might be someone prepared to do these more marginal things."

The press, so instrumental in transmitting this simple deed across the world, was itself in awe. Many acknowledge they were no different from the vast majority at the time, unsure about this terrifying illness being presented as a new plague. Richard Kay was at the Middlesex Hospital that day. "She had this incredible following around the world, but that was largely because of her beauty, her fashion, and because she was physically unlike other members of the House of Windsor. But she wasn't particularly involved in the early to mid-1980s in any particular charities beyond those normally associated with royal princesses, nothing controversial. The royals shied away from that." The handshake took them by surprise. "None of the press was expecting it. AIDS then was characterized in a lot of the press as the 'Gay Plague.' You could almost feel the taboos being broken. I think of myself as a reasonably liberal, open-minded person, but nonetheless, I was pretty amazed. It's easy to think now: 'It was just a handshake,' but God, it was an amazing handshake. I know it's a terrible cliché but it was a ground-breaking moment and when people write about what made Diana what she was, that moment was one of the building blocks."

"I was absolutely amazed," says photographer Arthur Edwards, "because up to then AIDS was a really bad word. The following day the pictures were all over every paper: Diana with these AIDS patients. She chatted to them, joked with them, and generally made them feel good. This was her magic. People were amazed to realize this wasn't a disease you ran away from; it was perfectly safe. And she was going against all the advice from the old guard at Buckingham Palace. I believe she single-handedly took the stigma out of AIDS."

Even had Diana's contribution been limited to that one gesture it would have been significant, but the handshake was no flash in the pan. Diana's involvement in AIDS evolved and remained an integral part of her life. Over and over again she would come back to a simple but necessary point: "HIV," she said, "doesn't make people dangerous to know, so you can shake their hands and give them a hug." She stuck with AIDS charities even when their politics became more complex in the 1990s. Indeed, half the proceeds of the $5.6 million raised by auctioning her dresses in the last year of her life went to AIDS charities. Many of her other charity interests intersected around AIDS, principally those concerned with drug addiction and homelessness. Professor Adler believes her whole involvement with AIDS was crucial in shattering the taboos. "People did not like the whole ambience. It was seen to be mainly occurring among gay men and it involved sex, all the things we are not good at handling but she actually cut through that. She gave it respectability and a profile."

Baroness Jay noticed a definite evolution. "The National AIDS Trust invited her to be a patron in 1989 and at that stage she was a bit shy. But she was not visibly shocked and that was very important for AIDS issues. At first she didn't speak much publicly, just very chatty and friendly at meetings, but then she started making speeches and that was enormously important. She was very good at conveying the impression that something was completely straightforward. And of course she was absolutely invaluable for fund-raising. Her intervention on AIDS can't be underestimated. She had good advice and she was very strong willed. That had positive and negative sides, but it meant that there was no stopping her."

Baroness Jay was also impressed that Diana was not only willing to take on board the difficult area of families affected by drug use and AIDS but also to relate to the people affected. "I was with her at Brenda House in Edinburgh which is designed for women who were HIV positive or had HIV kids or both. I have a very vivid memory of her sitting on the floor amongst some pretty strange young ladies chatting away about ordinary things. I never saw Diana ever have a problem connecting with any people she met. If they were grand she would be flirty and jolly and if they were young girls like this she would just be completely natural. Because she was the right age she could just connect with people of that generation."

In spite of the prejudice which surrounded the condition and the contempt in which many sufferers were held, Diana was neither afraid to be with AIDS sufferers or to speak out on their behalf as she increasingly did for families affected by AIDS. "A mother with HIV or AIDS doesn't give up the responsibility of caring for her children easily,' she said in 1992. "Often she is

the sole parent, the wage earner, the provider of food, the organizer of daily life, the nurse to other sick members of the family, including her own children. As well as the physical drain on her energy, a mother with HIV carries the grief and guilt that she probably won't see her healthy children through to independence. If she has passed on HIV to one of her children, she will have to witness their illness. Worrying as to what will happen to them if she dies first. Yet the biggest fear of the mothers I've met with HIV or AIDS is not their disease. They've learned to live with their disease. No, what terrifies them most is other people! These women still face harassment, job loss, isolation, even physical aggression if their family secret gets out." As ever, what Diana saw were the individuals—not categories or statistics. It was a blindingly simple approach but utterly rare for someone in her situation.

Typically, another side accompanied Diana's formal help—emotional connection with the people suffering from the condition. She made numerous private visits that were incredibly important for people suffering not just from the horrors of the illness itself but social ostracism and disapproval. Her sister Sarah recalls, "We went on a visit and it was quite early on in what I call, 'holding hands with AIDS victims.' There were about six young men with full-blown AIDS. They went to shut me out of the room, but Diana said, 'No, no, let her come in. She's my sister, and she'll make us laugh.' Well, she told jokes that were so dreadful, so politically incorrect and these boys, these young men, just thought it was the best thing ever. That was one of the few times that we were actually unchaperoned, for want of a better word. I can't remember what the jokes were, but I remember thinking: 'That is close to the bone,' or, 'hope no one gets me for this. But they loved it. And they retaliated with worse. And not just because she was a princess, but also because she was the sort of person they could have done that with anyway. She got into the room, she made a dreadful remark, sat down in a chair, and they were stunned. And she said, 'Well, come on, aren't you going to reply?' And they needed no second request. They were off. We had an amazing time there, in amongst which she was able to ask questions because she was interested and wanted to learn, and she genuinely cared."

"The people she met with AIDS," says Jayne Fincher, "often had a great sense of humor. She would be doubled up the whole time with them, laughing—she didn't have to do all the flirting and everything that she did when you saw her with other chaps. We went once to The London Lighthouse and what sticks in my mind is one particular man, a big chubby guy, doesn't look like the usual AIDS patient. He's sitting in bed, he's got all these CDs and he's got loads of aftershave on. She walks in and the first thing she notices is all the aftershave and makes some comment. There's a chair by the bed, but she goes and sits herself next to him on the bed, short skirt on, hitches it up and away they go. The rapport between the two was incredible. She's never met him before, and she was only in there for five or ten minutes, but the laughter from both of them. She was going through his CD collection. They just clicked instantly."

The London Lighthouse, which provided support and some residential care for people with AIDS, was an organization that Diana became more involved with over the years and she continued to make private visits there until her death. "She used to pop in at the middle of the night to see who else couldn't sleep at two a.m.'"[6] said Paul Theobald, who was a resident at The London Lighthouse. "She had a tremendously loving and generous heart, but she was able to convey that she had an absolute ease with people," says its former president, Christopher Spence. "It was the same with groups. I've seen her go into a group of people all nervous and jittery about her coming but within 25 seconds everyone had relaxed and real things happened.

She had this complete affinity for people on the edge. I was with her so many times with people close to death or on the edge and I never saw her fail. I never saw her fazed by what was happening to them. It was quite, quite extraordinary. There's an author who talks about the victim turned healer and I think that was true of her. In emotional terms she'd had a pretty awful deal. I think she had suffered terribly but she put it to the task of helping others. She liked to come to the Lighthouse because it met a need in her just as it met the needs splendidly of the people there. She was absolutely clear about it being reciprocal. The last time she came to the Lighthouse, just before she died, was a day when there had been some awful stuff about her in the press but as she left she said, 'Christopher, this morning I arrived in a filthy mood. And I'm leaving on top of the world. Thank you.'"

Jean-Paul Claverie met Princess Diana when as a member of Jacques Lang's cabinet he helped entertain her at Chateau Chambord in the late 1980s. Later he became a friend and in a new capacity at LVMH, the Moët Hennessy Louis Vuitton group in Paris, collaborated on various charity initiatives with Diana. "When she decided to help the recognition of AIDS she had an enormous problem with the establishment. But she told me: 'I have to do it. If I have the power to change the position in society of the suffering people, I have to do it. Because I have this power. Because of my position, because of many, many things. But because I have the power, I have to use it.'"

There was also the prejudice of the courtiers who surrounded the royal family; people who not much later began to make Diana's life miserable. "There was a lot of negative sniping in the background from the traditional courtier class," says former palace spokesman Dickie Arbiter, "who just thought this was not what royals do." Patrick Jephson comments, "There was certainly a fair rash of old colonels who would say, 'Why on earth does she want to speak to these dreadful people?' which was only a powerful incentive for me and, I guess, for her too, to carry on doing it. The only answer being they were actually a whole lot more rewarding, a lot more satisfying, a lot more fun."

Difficult though it may have been, the opposition she met and the criticism she received from some establishment figures did not deter her. Diana's friend and patron of The Child Bereavement Trust Julia Samuel says, "People are drawn towards things that interest them. In her case, it was the vulnerable and the weak and the unrecognized." In helping people who felt outcast and rejected, marginalized by mainstream society and terribly lonely as a result, she had found an area that touched a personal chord. In spite of the difficulties, she knew she could have an impact. And, says her sister, Sarah, "She loved a challenge."

Even more remarkable than her effect on public views of AIDS in the UK was the fact that she managed to do the same thing in the United States. "Before coming to London," says Derek Bodell, "I'd worked in the U.S. as a child protection social worker in Brooklyn. So I was there the time she visited an AIDS center in Harlem. None of the political leadership was willing to talk about AIDS at the time because Ronald Reagan would not mention the word. He wouldn't have it discussed. And her visit got huge publicity, television, radio, press, and did more than I think anything else in terms of putting AIDS on the agenda. The *New York Times* printed a leader the following day really taking the American establishment to task that it had taken a foreign royal dignitary to get discussion or to draw attention to a major public health concern in the U.S."

Dr Stephen Nicholas, director of Pediatrics at Harlem Hospital Center in New York, is convinced that Diana's involvement in the issue transformed the perception of AIDS in the United States. Neither he nor his colleague Dr Hegarty had any high expectations of what a visit from British royalty might mean. They and Harlem were in for a fantastic surprise. "The first time Diana came was in February 1989. I had started the pediatric AIDS program here at Harlem Hospital in 1985. Many of these children with AIDS had been abandoned. Most had parents who were either sick or out on the street using drugs, not able to care for their children. They desperately needed foster parents. But even by 1989 there was still considerable fear of children with AIDS and fear of contagion, not to mention the stigma. No matter what you do, this is still a hospital. We had steel barred cribs, the children couldn't go outside. Many of them never saw flowers. It was just extraordinarily inhumane. So [eventually] we found and renovated an old brick convent and turned it into a place called Incarnation Children's Center.

"I don't exactly know how Diana came to us except I believe she had seen stories in the *Wall Street Journal* about the plight of these kids. I knew she was famous and I had seen her picture lots, but I didn't have any personal thoughts about meeting her. It was one of the most exhilarating things that ever happened to me. She was wearing this beautiful red dress and she was just really genuinely elegant. And when I shook her hand—I meet a lot of important people and it's a rare person who doesn't just look at you and say it's nice to meet you—but I really felt that Diana was looking inside of me. It was a very charismatic, wonderful charm.

"She had this very magical way with the kids and they were immediately attracted to her. Then she did what I realized only in retrospect was so important: She had her picture taken with a child with AIDS. And, of course, that picture then went around the world. Oftentimes we don't realize the power of imagery, the power of symbolism, the power of this sort of very high profile visit. Most of humanity didn't have a clue that these kids with AIDS were stuck in the hospital. We opened our doors at Incarnation Children's Center the next month and, sure enough, we were completely filled, almost overnight, with kids needing placement. But the really extraordinary thing that happened is that people began calling, saying: 'I didn't realize about these kids with AIDS until Princess Diana visited Harlem Hospital and I don't think most people would be a foster parent, but I will be.' Suddenly we had a whole group of willing foster parents who wanted kids with AIDS. So over the next two years—and this is really the extraordinary part of the story—two-thirds of the entire city's 'boarder babies' with AIDS, about 160 children came through this little Incarnation Children's Center. Somebody's dubbed it the 'Ellis Island' for homeless babies. And they stayed an average of 30 days and then went into foster care. And at the end of two years, for all of New York City, there was a surplus of foster parents wanting kids with AIDS. I can't prove this scientifically, but I know in my heart that Princess Diana is the one who made this possible."

There have been disparaging remarks made about Diana "playing to the gallery" with AIDS sufferers. Photographer Tim Graham is dismissive. On numerous occasions in the UK and elsewhere he saw Diana demonstrate the same warmth after the press had stopped taking the photos. "She definitely understood the power of images, but it wasn't just for the camera. The photographers would be in a room for two minutes to do the picture, and then we'd all leave, but I know she would stay and talk to the other patients and pick up the other kids."

Marguerite Littman, who worked closely with Diana in her later years at the AIDS Crisis Trust, says, "She was somebody that people admired— and that's an understatement—who embraced and helped people who had AIDS. She made it OK, just as simple as that. But she didn't need the publicity. It's not like a movie star doing it, is it. There was no reason to take up something that the royal family wouldn't embrace. I mean they certainly didn't encourage her. So it seems to me that she did it out of compassion. I can't see any other reason for her doing it, at that point. If she'd taken it up much later, perhaps you could say this but she was right in the front line when it was not OK."

"Some people say to me now she didn't have that much of an effect," says author Andrew Morton, "but I'll tell you how much of an effect she had. Recently I was in South Africa and I went to Robben Island with a man called Ahmed Kathrada who was one of the original men jailed with Nelson Mandela in 1963. After 18 years or so at Robben Island, they were moved into a prison in Cape Town. At that time, prisoners with AIDS were segregated from those who were healthy. There was an awful lot of prejudice and fear surrounding these AIDS prisoners who were effectively shunned by everyone else. The Diana handshake, if you remember, was on TV and they were so overwhelmed by it, that they physically embraced these AIDS patients and nurtured them as a result. For Kathrada, and for Mandela and the other political prisoners, it was a profound change in the way that they behaved towards people with AIDS. Mandela himself says now that he wished he'd done more to help AIDS during the reunification. But that is an example of the genuine impact that Diana had on real people around the world."

It is remarkable just how many individuals affected with AIDS Diana kept in touch with. In Harlem she found Shamir. "He was six or seven," says Dr Stephen Nicholas of the Harlem Hospital Center, "had been on the ward for months and months and he was one of the most foul-mouthed children that any of us had ever been around, and most of it was sexual. Diana had gone down the hallway over to the other side of the ward. So there's security men with their things dangling out their ears all over and Shamir comes out of his room and runs up to Princess Di and jumps up into her arms and begins to whisper in her ear. All the secret service men were very worried about what's going to happen. Now we will never know what he said, but she began to kind of chuckle and sat him down and chatted with him. He went into a foster home in Brooklyn and she wrote to him a couple of times until he died." "She was absolutely superb," says the *Mirror's* royal correspondent James Whitaker, "with people with no hope in life. She made them feel good, and that's a hell of a good legacy to have left."

✳ ✳ ✳ ✳

STIGMA ~ Diana's contribution to the breakdown of prejudice against AIDS is one of the things she will best be remembered for, but there were many other areas where those involved feel she made an equal impact. Superficially different, the causes she involved herself with were all concerned with illnesses and conditions that mainstream society found uncomfortable or even repellent. What Diana brought to all of them was a concern about the isolation people experience when society shuns them. "She was always interested," says Professor Mike Adler, "in groups or people that were marginalized." Beyond the diseases or conditions, Diana in a simple but clear-sighted way, remembered that there were people doubly affected, first by a horrific illness and then again by loneliness. Talking of families affected by AIDS in September 1993, Diana said, "Their need is for understanding. To be allowed to live a full and active life. To be given the support to love and care for their children for as long as they can, without carrying the added burden of our ignorance and fear." "The biggest disease today," she said, toward the end of her own life, "is not leprosy or tuberculosis but the feeling of being unwanted." In Angola, only months before her death, she reiterated her concern about the prejudice and intolerance that surrounds those already struggling with disease and disability.

"I find through the work I do that the biggest thing the world suffers from is a feeling of intolerance. People are so intolerant of each other and things."

The late Reverend Tony Lloyd's experience of Diana was of someone very different from the frivolous, fashion-obsessed woman often portrayed in the press. Before Diana's trip to Indonesia, as long term director of The Leprosy Mission, he advised on the facts of the disease. He thought little more about it until he saw the *Sun's* front page: "Di To Shake Hands With Leper. Don't Do it, Di." In spite of the tabloid's dire warnings, Diana went ahead, not only meeting leprosy sufferers at Sitanala Hospital, but also unhesitatingly shaking hands with them. Behind the lens, photographer Arthur Edwards saw her sit on their beds and felt choked. "Leprosy is something we learn about from the *New Testament*, about Jesus and the lepers and having to ring bells and having to go round saying, 'Unclean, unclean.' All my life I've grown up thinking there's no cure. So watching her holding this man's hand—he'd lost all his fingers—and looking into his eyes, that was very, very moving."

The picture created an avalanche of publicity. Most UK newspapers and many foreign ones, too, carried the picture on their front pages. Those who worked with leprosy were delighted by the power of the image and by Diana's behavior. The hospital's doctor Dr Maartin Teterissa said, "The princess has done an enormous service to the world's 15 million leprosy sufferers by demonstrating that the disease is fully curable by drugs, and that it is contagious only through years of constant and prolonged contact."[7] Back home, Tony Lloyd took one look at the photos and wrote to her: 'You have done more for the education of the public about the stigma of leprosy than we have done in 120 years. Then I added a PS: 'Would you mind being our patron?' We got a letter saying she would be glad to become our patron, which was really wonderful. We couldn't have had anybody better."

As with AIDS, this was no one-off photo opportunity, but the beginning of a long and significant commitment Diana made to The Leprosy Mission. After Indonesia, Lloyd accompanied her on several overseas visits, including Nepal, Hong Kong, and Zimbabwe to help raise funds. Tony Lloyd was a man with a strong religious faith, but even he found Diana intense and unusual. "It was just this compassion thing with her that used to frighten me quite a lot. She looked at you and the world went away. She would lean on me for guidance, but she actually taught me a lot as well. I met Mother Teresa. She was four foot six and she knew you to the backbone in two seconds. There was no way you could pull the wool over her eyes. It was the same with Diana. She could judge people immediately.

"She also had an antenna for people's suffering. The princess would pick on the worst case in a leprosy ward, not in medical terms, but in terms of whether the man or woman had been rejected by their family which is something that happens quite a lot with leprosy and causes immense pain. She sensed that very quickly. She always homed in on the patient most in need, most isolated.

"But Diana was also great fun. She did these great impressions—I once saw her do one of Charles after he had broken his elbow—but I never saw her offend any one. She was always teasing me about things like snoring on the plane. I once saw her going into a leprosy ward, not the most joyous of places, but she had the place in a riot in five minutes. There was one old lady who asked her, 'How old are you?' And the princess said, 'None of your business, old lady!' The old lady had enough English to understand. And there was this woman with leprosy without any teeth just giggling like a schoolgirl. Then the Indian director told the rest of the ward what she'd said and they all started laughing. I've never seen anything like that before."

Diana stayed involved with The Leprosy Mission right up to the end. Shortly before her death, she hosted a meeting at Kensington Palace to plan a Cliff Richard concert on behalf of leprosy. "She did so much for The Leprosy Mission," said Tony Lloyd, "and her motive was absolutely 100 percent pure compassion. The stigma lepers carry is terrible and her stroking of their hands was genuine. She showed it often when she thought nobody, not even I, was watching her." On one occasion, Diana had a totally chance meeting with a woman in Angola, leaning against a mud hut. Lloyd knew they would not be able to communicate, but Diana just crouched down and stroked this woman's hands. "This lady wouldn't have had a clue who Diana was except that she was someone important from somewhere. I was starting to look for an interpreter, but Patrick [Jephson] just told us to stand back, and leave them alone. We stood there for ten minutes and the whole world could have gone away. Compassion just poured out of the woman. It was so strong it was frightening. It is when you meet a truly good person. She was an amazing woman. I don't think we will ever see her likes again. She was stunning."

❋ ❋ ❋ ❋

MENTAL HEALTH ~ Another area where Diana had a lasting effect was in the area of mental health. Her work in this area was much less public than her work for AIDS and leprosy, but no less significant. In fact she devoted as much time to the little-known charity Turning Point as any other. "Turning Point's 'clients'", says Patrick Jephson, "had fallen through every safety net provided. These people were absolutely at the bottom of the heap, but she devoted more of her time and more emotional energy to that charity than to any other. She wasn't there clearing up the vomit from the day release hostel somewhere in the north east, but she did turn up and she did get involved, so that did her great credit."

"Turning Point became one of her favorite charities, in terms of the regularity of visits, which was pretty much monthly for about five or six years," says Les Rudd, its former chief executive. "I think we connected with her because we were helping people who not only had substance problems, but also mental health problems, including serious mental illness. Her own experiences would have given her insight into some of those issues, and I think the more she met users of various services, the more that was evident for her."

Turning Point's Wendy Thomson was impressed with how easily Diana dealt with the most difficult situations. "Some of the people we worked with aren't easy but she was good at finding things to talk to them about without being patronizing. Because she spent a lot of time on her own she'd watch TV programs they'd watched so she'd speak to them about their programs and other things she thought would be helpful to them. And she was a laugh. She never showed any signs of being uncomfortable." Wendy recalls one visit. "This [center] was for people with serious alcohol and substance problems. They were coming out of the drunk tanks at night and being taken in there. Some of them had HIV as well and were in the last stages. There were people with gangrenous limbs because of injecting. They were in a bad way. On one occasion this guy had just come in and he hadn't been cleaned up at all. He was still looking very much the worse for wear and she sat down on the arm of his chair beside a bunch of other people and was quite happy to chat with them. I remember thinking a lot of people wouldn't do that."

"It surprised us all," says Les Rudd, "just how forthcoming she was about her own issues in the privacy of groups. On one occasion she went to a specialist rehabilitation hostel for very chaotic drug users, people who hadn't made any decision to become drug free but who were on methadone stabilizing their drug use. It was a private visit, no publicity, no press and she spent about an hour in a group. There was a lot of self-disclosure from everybody in the room, in relation to issues that had affected them in their childhood, in their lives, precipitating factors for drug use. And she disclosed quite a lot about her own family life and personal life."

Diana's work with Turning Point shows her willingness not just to visit those ostracized by mainstream society but also to be open with them about her own issues. It was an openness that actually touched, and in some cases transformed, the lives of individuals involved. "There are a couple of people she met, who couldn't believe how—'She's just like us, she's been through stuff just like us,'" says Les Rudd. "It affected a couple of people significantly, who just grabbed hold of their treatment program and ran with it. She really inspired them. A lot of their problems were to do with lack of self-esteem. They think they're unworthy. Then suddenly someone they've got on a pedestal reveals her life is not as sorted as it seems, and suddenly it puts their problems into perspective. Some people in Turning Point projects were a bit cynical about a royal visit until they met her. But afterward, there was a real buzz."

Significantly, it was at a Turning Point conference that Diana alluded to her past issues with depression. Les Rudd says, "It was just after the break-up, and she was very tearful. She was referring directly to her own experience." "Women," said Diana, "are always assumed to be able to cope. They may be suffering from post-natal depression, violence in the home or struggling in a daze of exhaustion and stress to make ends meet—but they will cope. It can take enormous courage for women to admit they cannot cope, that they may need help. Frequently they will attempt to survive it alone, falling helplessly into a deeper and darker depression, as they feel more trapped by the life they are leading. As their world closes in on them, their self-esteem evaporates into a haze of loneliness and desperation as they retreat further and further from those who can help them."

Diana's involvement with Turning Point was courageous on several levels. As with AIDS and leprosy she was lending her glamour to issues around which there was serious prejudice. She even visited the most extreme cases. "Turning Point also worked in Rampton, Broadmoor and Ashwood, the secure hospitals, where the public think the really mad and bad are," says Les Rudd. "She went to all three. A lot of people would be scared to do that. She was meeting people who were very isolated and in very dire situations. It's very hard to get out of one of those hospitals once you get in. What the princess did was talk to them with understanding, making them feel normal."

Ted Unsworth, former chair of Turning Point, remembers one occasion at Broadmoor when Diana was invited to join a case conference. "The patient and the clinical team were there. It began as a rather staid affair, but she quickly engaged in the discussion and began talking to this guy and almost chaired the case conference. There was a psychiatrist there, who was the medical officer in charge of the case. Afterward he said he was amazed that somebody without professional training was able to key in to what was going on and make a useful contribution."

Those who accuse Diana of press manipulation get short shrift from the Turning Point staff who feel her highlighting of mental health issues was invaluable. "She didn't have to grab the media's attention," says Rudd, "but when she felt she was able to direct it in some way that was going to be positive for the causes that she supported, then she would do so. She was very well aware of the capital that she carried in terms of her ability to raise funds, raise profile. Some people might call that media manipulation, but I would say that she saw it as a resource."

Both Les Rudd and Wendy Thomson were particularly impressed by the fact that Diana was prepared to champion unpopular causes even up to the political level. The public knew nothing about this. Les Rudd says, "She did quite a bit to shift the political agenda on health during that period, which isn't so well known. The Tories produced a White Paper, *The Health of the Nation*, in 1992 and it took on board the key areas for prevention work: The drugs agenda, the substance abuse agenda, HIV/AIDS, mental health and suicide. Diana was able to sit there with them and challenge them with good, proper, informed questions. That's behind the scenes work, which was as important as the more public work that she did."

"We went with her to the government a few times," said Wendy Thompson. "She claimed she wasn't an educated woman, but I found her very bright and sharp and she understood the issues. We'd go with a brief set of questions and she'd ask them about it and come back at them if she didn't think their response was much use. The palace was very nervous about her doing that."

"I found her a remarkable person, really," says Ted Unsworth. "She did an enormous amount of good work for our particular field. She once said to me in Birmingham, 'Had I had a normal life, I would have wanted to be a social worker.'"

❋ ❋ ❋ ❋

HOMELESSNESS ~ Along with the AIDS handshake, one of the other things everyone knows about Diana is that she took her sons to visit the homeless. But few know the background to the story of her ongoing relationship with homeless charities. Not only did she make a difference to the way homelessness was viewed by politicians and the public in general, but she also made a difference to the lives of some of the homeless themselves.

"The issues have moved on from youth homelessness now," says the Depaul Trust's Mark McGreevy, "but that was the dominant theme of the late '80s and early '90s and nobody in public life contributed as much as Diana to raising awareness of the issues. She also understood that homelessness is linked to all kinds of things to do with a young person's life, like drugs or mental health. Youth homelessness is not resolved, but there's been a lot of investment from government and policy makers, and it's an improving situation. Much of that is down to the influence that Diana brought to bear."

When Diana first became involved there had been a huge increase in homelessness but many people—both politicians and the public—were deeply hostile to people sleeping rough, tending to blame the individuals for their own misfortunes. Diana's concern for the homeless and later her commitment to tackling the causes of homelessness was unusual for a celebrity, let alone a member of the royal family. Says Mark McGreevy, "Living at Kensington Palace, it must have been something Diana passed every day and I think she was genuinely affected by it. She latched onto the issue rather more quickly than the politicians did, and she did an awful lot to bring the problem to the public eye."

Sister Barbara Smith, a nun belonging to the Vincent de Paul Order, was someone with whom Diana developed a strong relationship. She had come to work for The Passage Day Centre for the Homeless in Westminster in 1984. Two years later she was running it and it was there she met Princess Diana. The Passage then mainly provided shelter and some crucial services, including a laundry and a medical room. Understanding homelessness, says Sister Barbara, is not easy for those comfortable at home because although the homeless are often destitute, the causes of homelessness are not always directly to do with material hardship. "People became homeless because they needed to disappear. Maybe they'd been in trouble or they'd been thrown out or things had gone so wrong for them that they couldn't stick it any longer. A lot of the youngsters would be like that. But maybe for the older men and women, it was broken relationships, or that they'd been in trouble, or just couldn't take the pressure any longer of living on their own and getting these bills through the door. The day would come when they'd go outside and lock the door and threw the keys away and go to the street, because they couldn't take it any longer."

Diana, however, had no such qualms about involving herself in this unappealing and potentially controversial area. She asked to visit, and was introduced by Cardinal Basil Hume, to whom she was very close, and by John Studzinski, a founding member of the Passage Day Center. Sister Barbara recalls the first occasion. "I could not tell anyone at all that the princess was coming. It was a terrific security thing. The plain-clothes police came with sniffer dogs. Of course, my men weren't daft. They all knew there was something happening. They said, 'What's up?' 'Well,' I said, 'The cardinal's going to make an *official* visit. I know he's been across before, but this is going to be a very official visit, and because of who he is, the police are doing this blessed security check.' I said, 'All they're looking for is drugs and knives, you know.' So a couple of young ones came to me and said, 'Would you mind my knife for me?' So for that first visit I ended up with a knife in each pocket of my habit. I was only allowed to tell the staff the morning she came. She said she'd like everything to carry on as usual, and she would stay for an hour. In the event, she stayed about two hours. She always overstayed the length of time."

This was the first of several visits where Diana impressed Sister Barbara with her ability to relate to the most marginal of all social groups. "She'd stop and talk with anyone. And she never wore gloves. She would shake hands with anyone that she was going to speak with. On one occasion there was a lady here, I think her name was Margaret, and she had a doll and she always used to be doing her hair. I think it must have been the daughter that she lost. And she would sit in silence, she always sat in the same place, and sometimes she'd talk out loud and sometimes be quite angry in her talking. At odd times, she'd pick up her dinner and fling it on the floor. This particular time, the princess was working her way up that part of the passage, and I thought, 'What will I do when she comes to Margaret?' She's sitting there muttering away, her hands are absolutely filthy. Anyway, she came through the doorway, so I just said, 'Your Royal Highness, this is Margaret.' Margaret got to her feet, held out her hand and the princess shook hands with her. They stood and talked for about three or four minutes, and then Margaret just suddenly sat down, and the princess moved on. I was just amazed, and so thankful that I had introduced Margaret. She knew it was the princess."

Now, there was the man we called Santa Claus. He appeared and he just sat, "you can see from the photo—that is just appealing, isn't it? Look at her expression, that's not acting, is it? He had string tied round his middle. We used to try and get him sometimes to maybe get a new coat but if they didn't, well, they didn't. And he would look in the distance and talk a lot of rubbish. He went down Carlyle Place once with a box of matches and he put a match into everybody's Yale lock and broke it off, which meant that when they went home at night, they wouldn't be able to get in. Eventually he was knocked down by traffic and he was taken to hospital, so of course they went through his pockets, and he died, so the police then found out who he was, got in touch with his relatives who had been searching for him. He was a respectable man, and had brought up a very respectable family. And they said they would never have recognized him. His mind had just flipped, and he'd taken to the streets and was sleeping rough, in and out of night shelters. And then I could understand why he'd put a matchstick in everybody's Yale lock. I think, at the back of his mind, he knew he had a home somewhere and he couldn't get back into it, you know, his mind was locked against him. And to me that match in every Yale lock had significance then, as some sort of expression of the way that he was blocked out. I think it's the most beautiful picture I've ever seen. It's beautiful of her; it's beautiful of him. Compassion is absolutely written all over her face; he's got her 100 percent attention. She's sitting down, with her arms crossed, to give him time, she's not just holding on ready to go, she's there to listen and to stay.

"I think she was genuinely concerned about disadvantaged people, because ours wasn't the only place she went to. She had a very compassionate heart. Whether it stemmed from her own loneliness in childhood, and maybe her sense of rejection in the situation she was in, I don't know. She was such a rich person and yet she spent a long time with these disadvantaged people and was very natural with them. This wasn't for publicity; she wasn't preaching to anyone, she was just doing something she needed to do: To give. And the only thing she could really give was herself. And that communication with them was just listening to them, taking the trouble to spend time with them. And they knew she got nothing from it. It wasn't in the paper the next day."

When Sister Bridie Dowd took over The Passage, Diana continued to visit; indeed she brought William with her for the first time. "Oh, she was just wonderful with those people, wonderful," says Sister Bridie. "Her biggest problem was trying to give time to such a big group of people, because she'd absolutely give anyone who spoke to her undivided attention." The center got its name, says Sister Bridie, because it's basically one long passage. "People sit along those tables, chatting or playing cards or eating, whatever's on at a partic-ular time of a day." When Diana arrived, "they stood up and nearly everybody wanted to shake hands with her, or catch her eye. I think she made them feel that in spite of who she was, she took the time to come and visit them, even though they're so often considered good-for-nothings. Obviously, and I think it was proven to them, she didn't see it that way. She gave them her time."

Diana was involved in the beginning of the setting up of a center for the young homeless, the Depaul Trust, again with Basil Hume and John Studzinski. "The cardinal came along and he was fantastic with Diana," says Mark McGreevy. "He used to treat her like a head girl at a public school, that kind of relationship of being able to talk very respectfully. They seemed to get on really well together. But the cardinal was a bit like Diana. He much preferred to be not in front of the press and the spotlight and actually in the background, so at one point I had the cardinal talking to all the kitchen staff in one room and Diana hiding on a landing talking to young people. Nobody actually talking to the funders, but they were both fantastic.

"There was also Heidi, who slept rough on Victoria Street. Heidi had real problems, God bless her. She couldn't bear to sleep in a bedroom, so we set up a bed in the office in the building. We drew straws as to who would meet Diana, because we were bringing up six people from the world press into this room. One part of me was hoping Heidi didn't win because she was a bit of a loose cannon, but of course the way the draw went she did win and she was fantastic right the way through the formal session. When the press left and we were sitting there, she pulled out a mug from the royal wedding and said to Diana, 'You've changed your hairstyle since then, haven't you?' I thought, well, that's OK. And the princess laughed and said, 'Yes.' 'Who's the big-eared guy on the back?' says Heidi, and turned it around to her. She thought that was very amusing.

"The kids here can be very volatile, but I always said that Diana would be one of the best project workers that you could ever have within a charity. She'd be able to talk to them about things that interested them, but she'd be able to tell if somebody was actually spinning her a yarn; she'd keep it very grounded on what the issues were. Some of these young people were very aggressive, but Diana always said that she didn't want to be accompanied by one of us. She wanted to go down and have her chats privately.

"At one project we were taking people straight off the streets with all kinds of drug and mental health issues, and she asked to visit and the cardinal turned up to host it. The young people knew nothing about it, so as they arrived they'd walk in and there was Princess Diana. One young guy came walking in off the street and just walked in, looked at her and said: 'Fuck me, it's a Beadle!' He actually thought it was a set-up by the comedian Jeremy Beadle. She burst out laughing and said, 'I don't think so! Sit down, have a cup of tea.' With those young people she would be able to sit down and listen to stories, and use them very well in feeding back to us, and to other audiences, the kind of predicaments facing the young people. On that night, when she left she was driving her own car and they were keen to see her burn rubber, so she wound down the window and said, 'I can't do that, but watch this for a perfect three point turn!' Fantastic quality, very good people skills with very damaged people. We would have employed her as a project worker tomorrow.

"It must have been a tremendously difficult learning curve to talk to so many different people from so many different walks of life and be able to be respected by all of them. But if you asked me where she felt the most comfortable then I'd say it was probably in talking to those young people on the ground. 'I feel more comfortable at this end of the market,' Diana herself said the year before she died. 'But you have to talk to the people at the top to help people at the bottom.'"

✳ ✳ ✳ ✳

DYING, THE LAST TABOO ~ Perhaps because Diana's sympathy for those on whom society turned its back has become so familiar to us, few remember just how extraordinary these abilities were. Just as with AIDS and leprosy, Diana was never fazed by situations that many others would find offputting. Mary Baker, who worked for the Parkinson's Disease Society, was enormously impressed at the way Diana was able to see the human being through the disease. "I think her concern was utterly, utterly genuine. I remember once she went up to Blackpool on another sort of visit, to see a biscuit factory or some-thing, but she let the society know that she was up there so the Blackpool branch went with their little placard. As soon as she saw it she went straight into the crowd, straight to the wheelchairs, straight down on her knees. Some of PD [Parkinson's Disease] is very unattractive—the trembling and sometimes dribbling, but she didn't mind. She was naturally straight in there and she knew that a quick smile and the right words would cheer people up."

David Ireland, who had moved from Tottenham to work at Trinity Hospice in Clapham, saw Diana bring this quality to people who were dying when she was visiting a former member of her staff in Trinity Hospice. "She was just so good with this chap. And he was so clearly encouraged by her visits. It wasn't like somebody coming to pay a sort of 'pat you on the head, poor chap' visit, it felt like a meeting of equals. She had no need to make those visits. They were in total privacy, so the way that she behaved was not for the press or for self-glorification. She did have an ability to meet people where they were and talk to them in a way that clearly brought understanding or comfort. There is a comparison with her reaction to AIDS: A hospice, for some, has the same kind of stigma about it. I had people, quite close friends, who would never come and visit me in my office, which is right in the heart of the hospice. They'd always find excuses not to, people I knew really well. Whereas she could walk in there as if it were just walking into her own sitting room. One of my great mentors was Robert Runcie, who was Archbishop of Canterbury and who, in fact, married Charles and Diana. I talked to him after Diana's visit. He felt, too, that there was something about her that was very special. Despite all the bits that hit the press, there was, deep down, a person of great compassion and great sensitivity."

"Most people are very uncomfortable around death," says author Andrew Morton. "Diana wasn't. People are very uncomfortable about other people in grief. She wasn't. You can talk about her psychology from here to kingdom come, but she had that gift of empathy. She didn't do it for public show. Once when she was nursing Adrian Ward Jackson, a friend of hers who died of AIDS, she went up to another ward, and met a family of a man who had had a massive heart attack and died. She spent hours with this Arab family, comforting them. I once asked her why didn't she spend more time with people who were recovering from illness, rather than people who were, effectively, on their last journey. Her response was that she preferred to work with people who were honest and open and on their last journey in life."

Christopher Spence, ex-president of The London Lighthouse, who often saw Diana with people reaching the end of their life, and who now as chairman of The Diana, Princess of Wales Memorial Fund is engaged in work on palliative care, says, "Diana had an enduring commitment to people facing death and bereavement. She always focused her attention on life in the present and how to make it the very best it can be. She understood that the needs of others at the end of their lives, as well as of their loved ones, are not only medical but also emotional and spiritual—the need for relief from physical pain, as well as the need for love, resolution and peace of mind."

The extraordinary thing was that Diana displayed the same empathy for people across the barriers of language, culture, and religion. In many different countries, when she visited hospitals and encountered desperate and dying people, she exhibited the same intuitive connection. "She went to Harlem and she held babies there," says photographer Arthur Edwards, "She did the same in Sao Paolo in Brazil. I saw her holding lepers' hands in Nigeria and looking at where they'd lost their fingers. This woman was the first real hands-on royal we've ever seen. At the Peto Institute in Budapest there was this little girl learning to walk and Diana was there on her knees and the girl walked toward her and Diana was encouraging her to come and walk and show her how good she did it. And she was doing it brilliantly. Behind the lens I was thinking this woman has got the sort of magic that can get anything done."

Diana's visit to Mother Teresa's hospice in Calcutta in 1992 made a particular impact. Mother Teresa was not present on this occasion but Diana insisted on visiting the nuns' home and Mother Teresa's hospice for the dying. As always the press followed. "We went first to the sisters' home," says Jayne Fincher, "and as we walked in, they all burst into song. It's hard to describe the feeling but it was so beautiful and quiet with these women singing with these beautiful voices. Perhaps because of the horrors of Calcutta outside, it was like a little haven. As soon as Diana walked in her eyes welled up. Even the old hardened hacks of Fleet Street were getting all emotional. She sat there biting her lip, very tearful. And as we all came out there was a pot for the collection for the nuns, and all these Fleet Street people were all getting the money out, stuffing it in. Normally, they're so cynical, but they all suddenly turned to quivering jelly."

Again, at Mother Teresa's hospice for the dying, the accompanying press were overcome. Arthur Edwards noticed that "Diana went to each single patient and gave them some sweets, little sort of sweet-tasting stuff to make them feel better. And I can remember when she walked out of there that her dress was filthy, covered in mud and dirt."

On another occasion when Diana stopped over in Calcutta, she insisted on taking Sam McKnight, her hairdresser, with her, something for which he is now extremely grateful. "It was a five-hour stopover and I thought I would just stay on the plane, but she said, 'No, you're coming with us. You have to see it.' It was harrowing, but she was in her element just knowing that she was bringing some glimmer of hope. I'm standing there in an Armani suit thinking what a prat I am. I didn't even know this existed. It's so horrific. But at the same time I met all these amazing people who work there voluntarily. It blew my mind."

❋ ❋ ❋ ❋

OUTSIDE THE BOX ~ There were numerous charities or charity events to which Diana lent significant support throughout her life but to which she had no formal association. Many demonstrated her willingness to think outside the box and take on unconventional, sometimes controversial, causes. Musician and composer Jean-Michel Jarre, for example, experienced a great deal of support for a concert he was organizing in London's Docklands on behalf of AIDS charities which ran into all sorts of arcane political difficulties. "There was a 'problem' with the Borough of Newham. This borough at the time was extremely left wing, and was resisting the Thatcher program of developing the Docklands. And they saw this project being a project coming from that side and, actually, it was exactly the reverse. My project in the Docklands was to put a kind of spotlight on a place, to link it with the history of the country, from Dickens, the London docks, the East End, and also to consider the people working and living there for centuries. It was a tribute to them and not the reverse. But they wouldn't give the license" Diana had not to be seen to be too partisan, but gave Jarre a great deal of background encouragement. When he finally quelled the fears of the locals and got permission for the concert, Diana immediately gave her public support.

The delays caused the summer concert to become an autumn one and on the day it poured. "We had pouring rain, freezing wind, and the stage was on the water. The storm was so big that the navy came and decided that we would follow, on stage, the same regulations you have to follow on the boat. You have to have a lifejacket. I had people from the London Symphony Orchestra and other musicians in tuxedos and dinner jackets, and these orange lifejackets on top. The whole thing became totally absolutely crazy. But the project is still a record in the UK for the biggest concert, paying tickets, in the history of pop music. And the princess was really supportive. She went on stage in pouring rain and then we had a party. This place doesn't exist anymore, they blew up all the warehouses and all the buildings, and actually part of the implosion was supposed to be part of the project. So she got the message from day one, and really supported the whole thing from an artistic point of view. She definitely had an unconventional way of being interested in anything. She was not an intellectual. She had a more intuitive approach to lots of things. She was certainly very informed and interested by lots of different aspects of life, and mainly culture."

Esther Rantzen, who drew Diana into an involvement with the new charity ChildLine, also recognized Diana's readiness to support unconventional and perhaps risky causes. "She was very important for people who were starting radical new charities—be it for landmines, AIDS, homelessness or indeed in our field of child protection. She wasn't somebody who would only support something if it had a century of proven track record behind it."

At the time, ChildLine was a new and controversial charity: "It was a very new and different approach to child protection. That children would access the help they needed when they needed it in the way they needed it. And, in a sense, they were in control, therefore, of their own protection in a way that there never had been before, because always before adults had referred them. Some people regarded this as a dangerous new concept. [Diana] understood at once what the charity was about. She showed an enormous sympathy and understanding of the way abused children feel and gave tremendous support to us from then on, until she died. Children were a clear priority for her and she instinctively understood them."

"She had a unique place, both in the public's affection and in terms of her own very special kind of glamour, so she was able to draw attention to our work in a way no one else could," says Esther Rantzen. Like many of the other controversial issues she championed, sexual abuse is also surrounded by ignorance and stigma, with victims often shunned because people think they are lying or because the subject (and especially the effects on its victims) are so unsettling. "When she took on ChildLine," says Baroness Howarth, a founder director of the organization, "she wasn't afraid of what was being said about it—you know, that it was encouraging children to 'invent' things about their parents. Most of the nation didn't want to know about sexual abuse—they still don't now—but she didn't mind being associated with a controversial charity. Maybe she didn't mind risk in some way."

Hereward Harrison, who also worked for the charity at the time, remembers her early involvement as an almost "magical" time: "Before any reports about her or her life and before the *Panorama* program. There was never a visit that caused more interest, more genuine enthusiasm, than her visit. She arrived in those days looking tremendously elegant, and we all felt very good. She was never formally our patron, but she was able to help us in so many different ways."

Both Esther Rantzen and Hereward Harrison were struck by Diana's exceptional qualities with people. "She had a way of talking to children who'd been to hell and back that put them at their ease and allowed them to talk frankly about their experiences without being frightened. I remember a couple of boys who had had the most terrible experiences who had come to meet her at ChildLine's premises and they brought a camera, but they didn't dare suggest a photograph, so she said, 'Is that there for a present? Someone want a picture?' And she had a picture taken with them and, of course, it's something they'll always treasure."

Hereward Harrison particularly likes one photo where Diana is talking to a volunteer about a call she'd just received from a child. It sums up for him why she found it so easy to relate to ChildLine. "Listening to those in pain was crucial for her. Look at the expression on her face. This isn't a mock-up. She's feeling the pain. 'I understand people's suffering, people's pain,' she once said, 'more than you will ever know.'"

The late Reverend Tony Lloyd thought she could empathize because "she felt she was an outcast in some ways, in terms of family background. She just felt isolated. I was told by one of her equerries that at Kensington Palace she was surrounded by people who were just not on her wavelength. There were other royals and she never quite knew where she stood with them." "Who were the people that she embraced?' asks author Andrew Morton. "People who were bereaved, people who were dying, people with AIDS, people who were homeless, people with leprosy. Marital breakdown, battered women. It's not exactly the sexy top ten, is it? The victims of prejudice are

outsiders and she saw herself as an outsider, she saw herself as not fitting in. She said it quite explicitly in conversations. She felt a kind of empathy with those kinds of people because she saw them as part of herself. She never saw herself as an establishment figure."

❋ ❋ ❋ ❋

STRESSES AND STRAINS ~ The pressures of Diana's life at this time were extreme. If she lived up to the public's expectation of her appearance, she was accused of being obsessed with fashion. Although she enjoyed fashion and worked hard to achieve her groomed, glamorous look, she was always bothered by the way in which the media focused on it rather than the cause she was promoting. Mark McGreevy recalls the occasion on which she came to open the Depaul Trust's homeless shelter. "She turned up in this [incredible] outfit and the press outside were going wild and taking photos and we were on the front page of every single tabloid the next day. But the headline was 'Princess Thighana' and not one mention of the charity's name, except in passing." "She had a bit of a time struggling with the fashion icon thing," says her hairdresser and friend, Sam McKnight. "She didn't really want to be one, but she enjoyed it at the same time. She was a gorgeous woman. There's nothing wrong with showing it off and enjoying it, you know, but she didn't want to be seen too much like that."

"I remember she made a really important speech on leprosy," says her sister Sarah, "and the only thing that was written up the next day was that she had changed her hairstyle. She was so angry. She'd moved on, but she didn't consider that the press had. They weren't listening. In fact, she'd made a speech, a major, major speech, and she didn't enjoy making speeches. She was fine in a room, but to throw your voice and speak for some time and be judged on it was different. It's automatically assumed you've got to be good at it, but why should you be good at it? I can't remember her having too many parts in school plays. She had no confidence in doing it, but she did very well."

The pressures of Diana's public life were immense, as her closest staff realized. "It might be forgotten," says Patrick Jephson, "that for most of her royal life she shouldered a major share of the burden of public duties. She was also an incredible perfectionist. From the grandest state occasion to the most informal charity meeting she applied the same unwavering professionalism. She set the highest standards for herself and expected others to do the same. To work for her was to know that every success, however slight, was noticed and appreciated, just as no oversight however small could be hidden from her acute and increasingly experienced eye. The image presented to the world of beauty, poise, and informed interest owed much to her natural ability and instincts. But these were far outweighed by the commitment she showed to memorizing written briefs, researching personalities and a genuine desire to expand her own knowledge of a host of challenging subjects. Her courtesy was of the purest kind—it sprang from her inner conviction that those she was seeking to serve, and there sometimes seemed no limit to their number, deserved nothing but the best.

"One of the reasons that she was good at her job was she allowed herself to become emotionally engaged with what she was doing and the people she was seeing knew that. But to do that day after day was very exhausting for her at a time when she didn't have unlimited reserves of self-confidence to expand on their behalf." "It's what she got from it, one always worried about," says another former member of her staff. "Because, day-in, day-out, whether it was Barnardo's, very disadvantaged children, very ill people, whatever, it does sap your resources. She was always giving of herself. Regardless of what she was feeling like, she would always step off that airplane or train or get out of the car and give of her best."

"The miracle to me was not that she was a bit unstable sometimes," says Patrick Jephson, "but that she hadn't been in a mental asylum years ago. That's what I wrote in my book and I meant it. Given the provocation and the circumstances and the general highly sprung emotional tension she lived under, the miracle was how amazingly good-humored, generous, articulate and perceptive she remained." "The friends all knew what pressure she was under," says Lord Palumbo. "Every move she made, the press was continually hounding her. It must've been a very difficult life to lead. She was facing a battle with the Prince of Wales and she felt lonely and isolated. I often wonder how people who criticize her would have coped in similar circumstances."

The pressures of celebrity itself were incredible. Other people in the public eye were horrified at the sheer intensity of her exposure. Sir Cliff Richard, who saw her on and off through the years, says: "She was having a great deal of media problems, and at one particular dinner, she asked, 'What do you do? How do you deal with the press?' And I said, 'Well, I don't have to deal with what you have to deal with. But in the end you'll just have to come to terms with it, that there is no moment that's absolutely yours.' In showbiz, you can get away from it, but I don't think she ever could. We were skiing in the same resort once. She had a corner of the hotel, about three or four rooms, with the family. In her wing, the curtains were always drawn, always. Outside in the bushes and down the side alleys were cameras by the score, like guns pointing up there. It must have been an unbelievable pressure for her. I don't know how she coped with it at all. It's beyond anything that showbiz people ever suffer, almost certainly. I don't see cameras bristling at me from my front gate. Yes, if you happen to have a high profile, and if there's been anything controversial written about you by somebody, but even then, it's not a bristling army of paparazzi. I've never ever experienced that. She was almost certainly the most photographed woman in the world."

"She paid a horrible price," says singer Chris de Burgh. "There is this illusion about being famous and rich, but it is nothing more than that. It is an illusion. She showed us that, and dramatically. When you are out there in public and you are famous, it is a rare oxygen indeed, and it makes you feel that you are king or queen of the world, and everything is possible. It can be dangerously narcotic, which is why we have seen people who have been famous and are no longer famous shrivel, because they need that in their lives. I think that Diana was strong enough, she didn't actually need the adulation, but she certainly would have felt that center of attention euphoria that everybody wants you, everybody loves you, and she would have felt the opposite, as well. The door closes in the bedroom and you've just given everything you have to all these people, who've gone home with pocketfuls of love from you, and you're left empty. Not every time, obviously, but there would have been times when real loneliness would have kicked in."

The loneliness of the performer was exacerbated by the state of the royal marriage. Diana had been on her own pretty much from the start of her marriage, as Charles continued to live much the sort of life he had previously, keeping separate engagements from Diana. Her life was in some ways like a single mother. Behind the scenes, her marriage was not just in trouble but falling apart. Her friend, the MP Henry Bellingham, comments, "I suppose it wasn't that long before things did start going wrong with her marriage and when they did, the visits to Sandringham were more tense and difficult obviously because she was in the midst of a family she was becoming far from happy with. Her visits were really quite short. There was Highgrove to go to,

and Kensington Palace, but Sandringham wasn't ever a home. She used to go out with the family when they went shooting—I mean she used to enjoy going to lunch and taking the boys out—but she never had the same attraction to the place as Prince Charles did."

Janet Filderman, who gave Diana beauty treatments from the start of her marriage until her separation, thinks it is absolutely amazing it took so long for the difficulties to surface. "Right from the age of 21," says Janet, "Diana was aware of the fact that she wasn't loved in the way that she loved, or the way she wanted. She had been as a schoolgirl in love with Prince Charles and then she married him, and she was thinking, well, I shall love and be loved forever after and of course it didn't turn out like that. So consequently she was really desperate. She told me that when she was first taken to Wales by Prince Charles and she learnt some Welsh, she was really, really upset because he never said 'well done' or 'how clever of you,' or anything. She said, 'All I need is a pat on the back.' It was like a little girl wanting approbation. She never seemed to get it from the family at all, but it wasn't that they were mean and horrid, it's just that they're not used to it. They never did it to each other so of course they didn't do it to someone like Diana.

"Here was this young woman who was convinced that her husband didn't love her. Here was a young woman who was desperately, desperately unhappy and floundering around for someone to be everything to her and she to be everything to them and most of her amors were second best for her. She wanted Prince Charles and she wanted a home where she lived as a mother. The way it came over to me was that she was going inwards all the time, trying to decide what to do, how could she deal with it, and I once said to her, 'Look, if I were you, I would concentrate more on your outside work rather than inside. This way you will find some satisfaction.' I think she did exactly that. And she certainly beat the royals at their own game. She had to develop a persona and outlook for herself that would offset this desperate longing to be loved and what she did was convert all the energy that she was willing to give as the wife of Prince Charles into the general public. It was her lifeline."

Derek Deane, to whom Diana talked, says he thinks "she didn't understand what she was getting into in the first place. When it hit her what she was in, she couldn't go out. So then she was thrown to the slaughter and she was much too emotional to be able to put that aside and get on with her life as a royal princess within a marriage that doesn't work. If she'd been much more calculating, much more greedy, much more self-orientated, she could still be up there now, but she wasn't that type of person. She was emotional. She needed and wanted love, and she was just desperate to be loved, and she never was."

Detractors of Diana have tried to paint a picture of someone who was "paranoid" within her marriage, obsessively jealous and focused on her disappointments. One look at the sort of charities that Diana involved herself with, gives the lie to that. One of the charities she gave most time to was Relate, formerly the Marriage Guidance Council, a charity which is primarily about helping people understand the dynamics of their relationships and giving them the self-esteem to help make them better. This was no half-hearted involvement. It was one of her biggest commitments and many noticed she became very interested in counseling. According to ex-director David French, even if she didn't associate herself with the charity explicitly to help with her own problems, she was smart enough to know how to use her experiences to help herself: Hardly the actions and words of someone who wanted to dwell on her own disappointments.

"When she became patron of Relate in 1989, the state of her own marriage was already being discussed in the press. And I think the view that most people took at the time was: 'Well, that's a brave thing to do, to talk on that particular territory as patron.' If she'd left it a couple of years longer, she probably couldn't have done it. The public perception would have been: 'Well, she's gone to them because of her own marriage.' But nobody at that stage thought her own marriage was doomed.

"I really don't know how much she was explicitly influenced by the proposition: 'If I go and work with that lot, it'll help me.' Which is not to say that she didn't quite quickly engage with it and put herself into positions where she would be able to learn from the experience. I'm sure she believed passionately in the place of marriage, particularly in relation to children. She was hugely close to both her children and immensely conscientious about them. In fact my perception was she was getting more and more conscientious as she could see that the parental relationship wasn't what it might have been, and she became more and more concerned to ensure that her children were going to be OK.

"Undoubtedly she got something from her involvement in Relate. What she would be offered when she came on visits, whether it was at Relate's national center or one of our regional offices would generally be some variation on a group session of some kind, which is absolutely part of the life of Relate. Typically there would be a group of six or eight or ten counselors doing case studies. So she'd sit in on a real-life case of marital problems. And she'd participate, but even when she wasn't participating, she was hugely engaged and, of course, interpreting it all, in relation to her own situation because that's what every member of that team would. She wasn't a counsellor, so she was probably less well equipped than most of the other people in the room to, as it were, judge the boundaries between the private and the professional. And occasionally she'd come straight out with something and you'd get an insight into her own situation, which was not always very happy. But it was learning of a kind that she soaked up there. It was very practical. It was 'people learning.'

"One of my close colleagues in Relate at the time, the queen bee of the counseling system in the whole organization, a very experienced counselor herself, quite spontaneously, after the first time she met Diana said: 'She would make a brilliant counselor.' And one just heard that repeated so many times by counselors when they met her. I'm sure she knew it about herself; the feedback was always so good. I think she would have found it very rewarding."

"She sat in on many counseling sessions," says Ken Wharfe, her personal protection officer, "and here was a woman, actually, who was in a relationship and who probably needed counseling herself. It was pretty brave of her to get involved." Once, when Jayne Fincher was chatting to Diana she asked her, "What would you do if you weren't the Princess of Wales?" "I'd really love to become a marriage guidance counselor. I am a great listener and I feel I could help a lot of people sort out their problems."

She was terribly lonely. "I thought she was fantastic in what she did for all the charities she got involved with," says Jennie Bond of the BBC. "I feel that she needed to do it. I can't remember her exact words, but she said to me something like: 'It fills me up, but when I come home I'm empty. Every-one loves TLC [tender loving care], everyone needs TLC and it's something I know that I can do.' But when she came home, there was no one to fill that hole for her.

"On one occasion, coming home on a plane from a foreign trip, she asked me to go up to the front of the plane and we had a bit of a chat. She was snuggling under a little white duvet there and said she was feeling quite tired and I said, 'What do you do when you get home?' And she said, 'Well, I'll write some thank-you letters straight away.' I thought how different her

homecoming would be to mine. I would come home to the dog barking, my daughter running across to ask what gifts I had brought her, and the usual school run and all that, and she would go home to an empty palace—albeit a palace. I thought, Gosh, I'd rather go home to my little house." "The princess would go out to an official function," says Lord Palumbo, "and captivate everybody there and receive tremendous applause and affection, or she would go to a hospital and meet people who were ill or dying, and then she would go back to Kensington Palace—very often alone—and be served dinner on a tray in her room watching television. It was that I think she found disturbing; the adulation on the one hand and the loneliness on the other."

Jean-Michel Jarre, whom Diana had come to know quite well, sensed "a very deep loneliness. I talked about that and she told me how lonely she was, and suddenly we talked like close friends, and she told me about the long days and the formal aspect of her life. She was not criticizing even the system, and she was also not saying anything negative about her relationship with the prince, but you could feel that something was wrong there from the beginning. I had the feeling that she was a woman realizing that she's been betrayed. I understood, later on, how much that was the case. It was a kind of sadness, you know. Something really bad happened to this girl."

Many of the charities saw glimpses of this unhappiness too. "I know I became incredibly protective towards her," says Mary Baker, formerly of the Parkinson's Disease Society. "That's what she brought out in me. She was a very vulnerable person. All I know is I couldn't take my eyes off her. She had such a lovely face, lovely, lovely eyes, lovely expression, but with the smile there was the tinge of sadness. I can only say in all honesty, not with hindsight, but I was never surprised at what happened. I felt she was a tragedy waiting to happen. I didn't foresee her death or any claptrap like that, but I never envied her. I've always felt a concern for her and I have no reason to. She never moaned, never, never, never. It was always the reverse: 'I'm lucky, I see these operations, I travel,' but you still felt vulnerability. I guess it was the incredible honesty of her."

At English National Ballet where Diana often went to relax, Derek Deane encountered someone struggling to overcome that sadness. "Some-times," he says, "she came to Jay Mews in a very quiet, fragile way, emotionally worn out. She put on her act coming through the door and then of course once the doors were closed in the office the act stopped. I always said, 'Are you all right?' And she would say, 'No, not really,' or, 'I'm just coping,' or, 'Things could be better,' and then sometimes she'd open up a little bit about what was going wrong, but she always said without fail: 'I've got so much out of coming here today, you've cheered me up. You've helped me get through another afternoon when things are so dreadful at the moment.' Or, 'God, you've really given me food for thought about a dancer's life.'

"I saw panic in her and I saw deep, deep upset and sadness, but I never saw madness. She was so complex and there was so much in her life that I'm amazed she was as sane as she was. The pressure of being the most famous woman in the world, the Elizabeth Taylor, Jackie Kennedy Onassis figure and the pressures of that dreadful marriage and the pressures of the family and losing the title. These pressures were massive and I'm amazed that somebody as fragile as she was managed to survive it all—and not only survive it but actually do some incredible things on top of it, which is extraordinary, because she could have gone down a completely different route. She admits herself she wasn't the Brain of Britain, but if material things were her only passion she could have turned it into a Euro-trash princess in five minutes. But there was such a wonderful side to her that realized that her power and her position and her fame could do things for other people.'"

Ken Wharfe says the pressures of her life at this period were terrible. "There was the workload, there was also the pressure on her private life and although we managed to achieve a lot away from the media, there was tremendous pressure from within, from her own husband and within the royal circles." She was almost never free from what Wharfe describes as "the hubbub and almost 24-hour attentiveness that she'd get at Kensington Palace: Prying butlers, prying chefs, prying chauffeurs, prying policemen. . . . There were always people jockeying for positions. And it must have been nerve-wracking for her. It was bad enough for the staff around here to live with it. I used to think, Christ, I don't know how the hell you deal with this."

Of course that sadness and vulnerability added enormously to Diana's public appeal. Many thought her special charisma came from this combination of beauty, glamour and sadness. Chris de Burgh says, "I think what men found so attractive, and certainly I did, was her vulnerability. Not only was she gorgeous and feminine but vulnerable, an immensely attractive package. You just wanted to go in there and give her a hug and say, 'It's going to be OK,' but, you know, you couldn't."

Patrick Demarchelier photographed Diana several times during her life and they became friends. The first time was in 1986 at Highgrove, when Demarchelier took photos of Diana alone and with the children. "She had seen a cover of British *Vogue* with a girl holding a baby inside a coat. It was my son, actually. He was laughing and Diana loved that picture, so she called me. It was the first time anyone from the royal family had called me; it was very unusual to call a French photographer. She was a bit like a rebel . . . she liked to do things her way, not the traditional way.

"We had lunch in the kitchen. She was very casual, very nice, making sure everybody was happy. I thought Diana was fantastic. She was very open. She talked to everybody. She was very sweet. But what I loved about her was her smile. She had an amazing smile. When she smiled, it was like the whole world lit up. It was a very sexy smile, beautiful. She was very good in front of the camera, very natural, but at the same time you had to talk to her or she could freeze very easily. The best thing was to take her off her guard. That's why the paparazzi pictures are all so fantastic. I had to recreate that, to make her relaxed, happy, laughing. When I looked at the photos afterward I knew I had shot well.

"The first time I met her she had a lot of hair and a lot of make-up, with the blue liner on her eyes. The look was very old-fashioned. But the second time she came to me was in Frankfurt and we had the make-up artist and the hairdresser was Sam McKnight. So we cut the hair short. She looked fantastic with short hair and more natural make-up, more modern, young, beautiful. She looked much better with short hair. It's a beautiful face.

"Diana had magic. Everywhere she went people were in love with her. She was so giving and so nice to everybody. It shows in the images. You can see behind the smile something good inside. People think she was calcu-lating, that she planned everything, but she didn't—the charm is the natural way for her. People say she manipulated the press, but I think the press was in love with her. The way she photographed was the way she was.

"Diana was very photogenic. For the paparazzi she was big money. These guys used to work like a pool, a team. One would stay next to the helicopter, one would be in the harbor, and one would go to the beach to make sure they didn't miss anything. These guys made a fortune.

"She was one of the most interesting women I've photographed. She had no pretensions. She was a bit shy. When she talked to people, she would blush, little things like that made her even more charming. There are lots of beautiful people in the world, millions of pretty women, but she had amazing charm. People can be very pretty and have no charm: The way you look is the way you behave, the way you are inside. The beauty inside showed itself. She was very moved by people. You can see it on her face in the pictures. She wasn't like someone who went to these charities and didn't care. She really loved everybody."

"Deeply you could feel something very sad," says Jean-Michel Jarre, "and that actually added to the strong emotional impact she had. When you have this balance between happiness and sadness, or darker areas in your life, it suddenly creates a kind of density in your character, and she had that. So she was not at all this kind of little birdie people tried to describe her as—that's what, in my opinion, the Queen tried to describe—because it was not the case at all. She was definitely much more complex and much deeper."

"She had an air of calm understanding," says Hereward Harrison of ChildLine. "I don't think it's too far-fetched to say it was the sort of feeling that in medieval times people put down to saintliness—the 'Mother Teresa' touch, perhaps. Everybody commented on it. She was very calming, a person who really understood, but she was a princess; she had her aides, she was better dressed than anybody, she smelled wonderful. She wasn't of the people, she was definitely something else and she wasn't Mother Teresa either. I think she was an extraordinary person who, because of her extraordinary nature, had extraordinary naiveté, too. But disillusion happened. It happens to us all, but most of us grow up and get over it [away from public exposure]. What we saw was her actually experiencing the sort of disillusion that adolescents go through: that's why they're so bloody difficult. It's the growing up and becoming our adult characters. And you could see her going through that stage of growing up and witnessing the disillusion. All the fairy-tale stuff fell apart."

❄ ❄ ❄ ❄

SPEAKING OUT ~ "In the early days much of Diana's effort was directed to pleasing her husband. When it became clear that her success only aroused his jealousy, it was too late to draw back. What mattered most was the work and that consisted of pleasing the people she met and attracting media interest to the causes she espoused. She could use clothes to further both objectives. With the exception of her early years as royal fiancée and wife, the Princess of Wales was never terribly enthralled by fashion. It was the power of clothes that interested her. She had an instinctive understanding of their role in creating an image, of their power to communicate ideas and feelings. Diana's most eloquent use of clothes as a symbolic language was the commentary she provided on the breakdown of her marriage," comments Brenda Polan, fashion editor in the 1980s and 1990s for various publications including the *Daily Mail*, *You Magazine* and the *Guardian*.

There is a huge paradox in Diana's life. She was a visual icon and realized that she could use this power, but she was not a natural speaker, which is why, perhaps, she was attracted to ballet as a wordless language. She was, as her family and friends agreed, painfully shy about speaking and aware of her limitations. Public speaking was a huge obstacle for her, especially as she struggled to find a voice on the issues that really mattered to her. Anthony Duckworth-Chad, a relative, recalls, "staying at Balmoral in the cottage when we were up there fishing. She was quite newly married and William had just been born. She'd obviously done several official engagements, but she hadn't made many speeches. She was just about to make rather a large speech somewhere and, you know, she was going to huge trouble. She said, 'This one I really want to do myself, and get it right.'" James Whitaker, of the *Mirror*, remembers how in the early part of her marriage "she couldn't get the words right; she couldn't get the emphasis on the correct words. On one occasion in Australia she was making a speech and she knew she was doing badly and she was utterly enchanting. Suddenly, she stopped and she laughed at herself, and the whole room collapsed, because she knew she was doing it appallingly. In the room 80 percent had loved her before, now 100 percent loved her because of that. She could laugh at herself and really, really mean it."

Throughout her life she had help to write her speeches and took advice about public speaking. In the first years it was Richard, now Lord Attenborough. "In the beginning she was clearly nervous and my first task was to encourage a measure of self-confidence. She struck me as being genuinely shy but, despite this reticence, my overwhelming impression was of an enchanting, somewhat wicked sense of humor, most often applied to herself."[8] She ran through practice interviews with Dickie Arbiter and with Alistair Burnett. In the early 1990s the voice coach Peter Settelen helped her tackle her fears in a more radical way and find her voice.

Roger Singleton of Barnardo's says, "I saw her confidence grow, certainly, in terms of her public performance at events, but public speaking was really a major hurdle for her. Also by the time she was seeking to do more of it, the self-worth questions were maybe looming a little larger in her mind. Having got into the role of being a public celebrity on some of these things, she was starting to ask, 'Well, what difference do I make?' Writing the thank-you letter after a visit was always challenging because what I really wanted to do was persuade her that what she was doing had a real value."

Diana's speeches were often quite simple, but those who worked with her knew that she always made sure she knew exactly what she was talking about. "She was very good at finding things out for herself," says Mark McGreevy of the Depaul Trust. "A lot of people are satisfied with briefing notes on an issue and then feel comfortable getting up to give a speech. She always wanted actually to talk to the young people themselves and the frontline workers and form a judgment from that. When she was going to give one speech on young people, vulnerability, and homelessness, she visited one of the hostels and spent a lot of time talking one to one to young people and then invited the project manager back to Kensington Palace to work through what she was going to say. She wanted to be sure that she was echoing what was genuinely happening, authenticity."

Wendy Thomson at Turning Point witnessed someone who, however much advice she took, always made the issues her own. "Speech-making was always difficult and something which she had to work at to overcome. From being looked at and being silent, to being a person with a voice, that happened in this period. She'd practice and practice her speeches—you'd see all the annotations and underlining and pause marks. She had a speechwriter, but she had to be given things that she felt was right and she could believe, so you could just see how much she was putting into it."

Diana's struggle to find a voice was also a struggle to communicate through the causes she had taken up. In 1992 there was a European Drug Prevention Week, and DrugScope (then the Institute for the Study of Drug Dependency) held a special conference. As Harry Shapiro of DrugScope recalls: "It was a big event and Diana was the keynote speaker. The first thing to say is that she came on our stand and that was really great, because it kind of showed everyone that she was our patron. Again, tons of media and all the rest of it, as you can imagine. We'd written this speech for her, which pulled out the issues about drugs that we wanted said—and she basically threw it away. A few of the bits and pieces that we put in came out in the speech, but instead of the dry policy issues it was much more about families and people who are hurt and all the rest of it, in relationship to drugs, and people's

responsibilities in looking after each other. Clearly it was much more from the heart than what we'd written. Within about three years all of that stuff started coming out about what a miserable time she was having. And maybe other charities will say the same that somehow our occasions were used to give some sort of vent to what she was feeling, where appropriate. She certainly did it in this case. It was all about families and looking after your kids."

Remarkably, by the time the problems in her marriage were becoming public, some of the speeches Diana gave revealed her close identification with the causes she had espoused. "We did a 'women and mental health' event once with Miriam Stoppard and Libby Purves," says Wendy Thomson, "which I think was risky for the princess, given the kind of things that were being said about her at the time. Miriam Stoppard's thesis was that women's problems are men, really, and she had quite a lot of research to back it up. And in the back room beforehand, Libby and Miriam and I and the princess went through what we were each going to say and the princess was a riot. She was just going up on stage and she said, 'My heart is in my throat, you know, I just don't know if I can do it.' And I said, 'Don't worry about it—they'll think you're wonderful. You're a princess.'

"Diana was quite feminist in a way in her thinking. She couldn't say the things that Miriam was saying, but certainly I think she largely agreed with them. Libby Purves had gone through a very serious period of depression as well and the princess understood these issues and had dealt with them. As women, the four of us had a really good conversation, but laughing and saying things like: 'Really, if it wasn't for men everything would be fine,' and 'Well, don't think I don't know!' and she'd roll her eyes the way she did because I guess she was struggling in that area at the time."

There can be little doubt that Diana was struggling to express her own problems. All the speeches she gave in the period leading up to her separation touch on things close to her experiences. The struggle to keep sane under the pressures and expectations put on women, the pressures of perfectionism and low self-esteem, the tragedy and loneliness of being marginalized and finding yourself alone. "Isn't it normal not to be able to cope all the time? Isn't it normal for women as well as men to feel frustrated with life? Isn't it normal to feel angry and want to change a situation that is hurting?" she asked at a conference in 1992. "Perhaps we need to look more closely at the cause of the illness rather than attempt to suppress it. To accept that putting a lid on powerful feelings and emotions cannot be the healthy option. That to offer women the opportunity to explain their predicament sooner, could be a far more effective use of limited resources, rather than wait until their strength to survive has been sapped."

This was not using charities but it was certainly identifying with them. "What affected her most personally she connected to most personally," says Julia Samuel, friend and patron of The Child Bereavement Trust, "and that then had the most impact publicly. It was a full circle." The public reaction made it clear they understood, recognizing that Diana was involved with a cause not just because she cared about it, but also because she identified in some way with the people suffering. It won her huge respect. "She showed great personal courage," says Sir Brian Hill, ex-chair of Great Ormond Street Children's Hospital. "I escorted her to a speech at a conference in London on eating disorders. That was the occasion when she made public her own problems with anorexia. And we walked into this huge auditorium, and she was obviously nervous, but when she got to the podium she spoke with terrific confidence and also deep sincerity. And that was a very powerful, courageous sentence she made. We knew she was going to speak about it, but not in the way that she was going to do it, or the amount of publicity it would attract.

When she left, and it was very strange, just the three of us, and she behaved like a schoolgirl at the end of exams, very excited and very relieved. She was a very young person for a few minutes."

The years prior to the separation were marked by Diana's struggle to find a voice. This was partly to explain herself, as she felt the public, not understanding her situation, might misjudge her. But she also wanted to speak about the issues she had embraced and which she felt she could influence; she wanted to be more than the silent visual icon. To do this involved overcoming formidable obstacles. In the case of public speaking, it meant overcoming her fears and self doubts.

❊ ❊ ❊ ❊

DIANA AND DANCE ~ Diana is best known for charity work in the area of human health and welfare, but one of her most significant commitments was to the arts, particularly dance. She was involved as patron of an established ballet company, English National Ballet (ENB), but was also an active patron of other smaller dance and performance-based charities such as the Benesh Institute and Chicken Shed. ENB was one of the patronages she kept on, and her involvement in fact increased in the last years of her life. "It was a growing relationship that got stronger," says Daniel Jones, a young dancer who had known Diana on and off since meeting her as a 12-year-old at the Royal Ballet School. "It was huge for us, because we had someone up there who was our patron who so loved what we were doing and had a close relationship with everybody in the company. It was great." "Some charities might have wondered: 'Why ballet? Why not us?'" says another dancer, Louise Halliday. "But she had a huge respect for ballet as an art form, for the people involved and what goes into the profession. She recognized that her charity world wasn't just to make people physically well. It was also about making people emotionally well. She saw that ballet could have that transcendent quality so that even if people were ill or had problems in their life—as she had—it provides you with an escape."

Diana became patron of ENB in 1989. But she had been much involved with the company before that when it was known as London Festival Ballet. Peter Schaufuss was the artistic director from 1984. "She came to performances and gala events, but also used the downstairs studio to dance every morning. She would back her car onto the door to the downstairs studio and go in and do her class from nine to ten whenever she could. When she came to the studio, she didn't want to be treated like a princess. She felt comfortable in the artistic environment, and made everybody feel very relaxed. If she came to watch a rehearsal she'd be very friendly with the dancers. She had a real love for dancing. I was very fortunate to be the first person to take her to a discotheque in the mid-'80s—officially. She was the guest of honor at a function when we were still London Festival Ballet. Peter Stringfellow gave us the Hippodrome and we had a huge fund-raising party there. There was a sit-down dinner and everyone was dancing."

When Diana first started dancing at ENB's studios, Princess Margaret was still patron. "We had a function in Bradford for the European Union, and Princess Margaret was guest of honor," says Schaufuss. "She pulled me aside and said, 'Peter, I think I should step aside and Diana should take over as patron.' She knew how much Diana loved the company and the ballet. I already knew, but that was her official way of doing it."

"Princess Margaret stepped down," says Schaufuss, "and we had a stepping-down occasion. It was very nice. As part of that process, we also changed the name from London Festival Ballet to English National Ballet, so it

was a whole change of image for us. It was the right thing for the company, because with Diana there were tremendous possibilities for the company in terms of prestige and fund-raising." According to Schaufuss, he had a much more direct dialogue with Diana than with Princess Margaret. "It was much easier to work with Diana as a patron. She had a daily class in the building. Sometimes she couldn't do it because she had commitments all over the country, but on a regular basis I knew she would be in the building so you could talk much more informally and openly to her about all kinds of things. I danced many times with Princess Margaret at those functions we had, and she loved that kind of dancing, but with Diana it was a much more informal relationship. Diana could really understand the technique and she could appreciate things that were going on, on stage, technically, in a different way. Not as a professional dancer, but as a good amateur."

"Princess Margaret and Princess Diana got on very well," says Derek Deane, who became artistic director of ENB in 1993, and knew both of them well. "There were a lot of similar traits in their characters. Princess Margaret was sharp; Diana could be sharp. They were both sharp-witted, great sense of humor, a love of the ballet. Princess Margaret was also very insecure in her own way and covered it up basically by being rude to people. Diana was very insecure and covered it up by being the princess of glamour. Princess Margaret was more intellectual, but both were quite instinctive and very stubborn. At first Margaret took her under her wing. She didn't think that Diana had a clue of what she was letting herself in for. I think she tried on many occasions to help her through difficult patches because she felt sorry for her."

Peter Schaufuss believes Diana made the ENB a second home partly because she identified with performers but mainly because of her absolute love of ballet. "She admired dancers. She knew how difficult it was to go out on stage and do something in her own way, and we also have to go out on stage, in our way, in front of an audience. That's also why she was very relaxed in the ballet studio or around dancers or myself. She didn't have to act a role. She could just be Diana. Diana loved many art forms and culture, but ballet had a special place in her heart. Dance is a language without words, a language you can perform anywhere throughout the world, across boundaries, across everywhere. She felt it was a universal way of communicating, a way for her to express herself without any words. Also, when she was alone in the downstairs studio, perhaps it was a freedom. Sometimes when those pressures were high she could just go and take her ballet class, or go to a ballet performance, or go and watch a rehearsal, and it would be a different world. She could find a place of freedom in the middle of all the restrictions and demands."

The dancers at ENB could never quite believe their luck in having a patron so wholeheartedly involved as Diana. "Quite a few people in high society have things to do with ballet," says Daniel Jones, "but not many have quite such a close association with the dancers as Diana." "She totally wasn't in it to be 'the patron,'" says Jo Clarke, one of the dancers. "She absolutely loved it here and loved what we did. Once she turned up on Valentine's Day with a heart-shaped cake. It was just an excuse for her to show affection, almost as if she was grateful."

ENB was housed in Jay Mews, a ten-minute walk from her home in Kensington Palace and Diana obviously looked on it as a comforting social environment and as a sort of therapy. To the amazement of the young dancers who joined the troupe, "Sometimes she'd just walk in and watch a rehearsal unannounced and we'd look round and think, God, Princess Diana has just come in the room. Princess Diana is here."

Once they overcame their shock, they quickly got used to it. Dancers like Alice Crawford formed the impression that "she almost preferred coming to watch rehearsals and seeing behind the scenes. She loved the shows but she especially loved chatting with us all and finding out how we were feeling." They were all amazed to find how easy it was to talk to her, partly because of her personality but also because of how well she understood the life of the dancers. "She spoke to us not as if she was Princess Diana," says Louise Halliday, "but as someone who was really interested and really friendly. Other people ask things like: 'What is it like to dance on stage?' But she was more like, 'Are you tired?' 'God, you must be tired.' 'When are you going to get a day off?' 'When are you going to get out of here after the performance?' She came over as someone who knew exactly what our lives were like."

"The great thing," says Daniel Jones, "is that when she came here no one froze. People were quite natural with her. I don't suppose there were many environments she could walk into and not have any reaction. We literally would not react in any way. She'd come into the studio and we'd carry on with what we were doing." "It was never in the slightest intrusive," says Jo Clarke. "You never had to change or behave differently. You'd all just carry on and there would be Princess Diana sitting in the corner. She never demanded any attention."

Louise Halliday is convinced that Diana got a huge amount from these unannounced visits. "She used to just come in and get to know people. It was escapism for her. We weren't ill. We were just healthy human beings. It must have been quite depressing for her to reflect on the places she'd been to but this was uplifting, because you could see she really enjoyed it. She had a real love for the ballet and a particular fascination for the lives of dancers."

Derek Deane had first met Diana "when she was really young with Charles and I was still in the Royal Ballet and she'd just become the Princess of Wales. She was this terribly shy thing, although always lovely with a great sense of humor." When Derek first joined ENB as artistic director in 1993, he found Diana was "a bit reserved." "I'm quite gregarious myself and quite a big personality and so when I first met her she was very standoffish and very reticent. Then as time went on she got to know my character and she got much more relaxed. We had a very similar sense of humor. When she came to visit we used to have sandwiches in my room and close the door.

"She saw ENB as a place she could get inside and have people around her with whom she could relax. If everything was going well in her life and she was riding on the crest we wouldn't see her so often. If she was very depressed and very upset and very tired, we'd see her at Jay Mews more. She said to me a lot, "It's so marvelous to come in and watch rehearsals for a couple of hours. I adore ballet so much, it's one of the very few things that can completely take my mind off everything else I have to deal with. I feel comfortable in Jay Mews. I feel warm. I feel I'm not out of my depth here.'

"Because she did ballet when she was younger, she was quite knowledgeable. So when we were in the room and I was shouting about dancers' feet and so on, she knew what I was talking about. I think a lot of time when she used to go to things she was very nervous because she was out of her depth. Also, she obviously related to dancers and the dancers with eating disorders. I used to talk to her about that quite a lot."

Diana's identification with dancers and ballet went deep. "Ballet," says Daniel Jones, "is a beautiful thing. It's the fantasy of perfection and that's what she dreamed of. But it was more than just a fascination with perfection—if it was, she would have just come to see the shows. She wouldn't have made so much effort to come and see the real hard work and all the nuts and bolts kinds of things that really makes it tick."

"She could tell we were all striving for perfection even when we're here and it's all a bit grubby," says Alice Crawford. "I think she identified with

us because she knew that when we perform before the public, we dancers feel we are maybe making mistakes whereas what the audience see is perfection. They aren't sitting there thinking, 'That was awful, that step was wrong.' It was the same with Diana. Everyone thought: 'She's beautiful, she's lovely.' But we knew underneath she wasn't happy and she had problems. We knew what was going on, but to us she was still this beautiful princess."

The dancers all noticed how Diana understood one problem ballet dancers face all too well: The pursuit of the body beautiful. "A huge part of this job is the ideal body and the extremes that people go to achieve that and she had an ideal of herself. It affects all of us. You get a lot of it in this environment," says Daniel Jones. Derek Deane describes how conscious, informed and open Diana was about the eating disorders that affect so many dancers. "Some-times she would look at a particular dancer and say, 'God, she's looking very thin.' And I would say, 'Yes, well, we've had problems with her again, but she's seeing somebody and we're organizing this.' And she could relate to this and had an enormous amount of experience there, so I think that was another reason why she loved being there. Not just from the 'point shoe' point of view, but also because there were a lot of emotions in her that she could see and understand in a ballet company situation."

Diana also found in ballet a realm of emotional openness lacking, or even prohibited, in her own life. "Ballet deals with universal emotions. On the surface they might be about princesses and swans who turn into princesses, but they're not really, they're about love and loss, rejection and betrayal," says Louise Halliday. "You can see elements of your own life being illustrated. Maybe Diana had a more dramatic life—she had these wonderful things and terrible things happening to her—so you can say maybe she saw more parallels, but it's a universal truth that people come to see ballet and feel something familiar."

"Diana was a very emotional person," says Daniel Jones, "and she probably found it very hard that that didn't go down very well in the family she married into. She never wanted to hide any of that but that's what they all feel they have to do. There's none of that here. If someone feels like crying in rehearsal, they cry in rehearsals and if someone's going through a trauma it all comes out. It's a very open environment. In order to create anything artistic you have to spark and you have to be honest about your emotions because otherwise it's just bland and there's nothing there. You have to feel love and feel hate."

John Travolta wasn't the only star to be dazzled by Diana as a dancing partner. Others included Clint Eastwood and America's current defense secretary, General Colin Powell. "I was chosen to lead her onto the dance floor to dance to *Cheek to Cheek* at a gala ball in Washington in 1996 which raised a million dollars for breast cancer charities," he says. "Although I'd met her previously this was the first time I got close to her. She made me more nervous that many military opponents but it was fine. I've always considered myself pretty nifty with the foxtrot, but she was niftier."

Sensationally, Diana also performed once in public, with dancer Wayne Sleep who she asked to partner her as a "surprise" for her husband. "She knew a lot about dance," says Wayne Sleep. "She would have liked to be a dancer. She wasn't quite the right shape, but she could have made it into a ballet company more on the jazz side. She'd have made a very good jazz dancer. And, of course, she was so glamorous, so she'd have been the leading light. Something more exotic, where beauty came into it, like on the catwalk.

"When we first met, I was on a roll. I'd just done *Cats, Song and Dance*. I was still with the Royal Ballet at that time, so I was doing West End and Royal Ballet, then my own show that autumn. She'd been to see my shows and we got rather pally when she came up with this idea that she wanted to dance with me for the Friends' Christmas party at Covent Garden. I went, 'No! I'm far too small and she's far too tall. I would be a laughing stock. She must be mad.' Then I thought, well, I'd better go along.

"It was a Christmas present. It was a joke. The idea for this dance was hers. The music was hers: Billy Joel's *Uptown Girl*. I've only just got the message, 20 years later, because I never thought of myself as a downtown boy. I thought she just liked the rhythm. None of them wanted her to do it. And, of course, that made her more defiant. Anne Beckwith-Smith [Diana's lady-in-waiting] was terrified. She didn't see the routine before we did it, nobody was allowed to, even her detective had to stay outside the door. So God knows what they thought was going to happen. It could have been a striptease for all they knew. Charles only learned on the day but he didn't know what she was going to do."

"She was hysterical with giggles just before we went on. She put on her other earrings. I made her wear very low heels. I said, 'You've got to do me one favor. The lower the heel the better!' I hadn't been back to the Opera House for three years, so when I came on I got a huge reception. I did a few big steps just to show off I could still do it. And then out she comes. Well, when she came on I've never heard 2,500 people all gasp at the same time. We nearly fainted with lack of oxygen. I made her do eight walks. Uptown, three, four, five, six, seven, eight, look at the audience, three, four, five, six, seven, eight, in order for them to register it was her. They all thought it was one of the corps de ballet girls doing a look-alike impersonation. Then I gave her another eight steps. I knew what the audience was going to think.

"So we did a little bit of ballet in the routine, we did a bit of tap and then we did a big kick line from *Chorus Line* at the end. It was perfectly up her street. And we made it funny. We did a one-up thing. She'd do a pirouette; I'd do a pirouette. She'd look at me, smug, push me down, and kick over my head and go there, and walk away. So it was hysterical. And then when we did the kick line at the end—because I know how to do a finale, darling—it brought the house down. And then she went: 'I want to do it again, I want to do it again.' I said: 'You're not. Leave them wanting more.' Because then the cameras would have come out, then they'd have seen the thigh, then they would have seen me between her legs, holding her up and running across the stage, gripping me round the neck, all that. They were all in such shock they couldn't even reach for their handbags.

"Well, she's never had applause for dance. She gets applauded; of course, she's a performer, they all are. But to be performing something you've always wanted to do in your career, at Covent Garden. . . . she made Covent Garden. And so she goes: 'This beats the wedding!' Which obviously not, but, you know. And that's the sort of jibe she came out with all the time.

"I think she developed self-confidence through doing this. The dance she did with me was the first time that she showed complete defiance of what they wanted. And it was something none of the rest could do. It gave her strength. I can do this and people tell me I could have done this if I wanted to do it, and that gave her strength."

"You see her as a shy person," says Anita Roddick, founder of The Body Shop, "but to get on the stage with Wayne Sleep and dance—I wouldn't do that to save my life. There were these bouts of unexpected courage, not just moral courage but courage to do this. It's paradoxical isn't it. She was shy and timid as a young person and, suddenly, the spirit's almost like it's unstoppable."

But it was English National Ballet that was the backdrop for one of Diana's own most dramatic moments. "It was the day the divorce came through, and she came in and she went, 'Oh bloody hell, it's all like this,'" says Derek Deane. "And I said, 'Yeah, I know. Well, never mind, what do you want?' 'Oh, I just want to see a bit of dancing.' So we went down and had a look at some rehearsals and there was this girl being chucked around and floating about and I looked at her and she just had a look on her face of: 'Oh, God, I wish that was me.' She had such a look of: 'Things would be so much easier if I had been a dancer and I had had a different life.' When she was watching rehearsals and things, I saw envy in her face because she loved it so much. But this wasn't envy, this was: 'What a shame I wasn't something else.'"

As always though, Diana's humor never deserted her. Jim Fletcher started his new job as the communications officer for the ENB on the day of the divorce. The world's media was in attendance. "My first day on the job was the day of the divorce and I was introduced to her. She turned to me and said: 'So you're the press officer. This is your first day on the job. And I come—on the day of my divorce!' And she laughed like a drain. She thought this was just the funniest thing."

It was ENB that also provided the backdrop for one of her last public appearances, for the gala production of *Swan Lake*. She had drawn in sponsorship for the production from Mohammed Al Fayed and Harrods, and one of the most enduring images of Diana remains her appearance that night in the simple blue shift dress designed by Jacques Azagury.

For this 1997 production of *Swan Lake*, Diana posed with the ballerinas for a promotional photo. According to Alice Crawford, "She felt privileged to be our patron. Whenever we had photos taken she would say: 'No, no, you come in front.' For this she had to come and sit in the middle of us and you could tell she felt uncomfortable; she didn't see herself as more important. It was a lovely occasion. We were all laughing and talking. It was after a dress rehearsal and none of us had make-up on. We were all looking sweaty and disheveled and she just looked perfect—as always. We were kneeling down and she was concerned because we had to kneel for so long."

Derek Deane remembers that this production was when Mohammed Al Fayed invited Diana down to France. "We'd done my big *Swan Lake* in the round and she was fabulous. I'd asked her to go on television for me and just say a couple of words. She only said about three lines, but she did it. I said: 'Thanks very much,' and she said something like, 'Well, that's all you're going to get out of me this year,' and then laughed and giggled. I was sitting next to her at the dinner and Mr. Al Fayed was on the other side and she said to me, 'What are you doing for your holidays this summer?' And I said, 'I'm going down to France again. Friends of mine always take this house near St Tropez.' She said, 'Oh, Mohammed's invited me and the boys down there for ten days in July.' I said to her: 'You have to be out of your mind! You of all people in St Tropez!' And she said, 'Well, he's got his own enclave and a private beach.' I said, 'Nothing is private down there. You could have fences 50 feet high. St Tropez is not private.' And she said, 'You're overreacting.' She always used to say to me, 'Derek, you're overreacting.' She said, 'Oh, it's going to be fine because nobody's going to know we're there.' I said, 'Have you been there before? There is a telephoto lens on every street corner. You'll never be able to go out.' 'Oh, don't be ridiculous,' she said. 'I'll call you, 'cause we're there at the same time, and once we've settled in you can come over.' And I said: 'I'm telling you now, this will never happen.'"

She was our greatest royal personality since Queen Victoria.

Paul Johnson

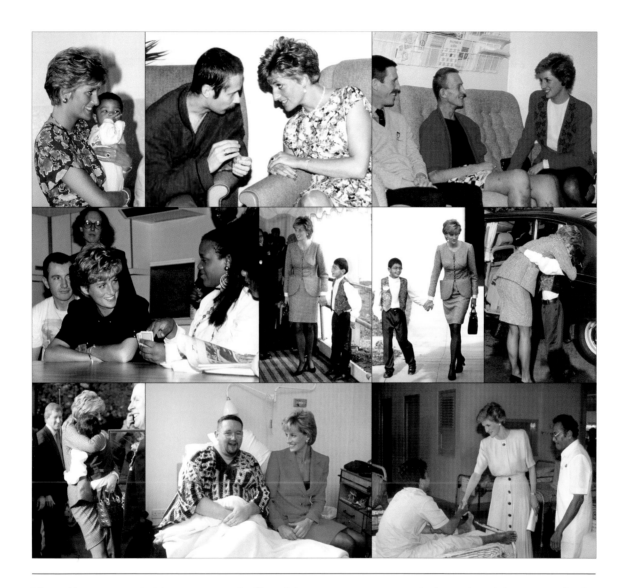

I found her a remarkable person, really. She did an enormous amount of good work for our particular field. She once said to me in Birmingham, "Had I had a normal life, I would have wanted to be a social worker."

Ted Unsworth

The trips I did with her made you either cry or laugh and there was very little in between. You either laughed with relief or happiness, or this lump in your throat sat there, and you just felt humble and lucky.

Lady Sarah McCorquodale

Her courtesy was of the purest kind—it sprang from her inner conviction that those she was seeking to serve, and there sometimes seemed no limit to their number, deserved nothing but the best. *Patrick Jephson*

26th October, 1990

Dear Ted,

You were kind to take the trouble to write, there was really no need as I quite understood your absence!

Les has been keeping me in order and his public speaking now has reached great heights!

I have missed seeing you on recent 'Turning Point' occasions, but hopefully our paths will cross soon, otherwise you may forget what your Patron looks like!

My warmest thanks, Ted, for thinking of me - I was very touched.

Yours most sincerely,

Diana.

8th April, 1992

Dear Ted,

I was so touched to receive your kind message on the death of my Father - I do miss him dreadfully as he was such a strong and positive force in our lives ...

Thank you for writing as you did and thank you for caring - it made all the difference at this difficult time.

With my best wishes,
from.

Diana.

Ted Unsworth, Esq.

22nd March, 1995

Dear Ted,

Your letter came as a very sad surprise, although I should have known that the qualities which made you such an outstanding Chairman could not be given exclusively to Turning Point for ever. I am so pleased for you - and hope that the new job, and all that comes with it, will bring every happiness.

I'm just one of many who will always have reason to be immensely grateful for everything you have achieved at Turning Point. Your active concern for those so often abandoned by hope will be remembered in hundreds of lives rebuilt with your help. And, never forget, the Patron will always recall with affection your special kindness and unfailing support, please keep in touch ...

With love from.

Diana.

March: 5th
1992.

Dear Sister Barbara,

You were so kind to write & I did appreciate the contents enormously... Thank you.

I am sad that the time has come for you to move on, but I feel confident that our paths

will cross in Glasgow! During my visits to the Passage & others you always made me feel particularly welcome & I did look forward to more occasions very much.

I will always have the memories of our meetings to reflect upon, Sister Barbara, & I do wish you all the best in your next vocation.

This comes with

My love & deepest admiration,
from.

Diana.

KENSINGTON PALACE

Aprie : 1st
1992.

Dearest Sister Barbara,
        I was deeply
touched to receive your
letter & all that was
in the contents.
    Thank you for writing
& thank you for caring
at this difficult time.

I miss my Father dread-
fully as he was such
a strong & positive force
in our lives....

    With my love &
heartfelt thanks for
your prayers & thoughts.

    from.
        Diana.

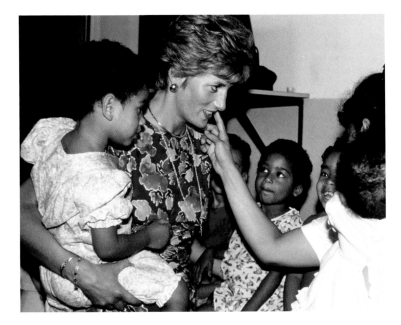
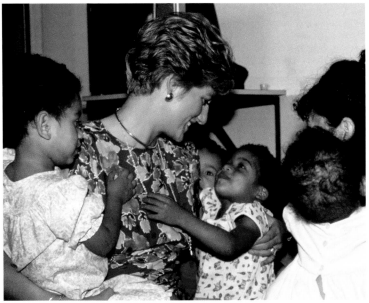
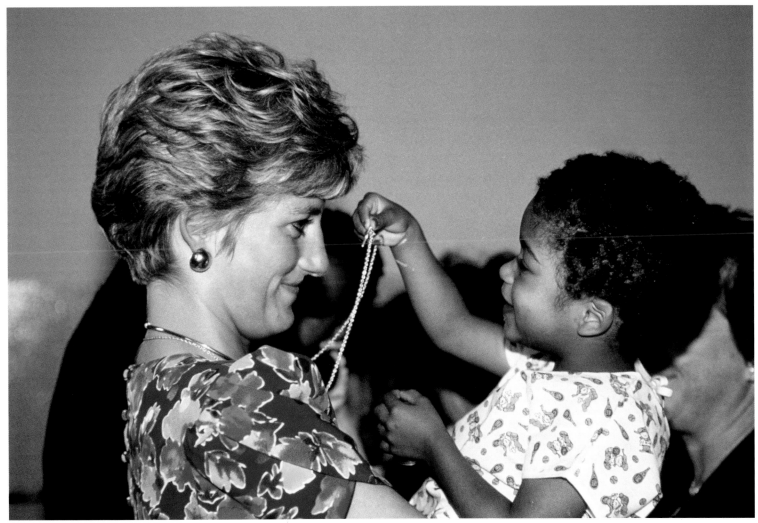

I saw her confidence grow, certainly, in terms of her public performance at events, but public speaking was really a major hurdle for her.

Roger Singleton

Lots of love Sam,
from Diana× 1991.

She saw English National Ballet as a place she could get inside and have people around her with whom she could relax. . . . . She said to me a lot: "It's so marvelous to come in and watch rehearsals for a couple of hours. I adore ballet so much, it's one of the very few things that can completely take my mind off everything else I have to deal with."

Derek Deane

I think she developed self-confidence through doing this. The dance she did with me was the first time that she showed complete defiance of what they wanted. And it was something none of the rest could do. It gave her strength. I can do this and people tell me I could have done this if I wanted to do it, and that gave her a strength.

Wayne Sleep

CHAPTER FOUR – THE IRREPLACEABLE

Diana, unquestionably, was unique in her approach to helping others and had a special gift with people from all walks of life which I doubt will ever be matched.

Kate Slater (née Menzies)

I will always be glad that I knew the princess, and always think of her in very strong and positive terms, as will Hillary. We can only hope that her work will go forward and that everyone who can will support her two fine sons and help them to have the life and the future she would want. She showed the world that people living with AIDS deserve not isolation but compassion, and that simple gesture helped to change world opinion, helped to give people with AIDS hope, helped to save lives of people at risk.[1]

William J. Clinton

Through 1992 and 1993 Diana continued with her intensive involvement with the charities and made some big trips, to Egypt, Pakistan, Nepal and Zimbabwe, the most popular representative of the royal family abroad. Yet the pressures on her during this period were considerable. Not only had she had to deal with the death of her beloved father in March 1992, but by then she had had to face the fact that her marriage was over. In effect Charles and Diana's lives had been lived apart for some time. Talking of her marriage leading up to the time of the separation, Diana later said: "We struggled along. We did our engagements together. And in our private life it was obviously turbulent."

But while the separation in December 1992 may have formalized the breakdown for public benefit, it did not bring either happiness or clarity for Diana. She said that the separation caused her "deep, deep, profound sadness . . . " However much support she got in public, her marriage breakdown caused immense private grief.

Catherine Walker was moved by the split in Diana's life between public adulation and private loneliness. "These were lonely times for her. People wanted to love Diana, the press wanted her image over and over again, *Vogue* had her on its cover, intellectuals wanted to analyze her and of course we designers dreamt of dressing her. The contrast between this wonderfully desirable image and the reality of her private unhappiness was too much for her to live with and her grief became my sadness. It was very hard for her after the separation. She had lost some of the love in her heart in her struggle to survive and her clothes became demure for a period for two reasons. First, she was vulnerable and upset and could only make a statement of how she felt through what she wore and second, I suspect, out of respect for her children."[2]

Diana was still officially within the royal family, but formal separation had left her role very unclear, something that was particularly problematic for foreign trips. "People's agendas changed overnight," said Diana. "I was now the separated wife of the Prince of Wales. I was a problem. It showed itself by visits abroad being blocked, by things that had naturally come my way being stopped, letters that got lost. Everything changed after we became separated and life became very difficult then for me."[3]

"No longer royal, yet far from being a commoner," says Jayne Fincher, "Diana was trapped between two worlds. She had lost the backing of the establishment. She had also lost the family life she had always envisaged with her husband and sons. But, despite all this, she remained a winner in the eyes of the world."

However ambiguous her status, in places where Britain's arcane royal protocol was less important, Diana's value and popularity was obvious. "She draws interest wherever she goes and whatever she does,"[4] said Anne Giscard D'Estaing, wife of former French president Valery Giscard D'Estaing. On her first visit to France after the separation, French *Vogue* carried a Demarchelier photo of Princess Diana on their cover with the headline: "Courage, Princesse."

Lord Hurd, then the UK's foreign secretary, was well aware of the situation. "She was very, very highly regarded abroad. She had this power of enchantment, put it that way. I've a vivid recollection of the European summit held in Edinburgh in December 1992, and I think it was while we were there or just a little bit earlier, that the announcement was made that the marriage was coming to an end and there was a separation. But Diana was there on the royal yacht *Britannia* when the Queen entertained all the foreign heads of government, and they didn't know what to make of this at all. She dispensed a sort of magic, really, partly because she was very beautiful, partly because she was very famous, and partly because she just had that personal magnetism.

There was no way we could guide her to carry out government policy, that wasn't the relationship at all. She was a phenomenon—but so far as Britain was concerned, overseas, a very good one.

"Diana was keen that she should be able to pursue her particular interests, particular charities she was involved with, overseas. And a problem arose when she was no longer a member of the royal family, as to how she should be received. Foreigners, people like the president of Egypt wanted to receive her, and they wanted to pay her honor. That was absolutely quite right, in my view, and we just had to make sure she was properly received, but that she wasn't representing Britain in any formal way."

Baroness Chalker, then Britain's overseas development minister, who had an affectionate relationship with Diana, was also well aware of Diana's cachet abroad. She supported her on several trips: "People were really ecstatic to see her. All those presidents that didn't meet her used to say, 'Why didn't you bring her here?' So she was very much wanted. She found it very hard to understand why, as she put it, 'the court' seemed to be so much against her. She knew she could do things for the de-mining campaign, she knew she could do things for leprosy; she knew she could do things.

"I remember her standing at the top of one of the foothills of the Himalayas and saying, 'Now I know what it feels like to be on top of the world.' We went to villages and, tall as she was, she would bend down low to go into houses with low doorways. She obviously couldn't communicate with the people. They knew she was some great queen from overseas, but they weren't quite sure who she was. She managed very, very well."

One solution to the fact that Diana was no longer representing the royal family abroad was for her to make foreign trips with charities. The royal family's loss was the charities' gain. Traveling with the British Red Cross, The Leprosy Mission and Help the Aged to Nepal in March 1993—her first solo trip after the separation—may have also crystallized her thinking about a possible future role. Diana's reception in Nepal reassured her that an international role was still very much on the cards, with or without royal support. To the press attending it seemed as if the whole country turned out to see her.

Her trip to Zimbabwe in July 1993 repeated this, attracting a huge level of press attention. One picture of Diana feeding children at the refugee camp appeared under the heading of "Di, the Dinner Lady" but it was the sort of attention to third-world poverty charities can only dream of. However absurd the headlines, Mike Whitlam, former director general of the British Red Cross, understood their value. "She really had the ability to attract ordinary people, people in positions of authority and the media. That combination was dynamite for a charity." Diana formally dropped patronage of the British Red Cross in 1996 but her relationship with the charity and with Mike Whitlam developed and she traveled with them to Angola for the landmines campaign.

If Diana thought that the intense scrutiny of the press might lessen after her separation, she was wrong. The tabloids continued to pore over all aspects of her private life and intrusive secret pictures were taken of her when she was exercising at a gym. In December 1993 at a conference for the charity Headway (the brain injury association) she delivered a speech that came as a bolt from the blue to many of her charities. She announced her intention to "withdraw" from public life, pleading to be given "time and space" so she could refocus her energies. "When I started my public life 12 years ago," she said, "I understood that the media might be interested in what I did. I realized then that their attention would inevitably focus on both our public and private lives. But I was not aware of how overwhelming that attention would become; nor the extent to which it would affect both my public duty and my private life in a manner that has been hard to bear."

It was a very dramatic speech, and many of the charities wrote offering their support and reassuring her just how much she had meant to them. Many were alarmed at losing the enormous benefits her patronage had brought. Although she didn't officially resign her patronages at that point, Patrick Jephson, her former private secretary, thinks she had pretty well decided at that point to reduce her charities to the six core ones as she did finally in 1996.

This decision has remained a controversial point in Diana's life, inviting very different interpretations. Yet all the evidence—including Diana's own words—is of a genuine attempt to escape press scrutiny and refocus her life and work. "I attach great importance to my charity work," she said, "and intend to focus on a smaller range of areas in the future. Over the next few months I will be seeking a more suitable way of combining a meaningful public role with a more private life." Certainly those charities she remained involved with and the new ones she took up in the following years bear out that publicly stated intention. "When the separation was announced, it was a tremendous release for her," says Sir Anthony Tippett, former chief executive of Great Ormond Street Hospital for Children. "I remember her saying, 'Now I can really donate my time and my energies to getting on with my work with my charities.' We were one of the fortunate beneficiaries and she never ever let us down in terms of continued level of interest and support for the rest of her days. No matter what was going on, Great Ormond Street was much in her mind."

"Downscaling her work," says Les Rudd, former chief executive of Turning Point, "was a really hard decision to make. She'd obviously built up a lot of attachments over time and there was an absolute need for her to ration-alize what she was doing. She didn't withdraw from public life; she focused her energies more effectively and identified herself even more with some very unpopular and politically sensitive things. The HIV thing at the time was going down . . . there was a lot of homophobic stuff. She stuck with the National AIDS Trust. The whole landmines thing at the time was totally unsexy, and how many really important people, governments, corporations took that up? Obviously, she had an interest in these areas, but the issue for her was also where she could make the most difference. On a world scale, not just locally."

"Over the years of her involvement," says Nick Hardwick, formerly of Centrepoint, "she visited our homeless projects about 40 times. She gave us a bit of a rest for about six months after her 'withdrawal' and then got involved again. All along I had the impression she preferred the private visits to the public ones and she continued to do those. But she didn't let us down with the public ones—even one engagement scheduled for three days after her withdrawal speech. We said to her, 'Look we've sent out the invitations, a lot of people are going to be very disappointed.' So after some time she agreed to come, but not to speak. Of course the media turned up drawing attention to her having retired from public life one day and doing this a few days later. It was very unfair because at that point, she would rather not have come, but she came because she knew what it meant to us and didn't want to let people down."

English National Ballet was the one non-health charity that Diana remained a patron of and in fact her involvement grew over this period. Vivienne Parry, who knew Diana through the charity Birthright (now known as WellBeing), saw not someone withdrawing from work but someone evolv-ing, leaving behind the fund-raising and devoting her time to the charities that could further this evolution. "Some of the charities had become terribly

dependent and hadn't developed other sources of income. So when Diana said that she was dropping them, they were pretty devastated. But her attitude was: 'Well, you know, they've benefited from me.' She was on a different path: The evolution of clothes-horse to grown-up, concerned woman."

When Katharine Graham, the writer and long-time publisher of the *Washington Post*, met Diana in America in 1994, she met a mature woman with her own focus and path. "If you spent time with her, you felt Diana's extraordinary strength, as well as vulnerability and her somewhat mocking ever-present humor. I asked her if she ever thought of going to college now that she was alone. She found my question hard to believe and commented with irony: 'I've already had an education.' She was right. Even though she lacked degrees, she had had a long, excruciating experience."[5]

Those who wished Diana would disappear from view were disap-pointed. She was emerging as a remarkable figure—a confident, compassionate humanitarian.

❋ ❋ ❋ ❋

TOUCHING INDIVIDUALS ~ throughout her life, Diana had enjoyed great rapport with people outside the charmed circles of royalty or aristocracy. She had a gift for meaningful communication with people even in the most difficult circumstances. Neurosurgeon Peter Gautier-Smith was astonished when he first met Diana in 1988 at the way in which she communicated with "a young man with severe head injury suffering from dysphasia—a speech disorder in which you can't find the words. These people are at a loss the whole time and may be very disabled, and when she said, 'Hello. What's your name?' he was totally defeated. Instead of being embarrassed or moving on, she said, 'Is that your walkman you've got there?' And he nodded. She said, 'Can I listen?' which she did, and she said, 'What's your favorite group?' And then in about less than a minute he was actually able to say some words to her and I thought that was a very spontaneous skill. The striking thing about her was that she actually listened to what you had to say. Some VIPs look over the person's shoulder at somebody perhaps more interesting, but she never did that. She focused on people, listened to what they had to say, clearly took it in and asked pertinent questions without being intrusive or going on too long. Those social skills were very remarkable."

Drawing on this aspect of herself grew increasingly important to Diana as she reached out to individuals across the heads of the establishment both in the UK and internationally and began to speak out on issues that she cared deeply about. It was these aspects that combined to create her unique status: a campaigner on humanitarian issues based on a deep connection with the people involved. "The emotional commitment is the new element Diana brought in," says Esther Rantzen. "And the fact is that when you have suffered, as many of the people she helped have suffered, the idea that someone is emotionally in touch with you is healing."

Vivienne Parry noticed a shift of balance away from being someone who merely lent her presence to openings, and fundraising events. "During the period that she was involved with Birthright, Diana became more and more interested in doing things that were less fussy. She didn't want to be noticed for what she was wearing all the time, and we began to do more events with her that were orientated round people who had problems. I always remember one particular lunch we held during the week when the first serialization of the Andrew Morton book was out. She was beside herself. She was terribly anxious and wasn't really concentrating well. Then there was a private reception and she met a woman who had had something awful, like

13 miscarriages, and then had gone on to adopt all these children. As she told Diana, she just burst into tears and Diana put her arms round her and completely put this woman at ease. It wasn't in any way forced, but she had that knack of being able to go right in and say exactly the right thing to people. You know how you don't know what to say to someone in distress? Well, Diana did know what to say. Increasingly, knowing what to say and knowing what pleasure and relief it gave people, became a way of validating herself. If no one else was telling her what a good job she was doing then, actually, ordinary people were telling her."

"Diana, unquestionably, was unique in her approach to helping others and had a special gift with people from all walks of life which I doubt will ever be matched," says Kate Slater (née Menzies), a close friend to Diana.

Ken Wharfe, as Diana's personal protection officer, was closely aware of Diana's intuitive connection with the people. "You can't dupe people out there. They felt for the first time that here was somebody different. Instead of getting out of a car and walking down a line of metal barriers, she identified the poor woman that had probably only just been able to get there. Diana would dig her out from the back and have a word with her. Ken Wharfe also knew exactly how much private visiting Diana did. "There were many things that we did outside of the glare of publicity and nobody ever knew about them. We went often to Basil Hume's day center. I remember them cautioning us saying, 'You know we get some very funny people in here. Just be careful. They do swear a lot and get violent.' Once there was a guy there who was still drunk from the night before. I think the princess had given him an old tweed jacket she'd dug out. He turned around and blasted off this mouthful of expletives: 'Keep your f---ing jacket!' But it didn't bother her."

Ken Wharfe admits to some uncomfortable moments from the security point of view. "When the Prince of Wales broke his wrist in a polo fall, he was in a hospital in Nottingham. It was quite bizarre to see the prince sitting at the end of this unoccupied ward in his bed. The princess went in, and I stood outside but the conversation wasn't lengthy. I said, 'You ought to spend a little bit longer than this, Ma'am.' She said, 'I can't, it's just too painful. I'm going to go and have a look at a ward in the hospital.' I said, 'This is not a good idea, but if you insist, let's clear it first.' So we spoke to the hospital sister and she said that if the princess could just come into the intensive care ward on the way out, it would be fantastic for the parents of the patients there. So we went to the intensive care ward and there was a young man who had been injured in a motorcycle accident. He was on a life support machine. His family were there and she took this guy's hand and said to his family, 'Look, I hope he's all right. What's your address? I'd like to know what's happening.' They exchanged addresses . . . and, well, this guy, Dean Woodward, made a remarkable recovery."

"Later, at Sandringham, she said to me: 'Ken, can we go to Nottingham to see these people, the Woodwards, because their son's having a party?' And I said, 'Well, if you must, we'll do it.' I didn't have a chance to go and look at it, but I sent a colleague who said it was fine. So we turned up and, of course, the whole street was out and it all came out in the local paper the following day. Then we had this whole abuse in the national press about why the princess was doing this. Actually it was a genuine wish on her part to do something—contrary to what people said, there was no ulterior motive."

The relationship Diana had with the Woodward family was typical of her unusual approach. Dean Woodward had been in a coma as the result of a serious road accident and his mother, father and young wife were keeping vigil at the Nottingham hospital when Diana came upon Dean's mother in the corridor and asked her why she was crying.

"In intensive care," says Dean's wife, Jane, "there was me, Dean's dad and mom, and in walked Princess Diana. We were like rats cornered. We thought, 'Oh, my God, where are we going to go?' But she came in, and broke the ice. We never felt uneasy or anything. We just felt it was like another person with us." After that initial visit, Diana called in on Dean every day, developing a warm relationship with his mom, Ivy. When Charles left the hospital, she followed Dean's progress with telephone calls and letters.

To everyone's relief Dean emerged from the coma and Diana telephoned and wrote to his mother to follow his progress. Dean was transferred to Lyndon Lodge to recuperate. "I was having me dinner at Lyndon Lodge, in the grounds of the city hospital and the receptionist came out and said, 'Dean there's a phone call for you. It's Diana.' I've got a sister called Diane and I said, 'Tell her I'm having my dinner. Call back later.' When she called back I said, 'Hello, me duck.' I'd had a tracheotomy so couldn't talk properly. She said, 'Do you know who you are talking to?' And I said, 'Yeah, Diane.' And she said, 'No. You're talking to Princess Diana from Kensington Palace.' Unbelievable!

"She said, 'Are you OK? Is the family OK? Is there anything you need?' I said, 'Yeah. When you visited me, I was unconscious. Can you come and visit me now I'm awake?' And she said, 'Yeah, I'll come and visit you, but I don't want any reporters, just a casual visit.' And she kept her word and came to visit me."

The whole family gathered at Dean's uncle's house near the motorway when Diana came. "The future queen, as she was then, came in with her arms open, gave me mum a hug. 'Hello, Ivy!' First name terms! 'Hello, Ivy. Hello, John'—to me dad. Then, 'Hello, Dean' and kissed me on the cheek. She was the most glamorous woman I've seen in my life. Her complexion was second to none. She sat next to me talking to me and I can remember sitting there twiddling my fingers—I couldn't believe it. She had both my children sat on her lap and she was talking about William and Harry. I said to her, 'We're just Joe Public aren't we? Why us?' And she said, 'It could have been anybody whose mom I saw crying outside, but it was your mom and that's why I've come to see you and kept my promise.'

"She wrote to my mom about four times, because she got quite friendly with her. She sent cards, phone calls, Christmas cards. She was a very, very terrific woman, she really was. Diana was bringing the royals and the public closer together and I don't think the royals agreed with that, but her being there made my mom feel better. Because me mom knew she wasn't the only one worrying about my accident, if someone like Princess Di can come and visit me. My mom said it gave her a boost, gave her energy."

Uniquely, Diana broke with royal protocol that keeps a distance from the public. She often followed up on encounters with people through charities with personal letters and contacts. When she did visits for Turning Point says Wendy Thomson, "There was always the formal exchange of us thanking her and her writing back and the notes between the members of palace staff. But the more interesting stuff was the stuff she did for individuals—it was always spontaneous." In 1994, Jayne Zito, whose husband was murdered by a schizophrenic, traveled at Diana's invitation to Carstairs high security mental hospital—in recognition of their joint interest in mental health problems. "When we got back in the car after the flight back," says Jayne, "her post was waiting for her. I think I asked her how she managed, because I was getting a lot of letters from people, but she just was very open to that kind of communication with the public. She could empathize with people and was very moved by what they said in the letters to her; when they expressed themselves and gave thanks to her, it meant a lot."

Maria Dorrian was one such correspondent. She met Diana through the women's health charity WellBeing (formerly Birthright) in Scotland and like many other members of the public, felt sufficiently familiar with Diana to write to her. "When she had problems, I would write to her, just to let her know that we were thinking of her. I wrote to her the day before the divorce and a personalized reply came back two days later by registered mail. I couldn't believe it, because there was this very busy person going through a very emotional period and she was still taking the time to write to people. In the letter, I said that it wasn't the title that makes a person, it's the warmth which they have within and that we would always continue to love her for what she was." Typically Diana responded promptly and personally, saying, "she had been very touched and she wanted me to know how much it had meant to her."

Often personal relationships developed. Diana became close to the little Bosnian girl Irma Hadzimuratovic who was lifted out of Sarajevo in 1993 with severe injuries caused by the shelling. While she was in Great Ormond Street Hospital, Diana visited her regularly and when she died in 1995 Diana spent time trying to boost the morale of the nurses who were so upset by Irma's death. Sometimes relationships developed out of letters, as with Helena Best, a woman whose family was tragically affected by AIDS. Helena's daughter Rebecca Handel had been infected with AIDS through a blood transfusion in 1981. Her own little daughter Bonnie also had the virus. At a time of ignorance and prejudice the family kept the cause of the illness hidden, but in 1993 Bonnie, having seen that Diana had written to another little girl, wrote to Diana herself. Diana responded immediately. Later, attending a World AIDS Day event, Rebecca met Diana and thanked her for the letter her daughter had treasured. On learning the little girl was very poorly Diana set out to visit her, only to find she had died a few days before. After that, Diana invited Rebecca to Kensington Palace which turned out to be just days before Rebecca's own death: "What the princess did for Rebecca and Bonnie," says her grandmother Helena Best, "was to show them they were just as important as everyone else in the world, and in her own life. She made them feel worth something, and that meant so much."[6]

"I feel close to people whoever/however they are," said Diana. "We are on the same level, on the same wavelength. That's why I annoy certain circles. Because I am closer to the people downstairs than the people upstairs and they don't forgive me for that. Because I have a really close relationship with the most humble of people. My father always taught me to treat everyone as an equal. I have always done that and I hope that Harry and William have taken it on board."

David Ireland, appeals and PR director of the charity SeeAbility, witnessed Diana's instinctive empathy with people on a number of occasions. He'd seen her rapport with people as a newlywed on a walkabout. He'd witnessed her consoling a dying friend in a hospice. But he was most startled by her interaction with the profoundly blind at a SeeAbility residential center in Leatherhead. "She, again, showed that same sensitivity with a group of people, whose disabilities can be pretty disarming, even for those who are reasonably well qualified to meet them. These are people who are vision impaired, some of whom have low disability, and some of whom have quite bizarre challenging behavior. Some are people who aren't easy to get alongside and many people don't quite know where to begin. You've got no eye contact. They may be quite slow in their understanding of things and may not necessarily pursue a totally logical conversation. But I was fascinated to see that despite all the pressures on her, once she got away from the public eye she was still able to sit alongside people and somehow engage with them. And the social workers and people who are very politically correct found themselves saying: 'How does she do it?'"

Diana had a particularly powerful effect on the life of Chris Anderson, a resident at the SeeAbility Centre. "I had met her once before at a reception at Kensington Palace," says Chris. "She was so friendly and kind. It was as though I had made a new friend so it felt natural for me to invite her to visit our residential center. When she arrived she came straight over and said, 'Hello, Chris. How are you?' I'd always wanted to know what she looked like and I asked, 'Is it all right if I touch your face?' Everyone was very surprised. I asked because her voice sounded kind and warm. I probably wouldn't have done that to the Queen, but Diana just laughed and said, 'Of course!' and knelt down so I could reach her very easily. I felt round her nose, eyes and mouth. In my fingers I can still remember the way Princess Diana's face felt. It was small and her skin was very soft. Though I am blind I knew she was very pretty. It made me feel very happy and special that she let me touch her like that. The picture was in all the papers the next day."

Diana had this effect with people she only met very briefly. She only ever visited Walsall Manor Hospital once, but won devoted followers among the staff. "It was a special feeling and a privilege that she was coming, because she was so well loved and liked," says Pat Mason, one of the catering staff. "We felt honored that it was Diana that was coming to open this hospital, because of the aura she'd got. Everyone loved her." "Her grace, her poise, she was just more than you ever thought she was, from seeing her on television," says Julie Watton-Butler, support services manager. "Although we worked incredibly hard for days and days beforehand, it was as if we were floating on air all day, and we wanted to capture that and put it in a bottle." "She gave the impression that she wasn't just there for the collar and ties, she was there for the normal people," says Marilyn Griffiths, senior support services supervisor. "She was for us, like, for the people" says Pat Street, another of the catering staff. "There'll never be anybody else like her."

"She had the ability to make people feel she'd spent a lot of time with them," says Vivienne Parry. "It was no surprise to me when she died to see that number of people, because if you'd ever been on those away days, there were huge crowds, I mean, just enormous. People's reactions were always the same. We would get all this agitation beforehand: 'I need more time with her,' and I would always say, 'Look it's fine, don't worry about it,' and it was like a record. People would say, 'She spent such a long time with me.' Actually she hadn't spent any more time that had been allotted, but she had that gift of being able to do a one-to-one conversation. And also, I think, the other thing was she was able to talk about the little things in life, how William had done this, or bath time for the boys or how she loved beating custard, so it became a very normal conversation. It wouldn't surprise me at all if, in five or ten years' time, suddenly a family comes up with boxes and boxes of correspondence from Diana, to somebody in their family, who perhaps has now died. She got a huge amount of pleasure from talking to ordinary people. The surprise is not that she spoke to them and trusted them, but that they never revealed their conversations."

Soon after Diana's death Susan Hill, the novelist, decided to put together a little book, *The Day I Met Diana, Princess of Wales: The People's Stories*, donating the proceeds to charity. She asked newspaper columnists to mention it and sent round-robins. The response was amazing. "Sacks of mail came every day and every evening I sat on the chair in the drawing room reading the letters. There were so many that were so touching. One evening my husband came into the room, and said, 'Look at you with tears running down your face!' Her worst enemies could not have failed to be moved. The power she had was extraordinary.

"'I suffer from the eating disorder anorexia,' one girl wrote to her anonymously. 'For so long such illnesses have been swept under the carpet or ridiculed. But Princess Diana showed such courage in speaking out that I took strength from that courage.' When she was very ill in hospital she wrote to Diana. 'I don't know why, exactly. At the most I expected an acknowledgement. I actually got a handwritten letter. This came following a phone call. As I was in hospital my mom took the call and spent 20 minutes talking to the princess who offered to help and support my mom over my illness.

"'A further surprise was in store for me—an invitation to Kensington Palace. Not only was she kind and helpful and her advice and inspiration invaluable, but the whole act in itself was worth more. This busy lady made the effort to spend time with me, to help and also entertain me in her home and not one member of press knew. That she considered me still means so much to me and my family."[7]

Even when abroad, without a shared language, Diana often connected deeply with ordinary individuals. "Diana came to the Mashambazou AIDS Hospice in Zimbabwe," says Sister Margaret McAllen. "The local Zimbabweans knew of her as a princess from a foreign land, but somehow she touched the hearts of everyone here. She was full of compassion. She took her time with everyone even though her entourage wanted to hurry her along. She spent time with one young mother in particular, a woman called Egipher, who was dying and who kept asking what would happen to her children. Diana sat with her, held her hand and listened. After she had gone, Egipher said she seemed to understand what it was like to suffer. She wasn't afraid of the dying. She seemed to give them energy just by listening. And I believe spending time with them gave her strength. And she was also a very spiritual person who believed in the power of prayer. I think Diana was a healer: she knew that a smile, a touch can make all the difference to someone in need."

Stories like these, says Susan Hill, "reveal her as generous with her time, and unhurried with people who wanted to tell things to her. They reveal someone who laughed a great deal and made others do so. They reveal what an impact her beauty made on everyone. Her warmth, her sparkle, her enthusiasm, her presence—an aura—a magic, all is here. Her loving and utterly genuine concern for people in some way in distress shines out. Of course a large number of her visits to hospitals and hospices were official and public, but very many were not. The hours spent sitting at bedsides and on beds—the surprise telephone calls and trips to the homes and hospital rooms of people who needed and had appealed to her were unknown to the media. So many of the letters give the lie to the criticism that she only did it for the cameras."

❊ ❊ ❊ ❊

QUEEN OF HEARTS ~ "I'd like to be a queen of people's hearts, in people's hearts," said Diana famously in the *Panorama* interview with Martin Bashir in 1995, "but I don't see myself as being queen of this country. I don't think many people want me to be queen. Actually when I say many people I mean the establishment that I married into, because they have decided I am a non-starter."

One incident in Diana's life that has been much misunderstood was when a photograph appeared in a national newspaper of her wearing a surgical gown and mask while watching a heart operation at the Royal Brompton and Harefield Hospital. The publicity around this photograph caused Diana a great deal of distress. But behind the photo lies a story about her close involvement with the Chain of Hope. This was not one of her patronages but, along with other causes at the Royal Brompton, became something to which she devoted much time and energy.

Professor Sir Magdi Yacoub, one of the world's top heart surgeons and founder of Chain of Hope, first met Diana when she was visiting a patient at the Royal Brompton. "I was immediately very impressed by her. I had walked into the patient's room and recognized her. So I said, 'I can come back.' But she insisted that I take precedence and that she would wait outside. I thought, 'This is an extraordinary person.' Later we got talking, and she was very interested in the work and we became friends. She used to ring me for a chat even when I was away at international meetings. She was just a very warm person."

Diana in return was impressed by Professor Yacoub's new British charity Chain of Hope, originally set up in France, to treat children from all over the world who suffer from heart disease but are unable to receive adequate treatment in their own country. The charity works on two fronts: It sponsors children and brings them for operations at the Royal Brompton and Harefield Hospitals, and it also sponsors groups of heart surgeons from the UK who volunteer to travel out to poor countries, like Mozambique and Jamaica. There the surgeons perform operations and help train local doctors.

"Everybody here does the operation for free," says Professor Yacoub. "The NHS [National Health Service] charges us the cost so we have to find three and a half thousand pounds for every child, to give to the NHS. In fact Diana funded some of the children herself."

Arnaud Wambo from Cameroon was one of the first children brought over by the charity and Diana became closely involved with his case. Six years old, he had a rapidly degenerating heart condition and would have died within two years had it remained untreated in his native Cameroon. Diana met Arnaud and his foster caregivers, Hans and Ursula Murmann (recruited through Chain of Hope) as soon as he arrived, alone, in the UK. She visited him in the run up to his operation. "People said she was posing for the media," said Professor Yacoub. "Actually she turned up at seven in the morning, herself, driving herself, so she must have left home at six, to see the child before he went to surgery, and to comfort him, to hold his hand."

It was this involvement that led to her attending the heart operation. "She always wanted to do more for people and wanted to understand exactly what the child was going through. She used to quiz me in a very methodical and intelligent way. She wanted to understand how their illnesses related to structural changes in the heart and how that could be corrected. She wanted to see it all and understand, but if she came into the theater she would apologize for distracting us in any way, and repeatedly say, 'Just ignore me.' And eventually we did ignore her. She always insisted: 'I don't want to be the center of attention in any way.' So it was the exact opposite of what the papers said at the time. She was so involved in the overall care of the child she would come, late at night, again, driving herself. At the time I pointed out that it was just not safe to be doing that on her own, but she would say: 'I want to see the child. I am all right.' Her dedication was total."

The famous photos of Diana in an operating mask "came about entirely by chance," says Professor Yacoub. "Sky TV wanted to film an operation. Diana had asked to see the operation not knowing that Sky would be there. She walked into it and I felt responsible because she was very upset about the suggestion that she had make-up on specially and that she was posing for the camera. None of that is true. She was dressed in theater clothes [nurses scrubs], and she was totally, totally unobtrusive, but they made the program. There were a few occasions I've seen her very, very upset and this was one of them."

Professor Yacoub's daughter Lisa helps with her father's charity work and became close to Diana, bonding over a shared interest in development issues and philosophy. Lisa was also aware of the distress this episode caused Diana: "She did ring up and cry down the phone. She said, 'I can't believe they've turned it into a media story about me wearing make-up and earrings. They've missed the point again. They haven't focused on this poor child from West Africa, who needs surgery.' She was furious it was always her at the center. She said, 'Oh, I'm just getting in the way again.' And I said, 'You're not getting in the way at all, we're so grateful for everything you do.' She had quite low self-esteem on some occasions, but then she picked herself up really fast and a couple of weeks later she said, 'Right. When's the next operation?' And we said, 'It's another child, coming from Senegal this time.' And she said, 'Right, book me in, I'm coming to watch it.' She came and watched it. She was not going to be told, 'You can't come and watch an operation.' She really wanted to learn."

After his operation, Diana kept in touch with Arnaud's progress through his foster parents and invited them to tea in Kensington Palace, ten days after his operation. She also followed the progress and operations of other children from Mozambique and lent her support to the charity's fund-raising efforts. At a Harrods fund-raising dinner, at which her presence helped raise £250,000 for Professor Yacoub and his team, she said, "To think of thousands of sick and dying children around the world is distressing enough. Even more disturbing to know is that many of these helpless victims of war and poverty could be saved by routine operations—if only the resources were available in their own countries. I have seen for myself the work of Professor Sir Magdi Yacoub and the team of volunteers who together give new life to sick children. I have been moved by the results, witnessing once desperate children now leading happy, healthy lives."

Diana also involved herself with other children at the hospital. "She asked me," says Professor Yacoub, "something to the effect of 'Which of the children here is suffering most? Who could I help?' And I told her about 12-year-old Victoria, whose transplanted heart had been rejected for various reasons. She had been brought literally dying to the hospital—she was unconscious and her heart had stopped. At the time people said, 'Well, the brain will not recover.' But, no, the brain recovered, and she came back. But she'd lost the use of her kidneys because of being on a heart-lung machine. She was a lovely, vivacious girl, but on dialysis all the time so she was tied to the hospital for the next three to six months.

"So what does Diana do? She befriended her. You would find her, weekends, in Victoria's room, unannounced, unknown to anybody, no security, nothing. It was extraordinary. And they would sit there giggling for hours as their friendship developed. Once Diana said to Victoria, 'Show me your nails. Don't you use nail varnish?' And Victoria said, 'No.' 'OK,' says Diana, 'leave it to me, you know, I'm fashion conscious.' She came to the hospital and painted Victoria's nails a different color every week, so everyone in the hospital would wait to see what nail color Victoria had—not only her fingers, but also on her toenails. It brought a lot of happiness and hope to Victoria like you have never seen. In some ways she was more effective than the doctors in treating people. She would bring life into kids by her total determination. When we were trying to get a kidney transplant for Victoria she rang late one night and said, 'Diana here. What are you doing about the kidney transplant?' I said, 'We're trying.' 'Obviously not hard enough,' she says. 'Sorry, I'll do my best.' 'Thank you. Really, I appreciate it. I will ask you again.' So, Victoria had a kidney transplant in Oxford, and she was able to go home and back to school."

Professor Yacoub believes that Diana, far from being a frivolous person, was not just sharp and knowledgeable, but was also thinking deeply about her role in life and the contribution she could make. In letters, Diana

exchanged with his daughter she outlined the views and beliefs that sustained her; "Soaring flight . . . Free from internment . . . Lifting yourself above the ebbs and flow of daily life, and then acquire broader vision." She also wrote about creativity and compassion and "the greatest disease in the world." "The greatest disease," she wrote, "is not leprosy or TB, it is feeling unloved, and it needs to be addressed." But she often added light-hearted bits: "Here ends lessons from Kensington, ha, ha, ha, ha!"

Lisa Yacoub finds it hard to reconcile some of the portrayals of Diana in the press with "how deep and philosophical she was. We used to send each other quotes and messages and things. In one of the last letters I received from her just before she died, she said, 'I want to share this very meaningful quote with you and send you lots of love.' It was from *The Little Prince*. It said: 'I have to go now to the stars. And one day when you look at the stars, you will remember me.' It was almost prophetic. She was so intuitive and she was a healer of sorts; she was surrounded by a lot of light. When she walked into a room people's energy would change immediately. Sometimes my father would say, 'Oh, you're the healer here.' But she would always make a joke out of it. She would laugh things off."

"She had a massive compassion, really," says Professor Yacoub. "She could identify with people. And when she died, people grieved because the public know precisely who cares and who doesn't care. The philosopher, Karl Popper, has said all of us know how to identify the truth, the naked truth. You don't have to be educated to do that. To be specific, this is a human attribute: That we know the truth, identify the truth and what is false and what's not. That is why people around the world loved the princess and went crazy when she died. They knew what she stood for."

Susie Kassem was a close friend of Diana's in the last years of her life and Diana involved her in visiting patients at the Royal Brompton. Susie was convinced that "when you're actually involved in charity work you're told what to do and where to go and who to see and what they're all about. So it's all pre-organized, whereas this was spontaneous, so therefore she's not on ceremony if it's all so relaxed."

At the Royal Brompton, the two women became aware of the plight of Cystic Fibrosis (CF) sufferers whose best hope of survival is often a heart and lung transplant. Later, inspired by her contact with, in particular, the children with CF, Susie put together a book of their writings to which Diana wrote the foreword. Again Susie shows that Diana's hospital visits were very different from the image painted by cynical detractors: They were about friendship both for the patients and for Diana. One friendship was particularly important. It was with a young Greek man, Ioannis Kaliviotis, known as "John," a life-long cystic fibrosis sufferer who had been sponsored by the Greek government for treatment in England at the Royal Brompton. "Diana met him through one of the nurse nuns, Sister Elizabeth. John, at that point, was fairly unwell, waiting for a heart and lung transplant. Diana introduced me to him and we used to go fairly often to see him. Certainly Harry went there because I was there a couple of times when he was there and I've taken in my kids and my husband. John didn't speak any English at all when he arrived. He was a qualified lawyer in Greece. Very bright boy and, in fact, taught himself English when he was here. He was very charismatic. All the patients, a lot of people from the Middle East who couldn't speak any English, used to go into his room and just sit with him. We became very friendly with him and his family."

Tragically John died before his transplant. "Diana and I went to his funeral in Athens. He was just such an exceptional boy. You always believe that doctors and nurses must have to be devoid of any emotion for their patients, but the whole of the floor just was absolutely devastated. They were very, very attached to him."

"John was perhaps, the most courageous person I have ever known," wrote Diana just before her own death. "Ours was a friendship borne out of adversity because for almost the entire time I knew him he was lying in a bed. Not a day went by when he did not awaken with hope; his inner courage was quite inspirational. John arrived into my life in 1995 when I first started visiting the Royal Brompton Hospital. Two or three times a week over the next 18 months I was privileged to spend precious moments in his company. From those moments it is his humanity that I will treasure most. He showed no sign of anger, no trace of bitterness but touched us all with an aura of optimism and hope for the future such that I have never before encountered."

For Professor Yacoub, a scientist and rationalist, Diana's involvement with Ioannis was full of coincidences and associations. "She went by British Airways to Greece, but then she hired an airplane to go to the island herself to pay her respects to her friend. Totally unannounced. But she didn't realize that in the Greek tradition the coffin is open. So she came back—I promise you—with swollen eyes. She just cried her heart out for her friend. She felt it very, very deeply.

"But it is very strange and sad that one of the pieces of music played at her funeral was *Song for Athene*, that haunting, haunting tune. It was written because John Tavener was obsessed by Greek music and church music, and he attended the funeral for Athene, a 22-year-old girl knocked down by a car in London. He did what Diana did and went to the funeral to see Athene looking at him, dead. And John Tavener ran home and wrote *Song for Athene*. And it came to be played at Diana's funeral."

Susie Kassem was also drawn into Diana's wider involvement in the Royal Brompton. "One thing led to another, the chief of the hospital got wind of Diana's arrival on a fairly regular basis and asked her if she'd be happy to visit Rose Ward, the children's ward. She said she'd be happy to do it providing I came with her. And then we were all taken round the wards and introduced to lots of the children and babies. Once they realized she was happy to help in any way she could, they were very keen to get her involved because it made such a difference to the children."

"People are too quick to judge Diana's motivation when they don't know the facts," says Susie Kassem. "She just liked to help people in need. She's not unique in that respect, but because of who she was, it made it more difficult. I think that it was extremely admirable of her to go and visit people like that. It was amazing to watch her effect too. The kids' faces lit up like little stars that popped out of the sky. They just could not believe it. Once we went into the room of a young man—he was probably in his early 20s—totally unannounced. Nobody knew that we were coming at all. We walked into his room and he just looked. He was speechless. Diana sat on his bed and said, 'Can't you speak?' And he said, 'No.' Then she had to leave the room for two or three minutes. So I sat on his bed and he said, 'I was a dustman for many years and I used to stand on dustbins to be able to see her. And there she is at the end of my bed. How can I speak?' It was just so sweet. That's what she did, very low key, very quiet.

"It was amazing to stand back away from her and just watch the reaction. 'Fairy dust' I used to call it. She used to sprinkle her fairy dust around and give joy to people, whoever they were or whatever their situation was. Obviously the fact that she was who she was had an added impact, but I do believe if she hadn't been Princess Diana she still would have done the work because she was born to it.

"One day she met this little girl called Danielle. She'd had a heart condition—she may even have had a transplant. She loved ballet, this little girl, and Diana had had these wonderful little pink ballet shoes made as a birthday cake for her. Imagine how that little girl must have felt when Diana walked in with this birthday cake made in a pair of ballet shoes. Diana got huge pleasure from giving people pleasure and making the kids smile."

Danielle Stephenson who spent nine months in the Royal Brompton Hospital vividly remembers her friendship with Diana. "I'm really glad that I've met her. I have lots of really good memories." When Danielle was seven and early in her stay at the hospital she says, "I was told by one of the nurses that someone famous was in the hospital. We'd seen her on the television. I thought she was going to be all princessy and have her own castle and wear a tiara and be posh and everything. But she wasn't. I went up to her and said, 'Please come into our ward and meet the children.' We took her into the ward and she came to my bedside and we were sitting and talking to her and asking questions. I asked her if she sat on a throne and she said, 'Oh, no!' And I asked her if she wore a crown all the time, and she said, 'No, I don't do that either.'"

After the initial visit, Diana came to see Danielle often. "She'd bring me flowers and sometimes she lent me videos to make my stay less boring. She lent me *Annie*, which she said was hers, and *The Mask*, and a Michael Jackson video that belonged to Harry and William. I really liked ballet at the time and I'd given her my video of a ballet performance I'd been in to watch and one day she brought me a cake in the shape of ballet shoes. We talked about dancing sometimes, about *The Nutcracker* because I'd been to see it, and we talked about things like guinea pigs because I had some. Most of the visits were in the day, but sometimes it was in the evening and she watched *Absolutely Fabulous* with us because she liked that and I really liked it. We drew the curtains around my bed and me and my mom and Princess Diana would sit on the bed and turn the television up. I think she came to me because I didn't make too much fuss about her being a princess and because I was in hospital, she wanted to help out and sort of make it a bit better."

After Danielle left hospital Diana wrote to her and gave her a phone number. Danielle rang several times, keeping Diana informed about her health. "Sometimes it was just to tell her what I'd done and see what she'd been doing. It wasn't really when I was feeling low. I just rang her. Once I rang her and she asked me if I wanted to go to Kensington Palace to meet her and we all went up there. She gave us cake and biscuits and we sat on her sofa in her drawing room and there were loads of pictures of her and her family in there. She was just like a normal person, but she was exceptional for the fact that she put herself out for other people."

✳ ✳ ✳ ✳

INVOLVING HER SONS ~ Perhaps even more striking than Diana's own very hands-on involvement with people, was the fact that she involved her sons in many of her visits. Susie Kassem recalls that Harry came on visits to see Ioannis (John) at the Royal Brompton Hospital, and Professor Yacoub recalls how she brought letters from William and Harry to Victoria, and on other occasions brought them on visits to the hospital. "That boy is going to be a king," Diana said, "and he has to care about people. He has to witness first-hand the suffering of the people. He must come here."

On two occasions Diana went to The Passage Day Centre, once with just William and once with both boys. "She certainly wanted William to be aware that there was another side to life other than the one he was experiencing, and that no matter what people are like, they were deserving of respect." Says Sister Bridie Dowd: "I think she wanted them to know that there are people who just don't always have enough to eat, who were not well in life, who are excluded from mainstream society. I think she wanted him to realize at a very early age that there are other sides to life. He coped very well with it, really. She didn't hold him by the hand or anything, but at the very beginning he stood, not too close to her. Then, when he was comfortable enough he chatted with people in the day center. In the night shelter it was much more friendly, because it's a smaller place and Diana and William sat with people, and they joined in with the games and the chat. It was very normal, in abnormal circumstances. There was no special preparation done or anything like that."

In the 1995 *Panorama* interview, Diana was explicit that she wanted the monarchy and the public "to walk hand in hand" and that taking her sons on such visits was part of that process. "With William and Harry," she said, "I take them 'round homeless projects. I've taken William and Harry to people dying of AIDS. I've taken them to all sorts of areas where I'm not sure anyone of that age in this family has been before. And they have a knowledge—they may never use it, but the seed is there and I hope it will grow, because knowledge is power."

Some of her friends have remarked on the curious sense of urgency Diana had about introducing the boys to the real world. Jean-Paul Claverie comments: "She was devoted to her children. And after the separation with the prince she spent some weekends without the two boys and she told me how sad she was. And I've many, many letters from her expressing the importance of the two children to her. She was very involved in preparing them to be princes and she wanted to open them to the modern world and to make them sensitive to the problems of others."

❋ ❋ ❋ ❋

EMPATHY, TOUCH AND HEALING ~ Diana's behavior was so unusual for anyone, let alone a member of the British royal family that inevitably people have speculated on motivation. "I think she discovered in herself perhaps what she didn't know before she was married," says Lord Hurd, "that she had this extraordinary capacity of relating to people who were sad or in trouble in one way or another. Of course, it helped being a princess, but she actually had the capacity to bring comfort to people. The prime minister and I knew that, there was nothing bogus about it or publicity seeking. She had a vocation."

Many of the charities recognized that at the basis of Diana's ability to connect and comfort people was empathy. "She had an empathy with people who were damaged in some way," says Harry Shapiro of DrugScope, "because clearly she was, herself, a bit fragile and vulnerable and she could kind of empathize." "She enjoyed going to hospitals," said Malcolm Green from the British Lung Foundation. "She felt it helped people and it did. People felt their day had been blessed when she came round."

"I don't think she had a game plan," says her bridesmaid, Sarah Jane Gaselee. "I think she was really, really hurt by what happened. It was a nightmare, because she really, really loved him [Prince Charles], and her heart was broken. That kind of pain and suffering gives you a lot of empathy with other people."

"It is surely right to dwell," said Lord Deedes, ex-editor of the *Daily Telegraph*, "on the supreme quality of one who sought above all to help vulnerable people in society, and who did it so well. She was good at this because she herself was vulnerable. She knew the feeling. She did not set out to be a saint."[8]

"I'm a naturally suspicious person, but speaking from experience what I saw was genuineness, an 'emotional intelligence' I thought was off the chart," says Jerry White of Landmine Survivors Network. "I'd never seen such an instinctive and emotional read of emotionally tense or sensitive situations. Whereas other people would say, 'Oh, I don't know if she's that smart,' or, 'Can she write that speech herself?' Or, 'What is she really like? Is she really that bright? Does she really comment on world affairs?' I would say, 'You know, I don't know that I'm going to have a conversation about Descartes with her, but I have never seen emotional intelligence as high as Diana's.'"

"I saw it over a course of time in preparing for the trip to Bosnia with landmine survivors. I'm a cynic. I would have gone along with it if this was about staging for the cause, but I was pleasantly delighted to observe compassion in action that was as genuine a gift as I have ever seen. By the third day, at the end of our trip to Bosnia, I was just saying to our staff: 'Don't go in with her. Let her alone with the survivors. She will make it work, with a touch, with a smile, an embrace. She will be so appropriate and dignified in the face of that family's suffering, that all of you take notes and learn from this.'"

Julia Samuel was a good friend of Princess Diana who set up The Child Bereavement Trust, a charity that, with the aid of funding from the Memorial Fund, helps families who lose a child. It aims to help doctors and hospitals handle loss sensitively, because this has a big impact on the ability of families to grieve without regrets. Diana gave Julia a great deal of support when the Trust was launched and Julia feels it was Diana's own feelings of loss which allowed her to empathize so strongly with others' sufferings.

"She was personally very, very sweet to me. It was the first time I'd done a public speech, so I was absolutely terrified. My legs were shaking so much I had to hold them down with my left hand and sort of turn the pages with my right hand. And I could feel her willing me to do it right. She sent me flowers and talked to me afterwards. She was fantastic both as a friend and for the Trust and I feel hugely, deeply grateful to her for that. She gave of herself very freely: She came to the launch and she came when she had stopped doing public work. Her involvement meant that, for the Trust, we had a media response we would never have had without her.

"She'd had a brother who was born before her who had only lived for a few hours, and that was the connection for her with the Trust. She had a great natural empathy for understanding what parents were saying and feeling and she was able to communicate that level of understanding. Her genuineness completely came through with a look, with her body language, without necessarily having to say something.

"One of life's big tasks is how we manage loss, whether it's not having the parent, or boyfriends, or husbands, or jobs. There are different levels of loss. It's certainly not only death. I think she had had very deep experiences of loss that certainly had a big impact on her. So it was an area that she responded to naturally, although I don't think she ever really resolved what the issues around loss were, so she would instinctively respond to things, but never really resolved them for herself.

"She wasn't academic, but a lot of academics are fantastically stupid, aren't they? No common sense. Or they can't communicate. But she was clever, truly clever. I think she wanted to throw light on areas that other people didn't want to face. She felt personally nurtured in some way by meeting people, and the fact that her response to them had an impact, nurtured her need to make a difference."

Diana's exceptional abilities with the sick and dying were much in evidence in her visits to Pakistan where she stayed with Imran and Jemima

Khan and visited Imran's cancer hospital in Lahore. At the hospital, Diana came across a 7-year-old boy, Ashraf Mohamed, who was terminally ill with a brain tumor. In spite of the terrible state the boy was in—he had a festering tumor—Diana held him in her arms for half an hour. Imran Khan said it was as if she was holding her own child. Later Diana chose the photo of her holding the child as her favorite. "This little boy died. I sensed it before I took him in my arms. I remember his face, his pain, his voice. This photo is very dear to me. It's really a private moment taken at a public event—a private emotion transformed into a public display because a photograph was taken—a strange combination. Yet if I had the choice, it is still in that type of environment, with which I feel perfectly in sync, that I would prefer to be photographed."

Annick Cojean was the journalist to whom Diana said this. She interviewed Diana for *Le Monde* just before she died. Annick is convinced Diana's popularity was rooted in the authenticity of her image. Because Diana expressed those immediate feelings of empathy with touch they were visible and moving. "Photos evoke strong feelings in me," says Annick, "and I don't think it's possible to cheat with them all the time. You can cheat once with a smile but not all the time. You can't cheat the way she would put her hand on people's faces, for example when she goes up to an AIDS patient or she puts the palm of her hand on people's cheeks, like with an old lady in Bosnia. Very few people can communicate that kindness, that sense of contact. I think she had something special, a real sensitivity and connection to people who had suffered.

"For my interview with her, I asked her to choose one photo which best expressed what she was about. She chose one of the little Pakistani boy whom she is holding in her arms. Her eyes are shut. It is certainly not the best photo of her—it's even out of focus and rather poor quality—but she chose this photo and it seemed to reveal more about who she was and what she wanted to do. It expressed her care for suffering children.

"This is why Diana's approach was so rare. Her touch was intuitive, direct and personal yet, captured in an image and conveyed around the world, it could be enough to motivate a wider global campaign. Her touch, her empathy with the loss and pain an individual was feeling was an image that moved others to care too." "Yes, I touch people literally," Diana told Cojean. "I think everyone needs that, whatever his age. To put your hand on the face of someone in trouble or sick or grieving—that is to have immediate contact, to communicate with tenderness, to indicate your closeness to people. It is a natural gesture that comes from the heart—it has no advanced planning. And the truth is I feel near to people who are suffering, whoever they are. That is why I disturb certain people, because I'm closer to the lowly than the mighty, and they can't forgive me for that. No one can dictate my behavior to me. I work by instinct. It's my best advisor."

❋ ❋ ❋ ❋

MOTHER TERESA ~ Although Diana's visit to Mother Teresa's hospice in Calcutta in 1992 was the high point of her trip to India, she was sorry to have missed Mother Teresa herself not least because two other previous attempts had also failed. Immediately after this visit however, Diana went to Rome specifically to meet the nun who was recovering from a heart condition. After that they met again in London and once again in America just before their deaths. "I admire her," Mother Teresa said of Diana. "She is doing God's work here on earth. She is deeply concerned about many issues that concern me, particularly the poor and underprivileged."⁹

The connection Diana made with Mother Teresa was one that resonated for many. "As far as I could see," says Ed Matthews, of United Cerebral Palsy, "she had become very close to Mother Teresa, in her increasing involvement in world health problems." "The outside media would look at the photographs and say: "Oh, this is a photo-op, look at them, they look so different," says Jerry White of the Landmine Survivors Network. "But I think Diana identified with Mother Teresa even though the packaging and circumstances were completely different. I think she identified with a person of compassion with a high emotional intelligence, with her concern about suffering, and social injustice. They were both imperfect and complicated individuals, but I think they could understand and feel the stream of the same emotional gift. That's why, when I look at pictures of Diana and Mother Teresa, I think of them as similar, in recognizing, in each other, the same gift. Those pictures of them holding hands, it's peer support." Diana once told the late Reverend Tony Lloyd of The Leprosy Mission, that Mother Teresa had reassured her that she valued her work. "Mother Teresa said to her," said Reverend Lloyd, "'you couldn't do what I do and I couldn't do what you do.' Which I thought was an absolutely perfect way of summing up the relationship."

There are many who think that there was a strong spiritual element in the charity work Diana chose to do, which increasingly concerned her being with the seriously ill, disadvantaged or dying. "Religiously I think she was a seeker," said Reverend Lloyd. "She went seeking down some odd paths, but she knew what compassion meant. It was so strong it was frightening. It is when you meet a truly good person." She certainly felt close to and drew inspiration from religious figures such as Cardinal Basil Hume and Sister Barbara Smith and had a close, affectionate and admiring relationship with both. For her part, Sister Barbara believes the private visits Diana made to people in desperate circumstances or on the point of death had a religious motivation in the broadest sense of the word. "She must have got closer to God through it. There's no way you couldn't get closer to God through that because, as you know, Jesus said, 'Whatever you do to the least of my little ones, you do to me.' That's what we'll be judged on at the end. 'I was hungry and you gave me food, I was thirsty, you gave me drink, I was sick and you came to me, I was homeless and you took me in, I was naked and you clothed me.' She did all that. I think she grew closer to God—she must have done, there's no way she couldn't.

"What else could it be about? She wasn't doing this for any personal gain either in the eyes of the public to boost her image or to prove to the world how good she was. She didn't have to do this, but she did it over and over again with people who were suffering, people who were suffering at the worst end of suffering. It's got to be love. And in the end, we'll be judged on our love. And I would say she loved."

By the time of their last meeting, Mother Teresa had become so important to her that Diana insisted on changing her schedule when she realized they were together on the same continent. Shortly after she returned from this trip in June 1997 Jean-Paul Claverie talked with Diana about the meeting. "She invited me to join her for lunch at Kensington Palace. She was just back in the morning from New York where she had been preparing for the dress auction. She had had a breakfast with Mrs. Clinton, and she was happy to meet her, but what was so important for her was having this meeting with Mother Teresa in New York. And when she told me what they had spoken about and the relationship with Mother Teresa, suddenly she began to cry, because she was so touched by this person and felt so close to her. She told me: "I have a position in this world. I'm lucky to have this position. And I'm here to help others. I can't stay in this palace without doing things to help others." And you can't imagine how sincere she was.

"What was important for the princess, I think, is that Mother Teresa understood her very well. And she admired Mother Teresa. For the princess, it was so important to listen to what Mother Teresa said, and to get a certain kind of recognition from her for her actions. They spoke about how to help others and how to speak to the dying. She was very interested in speaking about this problem, because it is the main problem for the people who are in difficulties. Their anxiety is about suffering, but also their fear of dying. And she was deeply upset by this problem and she spoke of that with Mother Teresa. And during this lunch—I didn't know, of course, that it was the last lunch, this was two months before the accident—she explained to me what was the problem of dying, after this conversation with Mother Teresa. And suddenly she began to cry."

"Mother Teresa and Diana had this incredibly strong aura of kindness and giving, which when you came close you could just sink in, this incredible, embracing aura," says Tokuo Kassai, whose company Aprica had decided to award the Naito Peace Prize jointly to Mother Teresa and Diana. "Mother Teresa said that it would be very welcome and very much in their interest to start joint activities. What a strange turn in life—this fatality. Within a week, two of the most important people in my life and the most incredibly powerful. Whatever they did and said was so powerful, a million fold, beyond comparison. Jointly they could have taken on the world for the better."

❋ ❋ ❋ ❋

A FRIEND'S PERSPECTIVE ~ Lucia Flecha de Lima, the wife of the former Brazilian ambassador to London was one of Diana's closest friends for much of her life and perhaps more than anyone else saw the richness of her character. She saw that Diana's charity work was, and remained, absolutely central to her self-definition, but she also saw the self-doubt. She witnessed too Diana's extraordinary abilities with people and saw how that was absolutely central to her sense of purpose. "Apart from her sons," says Lucia, "charity was the most important part of her life because she saw it as a mission. I think she had a very special power, almost like people who cure you with the hands. I'm not saying that she had this power or she ever thought about having these powers, but her presence has affected sick people in such a way that they would really get better because I saw that happen with my husband. My husband had a very serious stroke in Washington and of course I told Princess Diana and she took the first plane from London to Washington to be with us at that terrible moment. She was there all the time with us and there was a moment where the doctors were testing my husband and they wanted him to open his eyes and say something and I think he was too tired because he refused. And then the doctor asked my son to say something. 'Paulo Tarso,' my son said. And then Princess Diana said, 'May I try?' and I said, 'Of course.' And then she said, 'Paulo Tarso,' and he opened his eyes and almost sat up in bed. A true story, I'm not exaggerating."

On a lighter note, Lucia recounts another incident. "On the bed next to his there was a man from Washington, a very simple man who worked in a furniture removal company. He had to move very heavy things so he was a strong man, but he had had a stroke as well. When he arrived in the hospital he was calm, but the next day he started shouting, 'Nurse! Nurse!' The nurse arrived and he said, 'I am delirious again. I'm having visions!' And the nurse asked why he was so excited. And he said, 'I thought I saw Princess Diana in the corridor!' A wonderful story that shows the effect she had on people.

"She was very protective of her children; she loved them so much and she was so very proud of them. I wish they knew that. Of course she longed for personal happiness, but her real mission was to bring up her boys and to be always there for them.

"She touched people's lives in such a way that no one who ever met her was the same afterward. I saw it with some of her personal friends and I saw it with members of the public. It was her mission in life to bring relief to people in any country, in any position. In India, Angola, Pakistan. For her, people were people: I never felt she judged people because of their race or religion. She wanted very much to be a kind of British ambassador around the world, not for politics, but with the organizations for people's health and for the homeless, trying to bring peace and happiness to people. I think the royal family—and the world—had the chance to have the perfect Princess of Wales.

"She had a real spiritual depth, awareness, understanding dimension. Her trip to Angola was very distressing because she saw young children without limbs and things like that and it probably had the worst impact on her. Obviously she went to see people with leprosy and in misery when she visited Mother Teresa's home, but this trip to Angola horrified her because they were not sick people. They were normal people who could lead a normal life.

"She was not a religious person who goes to church, you know, but she was really very spiritual and she was struck by many religions. She was curious about religions, the strange ones, the normal ones and she talked to people, Buddhists and Sufis etc., so I think she was searching.

"She really had a wonderful sense of humor. She was able to make fun of herself and that was very special. It didn't go to her head being so famous. She had her problems but they were not all because of her fame or people watching her. On the contrary, it was because of her childhood, living with her father, but at the same time loving her mother was a conflict for her."

❋ ❋ ❋ ❋

THE LAST YEAR ~ The divorce between Princess Diana and Prince Charles was finalized on August 28, 1996, almost exactly a year before Diana died. Even in the context of Diana's remarkable life, this last year stands out as a remarkable time, with Diana recognized as an international figure both for beauty and her compassion. Painful though the divorce and loss of title was for Diana, she seemed to be emerging as a stronger person with a sense of purpose both for what she could do to help people and how the British monarchy could go forward. "The 'third stage' of her life," said William Rees-Mogg, former editor of The Times, was "the one between the divorce and her death. Diana was engaged in making a new life for herself. As a single woman she was enjoying a much freer social life; as a public figure she was making her compassion practically useful; she was continuing to be an excellent mother. Everything was beginning to fall into place. Nobody can say yet whether the death in Paris will have brought to an end the warmth and modernization that was Diana's contribution to the history of the royal family. A lot will depend on how well Prince William is able to overcome the tragedy."[10]

After the Panorama program in November 1995, Diana's popularity with the public increased. In the interview she had said: "I don't want a divorce. I await my husband's decision of which way we are going to go." That decision came quickly. "She got two letters, one from the Queen and one from her husband proposing a divorce," says Anthony Julius, who had acted successfully for Diana once before. "They came within a quarter of an hour of each other. The Panorama interview was in November and the letters came in January. She rang me up and asked me to act for her again. So I said, 'Of course, but I must tell you that I'm not a divorce lawyer. It will be my first divorce case.' She said, 'Oh, don't worry it's my first divorce, too.'"

"I never had any sense of her being a victim at all and right through the divorce which lasted about four or five months we were both—and she in particular—put under fantastic pressure just to settle. That required great strength of character and resolve. She knew her own mind and she was aware of her own power. She had a developed sense of the symbolic nature of her role. It was like a Russian doll. The icon was larger than the royalty but the royalty was inside the icon. It wouldn't have worked if she'd just been a grand woman going round doing good works. The pathos of her own position added to it: The extraordinary paradox of this very beautiful woman who had at the same time been rejected."

Anthony Julius talked to her at the time about how she saw her role. "Like all of us, I suppose, she was in the process of defining what it was she wanted to do with her life and my sense was that she was becoming more and more a person who was serious about not just charity work but about doing it differently. Her kind of activism, married to philanthropy, seemed to me to be something which was almost extinct in this country—you have to go back to the 19th century Quakers to find it—because what we have now in the culture, is on the one hand, big charitable institutions that give money and care and on the other, activists who are involved in politics and campaigning and all the rest of it. In combining both I had the sense that she was moving toward something which was quite radical and new."

Like others, Anthony Julius noticed how much Diana was vulnerable to people, often with their own agendas, trying to give her advice. "I thought she spent most of her life fighting off people who were seeking to influence her and I think maybe in the very process of resisting them she educated herself. I think she came to define herself against the influences that people sought to bring to bear. There is that sense that she in her life recreated the long march of womankind from the Middle Ages through to the late 20th century in one life, in 36 years."

In July 1996 Diana wrote to 100 of her charities formally to withdraw her patronage. "As you know, my personal circumstances, in particular my marriage to the Prince of Wales, have been the subject of detailed conjecture in recent months, and this will soon be formalized in the normal legal manner. Although I am embarking upon the future with hope, I also do so with some trepidation since there are a number of matters which I shall need to resolve." The divorce was finalized in August 1996.

In spite of the setbacks in her personal life, Diana was emerging stronger. Anthony Julius says they discussed the possibility of her setting up her own fund, something that she had previously discussed with Patrick Jephson. "In the last year of her life," says Anthony Julius, "we were talking about charity and foundations because various people made proposals to her. The direction her thinking was moving was rather than appearing at other people's functions and raising money for them perhaps an alternative might be for her to set up her own charitable foundation and have greater control over where the money was disbursed."

Certainly the charities she remained involved with and the new causes Diana took on confirm a perception not of someone who has lost the plot but of someone who with her extraordinary international appeal and intimate rapport with individuals was evolving a whole new approach. The late Reverend Tony Lloyd of The Leprosy Mission saw that "she visibly grew stronger between 1993 and 1997. When I first met her, she was a young, fresh new wife and not at all experienced. But in the last year of her life I could feel the strength, when she would take decisions on her own. She was making plans for the future. For example, she invited me to a fund-raising meal for about 12 of us, which included Cliff Richard, at Kensington Palace, and she was planning a concert with him for The Leprosy Mission."

Derek Deane, in whom she confided around the time of her divorce, encountered someone trying to evolve a separate and meaningful role in the world. "We had conversations, especially when the divorce happened. I said, 'OK, you are divorced now, what's the plan?' She was desperate for an ambassadorial role where she could use her fame and her position as she did with the AIDS and landmines to bring things to the public eye that nobody else could do. She always, without question, said, 'That's where I see myself.' I used to say, very cautiously, 'Yes, but what about the other side of you, you can't be giving all the time. What about getting?' And she used to say, 'Well, of course, if somebody comes along it'll be wonderful, but I can't just be sitting and waiting and, as you can imagine, it's very difficult for me because of who I am to find that person.' So we sort of washed the personal side of it. But her professional commitments were second to none. She really wanted to do good for other people.

"She certainly knew the power she had and wanted to put it to good use. She didn't want to flit about the world being the ex-Princess of Wales, she also wanted to be taken seriously. Of course she realized the labels people put on her, but she also knew that she just had to accept them. She just said: 'That's life. What can I do about it?' If she has to go to 200 receptions a year, people wanted to see her in different clothes. She's not Princess Anne; we're talking Grace Kelly. Nobody wants to see Grace Kelly or Princess Diana in the same frock twice. But her determination was not to lose her identity about how important she could be in the work she wanted to do.

"She could have just Euro-trashed herself into a stupor if material things were all that mattered to her. But she realized that her power and her position and her fame could do things for other people. And, of course, the country supported her. That was what kept her going."

Derek Deane felt she had a strong sense of purpose and urgency in the last year of her life. "This whole ambassadorial thing she wanted to work out with John Major and then Tony Blair really gave her a focus. 'But get in quick,' she used to say, 'get me quick, because there's so much going on I might not be available.'" She saw her life as having a working agenda. She had these six charities as her main concern plus the other things she wanted to concentrate on. She adored the ballet, but she was very business-like. From her divorce onwards she had a program with us, a five-year plan. She talked like a businesswoman. She said, 'What can I do for you?' or, 'What about going to somewhere like New York to do a gala? I can earn money for my AIDS things and we can mix it together. Leave it with me I can make some calls.' So it wasn't just English National Ballet, she was really trying to think ahead. I said, 'Listen, I know you don't want to hear this but thank you very much for doing this, 'cause I know what you must be going through.' And she said, 'Derek, it's just my job. I love you, I love the company, I love the ballet. It's my job. I'm the patron. That's what I do.'"

All the charities she was involved with have similar stories of substantial plans for the future. There were plans underway for Diana to continue landmine work with the Red Cross; a schedule for a trip to Georgia was being drawn up. Diana had also agreed to travel with Professor Yacoub's Chain of Hope charity to Jamaica late in 1997. Jean-Paul Claverie, cultural advisor to the Louis Vuitton company, LVMH, which supports various humanitarian programs, says that plans were relatively far advanced for collaboration between his company, the International Red Cross, and Princess Diana for a health education program in developing countries. Plans like this refute the suggestion that Diana was paying less attention to her charity work. On the contrary they reveal a strong sense of purpose.

BLOSSOMING ~ The complexities and pressures in the year after Diana's divorce and before her death are hard to grasp for ordinary people. Apart from these work commitments she was shockingly lonely. Jean-Paul Claverie received several letters from her in the last year of her life. "She suffered a great deal because she was so lonely. It's hard to imagine how lonely she was."

Even after the divorce, however, it was hard for Diana to socialize casually as her every action was scrutinized and examined by the press. The actions of the paparazzi and even some of the more mainstream press became more and more harassing. Photographers boasted of "spraying her down" and insulting her, hoping to provoke her to tears. As Sam McKnight recalls, "I went 'round there one morning and she was sitting on her bed crying. A car and a motorbike had turned up shouting out: 'You f---ing bitch, you whore,' and made her cry. I cried myself when she told me. She said she was really angry with herself that she had cried because in the paper the next day it said: 'Diana's having a nervous breakdown,' or something like that." "I just can't stand it," she once blurted out, "when I see them around all the time, it is like I am being raped." "Fleet Street, frankly, lost the plot with Diana in those latter years," says royal journalist Richard Kay. "There was an obsession with anything and everything she did. No one had ever had that level of scrutiny. I think we tended to forget that she was actually still a human being trying to lead a life, and it warped and twisted our approach to her."

Not surprisingly, Diana found more and more comfort in her private visits to the ballet or to hospitals. In her loneliness she knew her abilities to communicate and empathize with people's pain from her position could make a difference to their lives. "Nothing gives me greater joy than to try to help the most vulnerable members of society. It is my one real goal in life—like a destiny. Whoever is in distress and calls me—I'll run at once, wherever they may be."

There is a paradox in the last years of Diana's life. Although it was a time of loneliness and pressure, it was also a time when she was blooming. She was a single woman in control of her own life for the first time. The change was visible. Under the heading: "No More Royal Blues," journalist Brenda Polan wrote: "Butterflies should be bright. Especially butterflies newly emerged from the chrysalis. The Diana butterfly is different. The creature emerging from 18 months of confusion, contemplation, and reconstruction is less flamboyant than the one who felt compelled to wrap a cocoon of privacy about herself, but infinitely more impressive. The Princess of Wales has found her own style, an interesting amalgam of a cool, businesslike elegance and a mischievous flirtiness. She seems easier in her clothes as if there is no longer any conflict between who she is and who she appears to be. Any reader of the language of clothes has to conclude that here's a woman who finally knows, understands and likes herself and, furthermore, knows how to express her new found confidence in what she wears."[11]

"From the early '90s," says designer Jacques Azagury, "she'd been relying more and more on designers like Versace—international, sexy, haute couture. She always did have a great sense of style, and although maybe at the beginning she didn't always quite get it right, certainly toward the end of her career she was spot on with what was happening with fashion and how she wanted it to look. It was a kind of liberation.

"Toward the end of her life, when she wanted to change her look completely, she turned to me, and that's when she started wearing those very slinky, very sexy, more international-looking dresses. The first indication we had that she wanted to change her look was the night the *Panorama* interview was screened and she had to attend a function. We knew she wanted to wear black, which she was never able to wear before. And we had two dresses to

choose from. Immediately she knew which one she wanted. It was really just to make a statement, to say, "I'm still gorgeous, I'm still sexy." It was a lace-bodied empire line, very low cut, and then a georgette dress, fitted all the way down with a slight train at the back. And that was the first time we made something like that for her.

"She did definitely turn from a puppy to a gorgeous lady. Toward the end she was the most gorgeous woman: Her body was really toned. She lost a little bit of weight, she didn't really mean to, but still she had very womanly curves. As she matured, she became very much more beautiful. It'll be a long time before we see anybody like the princess again."

In the same period Diana told shoe designer Manolo Blahnik: "'I never wore such high heels but now I'm going to.' She started to have her own style identity the last few years of her life. She wore very simple shifts and dresses. She was a picture of beauty, and I do miss her image continuously."

Catherine Walker, the designer most closely associated with Diana's life, also noticed a change: "The demure phase was over and so was her marriage, but what I hadn't anticipated was how quickly she would change and begin wearing my sexier evening wear. By this time her looks and physique had changed dramatically since she had first come to see me as a pale, slightly plump, fragile-looking girl. Now she was tanned, fitter, more muscular. She had become a perfectionist, working very hard on her body because of the scrutiny it was under and to help keep her sane through her marital upheaval. I was dressing a real body, full of corners and the designs had to enhance this new beauty, not just hang from the shoulders. Perhaps because I was always trying to do something that helped her move on, she always came back. I wanted to go on providing all the answers I could. My dream from the beginning had been to deal with Diana as a real person—to me it was as important as the designing. I was aware from an early date that, in a way, Diana did not exist in people's minds as a real person but as an image. I often thought that it was one of the most unfair parts of her life. It's not possible for anyone to live, to survive, in that position." In the last months of Diana's life Catherine could see Diana taking control of her own image. "I felt thrilled. The real person had finally become strong enough to supersede the image."[12]

However vindictive parts of the British establishment, however merciless the British press, the rest of the world was hugely appreciative of this beautiful woman. The French were well aware of her global appeal. "I told Monsieur and Madame Chirac that the princess would come to the opening of the Cézanne exhibition," says Jean-Paul Claverie, "and Madame Chirac organized tea at the Palais de l'Elysée. She told me, 'I want to give a gift to the princess. Do you have an idea?' So we spoke to Monsieur Arnault head of LVMH and, at this time, we were just about to launch a new Dior handbag. So we suggested to Madame Chirac, 'Why not the new handbag?' And she said, 'Oh yes, that's a good idea.'"

"She presented this bag to Princess Diana and she immediately loved it. She wore it immediately and it became an enormous success. In our Christian Dior boutique in Tokyo, 4000 people were on the waiting list to buy this bag because they had seen it in some newspaper. Immediately it was called 'Diana's bag', or 'The princess bag.' Every woman in the world identified with her, because she was a legend and she was also so close to the people."

In Japan Diana was incredibly popular. On her third visit in 1995 she had endeared herself by memorizing a little speech in Japanese. "She was extremely warm-hearted and so charming," says Mr. Makoto Watanabe, Chamberlain to His Majesty, the Emperor of Japan. "We were all in awe of her. She was incredibly beautiful and her heart was shining outwards. The few times I have met her her beauty struck me." The separation simply increased interest and admiration for her. Juliet Hindell, a BBC correspondent based in Tokyo, said that "many women told me they had seen her first as a fairy-tale princess but later as a modern icon, an independent divorced woman getting on with her own life."[13]

In America Diana was also hugely admired. In 1995, Ed Matthews, chief executive of the United Cerebral Palsy Fund, invited her to New York to receive the International Humanitarian of the Year award. It was like "capturing lightning in a bottle." The dinner alone raised $2 million for an organization with a normal annual income of $1 million. "She understood more than anything else what to do with her station in life. I think she constantly struggled with what it meant to be a member of British royalty and how to make the most out of it to benefit society."

Diana's visit to Chicago in 1996 was a sensation. Phyllis Cunningham, then chief executive of the Royal Marsden hospital who accompanied her, could barely believe her eyes when they visited a city hospital in a very rundown area of town. "This was a city hospital, no private patients, very ethnic community. And the streets were absolutely packed. They were standing 50 deep and hanging out of windows. It was absolutely wonderful. And then when we got to the hospital itself and tried to visit, we were absolutely surrounded by people." "It was the biggest thing that Chicago had seen," says Pollyanna Benjamin, who worked at the British Consulate and acted as the royal team's secretary for the visit. "I've never actually been part of anything quite like that. It was just electric." Caroline Cracraft was head of public affairs at the British consulate in Chicago. "She was a wonderful representative. She was glamorous and had this amazing ability to connect with people." Both Pollyanna and Caroline were on call throughout the visit and enjoyed her company. They were particularly amused by one episode. "The phone didn't stop ringing," says Pollyanna, "and one man claimed to be Anthony Hopkins wanting to speak to the princess. You could tell immediately it wasn't him. He said he was calling from his set in Chicago. I said: 'Well, can I take your number, please?' And he said, 'No, I'm using the director's mobile phone, I can't give out the number.' Well, one by one the staff and the princess's entourage came in and one by one they all said, 'We've just spoken to somebody called Anthony Hopkins.' And then, lo and behold, the princess walked in and said, 'I've just spoken to somebody called Anthony Hopkins.' He had managed to get himself put through to the princess's private suite! We asked what she said and she said, 'Oh, I'm sorry, you've just missed the princess, she's gone out.'" We all sat around and laughed and I thought, 'Good thinking . . . toying with this mister. Little did he know.'"

For Henry Bienen, president of Northwestern University, whose cancer unit was at the heart of Diana's visit, it was a memorable time. "Chicago will always be a mixed bag. It's a big Irish town, so Brits are not always warmly welcome in the press, but she just got rave reviews. And I don't think there was a discordant note. Everybody thought that she was just sensational, very enthusiastic. It was a great PR coup, from all our points of view. There was a bald-faced headline on the front page of the *Tribune* saying, 'Northwestern University's . . . to Di for,' and so it was great publicity. For me personally, I mean, I've lived off that publicity ridiculously for years, just because it was such a splash for the university, and for its cancer center, you know. It gave a lot of very good attention to the research we were doing and it stuck in people's minds. She really acquitted herself terrifically well for all this. She was really consistent in her ability to be friendly and make people feel at ease."

"By the end of her life," says Jean-Michel Jarre, "she became a universal symbol, not an international one. International is just the smallest

common denominator between everything to be consumed by anyone. The universal is found by digging deep in your soul. It can be felt, or you can be understood by anyone, by the Chinese or by a Brazilian, by an Indian. It was the reason why, when she died, so many people reacted in such a genuinely strong emotional way." Christopher Spence says, "She was a symbol of a universal citizen."

❋ ❋ ❋ ❋

THE DRESS AUCTION ~ Some people belittled Diana during her life—and indeed afterward—for being a fashion icon, as if this proved she was insincere about the serious issues with which she involved herself. But public opinion can be harsh about women who look beautiful and especially harsh about those who appear to care about their appearance. "Even today," says Bianca Jagger, "there is a veiled prejudice toward beautiful women who are intelligent and committed. People have difficulty in accepting that it is possible to be beautiful, to have brains, and to be a person of substance." No one has ever been more confusing to these prejudices than Diana, who moved between these worlds with equal aplomb. Yet at the dress auction held in New York six weeks before she died those contradictions seemed to be contained in the one extraordinary person. Who else's dresses had become such desirable objects in their own right? Who else could have attracted such crowds? Who could have done this while in the same month undertaking a harrowing visit to war-torn Bosnia to meet and comfort people suffering the trauma of war? It's hard to imagine anyone else before or since who could in one event excite such interest, raise so much for good causes, and pay such a graceful compliment to her designers.

"What she looked like was more important than who she was in many of the tabloids: How she looked, her hairstyle, her clothes, whatever, but it's only in the later years that it was less about that and more about what her action was. It's still the burden of women that they're measured more by what they look like than what they say or do," comments Anita Roddick, founder of The Body Shop.

The auction was held in June in New York, an idea which Diana later gave William credit for. What made it possible, though, was a journey; the divorce, the loss of royal title, the changing style and priorities and the recognition that in spite of all these changes she could command interest and funds more easily than any other figure in the world. When Diana put forward the idea of the auction, she knew she had turned a corner. "I am extremely happy," said Diana, "that we can raise money this way for important charities. Yes, of course it is a wrench to let go of these beautiful dresses. But I am extremely happy that others can now share the joy I had wearing them. Life has moved into new and exciting areas. Clothes are not as essential to my work as they used to be."

Marguerite Littman was closely involved with the dress auction. Marguerite was a founding figure of the AIDS Crisis Trust. To begin with she organized film premieres, getting in sponsors for food and flowers so she could charge a good price for tickets. "I got to know Diana when she started coming to these events. Adrian Ward Jackson, who died of AIDS, was a great friend of hers and he was on my committee. He was the first one to ask her to one of our events and we became friends. She came to *Prince of Tides* with Barbra Streisand, and to all our big events. She supported us whenever she could." The two began to see each other socially. "We used to have lunch, sometimes at a restaurant or sometimes at Kensington Palace, but usually it was just the two of us. One morning she rang me and said, 'Marguerite, I'm giving you all my clothes.' I said, 'Why? Don't you think I dress well?' And she laughed and said, 'No, I want to get rid of everything and give the money to you.' Later she told me it was Prince William who gave her the idea.

"I went over to lunch and she said, 'Go down and look.' There were 400 dresses." They discussed how they should be sold and decided on Christie's as the auction house. Marguerite offered to do much of the background work for the events. But, "I told her she had to pay for everything for herself like her flights and hotel. I said, 'You just come on Concorde and arrive, don't stay for the sale, just be there for two days.' They thought it would be undignified if she stayed for the actual sale."

Christie's was the obvious choice of auction house since Diana's friend Christopher Balfour had already worked with Diana on AIDS Crisis Trust fund-raising. "I hadn't been chairman of Christie's for many weeks before I got a call from the Princess of Wales, who said she wanted to talk to me about something very private, so I went over to Kensington Palace. She said, 'I've got hundreds of dresses, which are so showy that I can't wear them again because all the press will say, 'Oh, she's brought out that old thing.' And I'm sure people would pay for them. And we ought to have a sale for charity and would Christie's do it?' I quickly conferred with my senior colleagues and we said not only will we do it, but we won't charge a commission. That will be our input into the charity. Meredith Etherington Smith got involved, and she masterminded the catalogue. We chose the best possible time of year, so the dresses could be shown in the UK. But we thought there would be more glamour if we had the auction in New York.

"I think she just suddenly realized that she was in a position to give a great deal more than she ever had thought she would have, at that time, to give. She suddenly realized that the dresses could be turned into a huge asset, because they weren't second-hand clothes, they were absolute icons, which people would pay a lot of money for, so why not exploit that for charity."

The auction was held in New York on June 25, 1997, preceded by a number of charity events where the dresses were shown in New York and London. "We held dinners, and one big cocktail party, so we collected money for charities just for people to be in her presence, and she was fantastically good with her busy schedule. If she said she was going to be at Christie's for an event, she arrived on the dot at 6:30 and she didn't leave until 8:30, so everybody was thrilled when they could say hello to her. In New York, we had a similar event the night before the auction, which was unbelievably crowded. And she was absolutely incredible. She knew everybody who was there had paid to be there, so she made herself available to everyone who wanted to talk to her. An awful lot of other stars would have said, "Look, I've had enough of this. You've got too many people here. It's a very hot night and I'm going home.'

"We were a bit worried at one point when they said that the main bidders for these clothes were going to be drag queens and they were going to be doing drag acts wearing these clothes in nightclubs and things. We did everything we could in vetting the would-be bidders, but there were a lot of people whom we just didn't know. There were names that never appear in our computer as bidding for anything at Christie's before. And what if they suddenly appeared in a nightclub in Chicago? But Diana was wonderfully matter-of-fact about that. "Well, if they've paid their money to the charity, as far as I'm concerned, good luck to them,' she said. We had to warn her that there were these rumors, and I was incredibly nervous. But, in the end, it didn't happen.

"I said, 'Do you think, what a shame, I'll never wear that again? She said, 'No. Because some of them I do like very, very much indeed and I'd love

to have worn again, but you know, it's difficult. They usually say, 'Oh, she didn't bother to have a new frock for this particular charity.' You know, she'd be criticized.

"I'd never been involved in an event like this. I mean, the crowds in New York, it really was like you see for an Oscar ceremony or something. There were police and the streets were lined, and you couldn't believe the flashbulbs when we got out of the car.

"Diana and I left for the UK on the evening of the sale on the overnight plane. British Airways, in their wisdom, boarded us first, she and me and her detective were somewhere 'round the back. The way the beds are put, they always look like double beds, although you can put a glass partition between you. I said, 'We're here sort of on exhibition, every passenger who walks on this plane has got to pass these two seats. We should have boarded last.'" And she said, 'Too late now, look, they're coming down the passage!' And we got absolutely in hysterics. Four hundred people stared at us, or however many people fit on one of those airplanes, and I've never been so embarrassed in my life. At least we hadn't got into our pajamas yet. Staying in The Carlyle with her in New York those two or three days was an absolute lark. They put us on a top floor suite for privacy. The whole auction, which I thought was going to be incredibly hard work, was just the greatest possible fun. It was as smooth as it could have been.

"The auction was a success beyond the wildest expectations of the organizers. Marguerite Littman had spent a month in New York persuading friends and businesses to sponsor flowers, food, drinks, mannequins to maximize the amount raised. But no one had any idea who would buy the dresses and, in our more anxious moments, whether anyone actually would. I didn't know any of those people who bought the dresses. I thanked them, but I didn't quiz them because they were being interviewed non-stop by the newspapers and TV. I gather that some of the people have given those dresses now to charity themselves. It's like a rolling thing, which is good."

The auction raised $7 million in one evening, making Diana one of the world's leading philanthropists. The money was split between the AIDS Crisis Trust, Britain's leading breast cancer hospital, the Royal Marsden, the Harvard AIDS Institute, and the Evelyn H. Lauder Breast Cancer Center at Memorial Sloan-Kettering Hospital. "When the AIDS Crisis Trust got the check," says Christopher Balfour, "it was a sum so much greater than we had ever been able to raise. Some years we raised up to half a million a year, but to raise millions like this, I said to Marguerite and the other trustees agreed, that really we were never going to be able to get another amount like this.

"I have always wanted to pay tribute to how wonderful she was at working with people. Everybody got involved with the parties we had to give for her, the things she had to do, the appearances in front of the television cameras, she had a nice word of thanks to everybody including the butler who would give us lunch. She was quite amazing at dealing with the people that were serving her in any way and there wasn't a soul at Christie's who didn't love her by the end of that year."

Behind the auction was also the story of Diana's relationship with Catherine Walker. Although many other designers were represented, the auction certainly highlighted her role in Diana's image. A deep-thinking, introspective, sensitive woman, she was a curiously appropriate designer for Diana to have found so early and their lives remained closely linked. The year before the auction Catherine Walker had herself been diagnosed with breast cancer and this was one reason why breast cancer was a beneficiary of the evening. For Catherine it was an intensely personal occasion. "When I was first approached about the auction of Diana's dresses at the end of 1996 my initial reaction was that I wanted to buy all my dresses back. Naively I had not understood what a major event lay ahead; I just didn't want them to be scattered around the globe. However, when it became clear that both charities involved were likely to benefit hugely I gave it everything I could. I watched Diana and Meredith Etherington Smith set about it with the same energy and professionalism that Diana went on to give to her work with the landmines.

"Typically, after the auction in June 1997 the princess invited me to bring the staff of my first workroom to Kensington Palace. She wanted to mark the occasion of the auction of her clothes with a private meeting with the people who had carried out the work. My staff was of course honored and delighted at such a personal meeting. In the space of a morning, 16 years of memories were raised and discussed. One member of staff who had made her maternity dress suffered claustrophobia. Diana was the first to notice. This one small meeting demonstrated the princess's ability to bring people together and make each person feel special in a most unique way."[14]

As ever, some of the press put the worst possible spin even on this occasion. "The last thing I did for her," says Anthony Julius, her lawyer, "was to sue the *Daily Express* when she auctioned a number of her dresses to charity and they ran a story that she was keeping the money for herself. She was furious about it, as you could imagine. They had been given some bogus documents that purported to show that she had some side deal. They were mad, they didn't ask her about it beforehand and we sued them and they paid £70,000 damages, which went to charity. They wanted to pay the charity direct, but I said to them: 'No, you'll give the money to us first.' The princess was very angry and she said, 'They don't understand what I'm about.'"

Mario Testino, who took a series of photos in March 1997, describes Diana's image as "a classic and eternal style. The princess," he says, "was heaven. I absolutely adored her; she spent the whole day laughing. She had a lot of style and grace; she was very attractive and at the same time unreachable. There was something noble about her. I think she is one of the most beautiful women I have ever photographed, because she had everything: the legs, the face, the personality, and a smile that lit up the room. She was quite wonderful. I have had the privilege hopefully to show the world the real person behind the princess. It was rather like being let in on a very private secret.

"I think she became an icon as a result of her many different qualities: Her beauty, her style, and her rank. She was fragile and confident at the same time. I have never seen a response quite like that. The basis of her charisma? She liked life and people."

❊ ❊ ❊ ❊

LANDMINES ~ In the last year of her life, Diana became involved in the cause with which she will always be identified: The campaign to ban land-mines. However painful the invasion of her private life, in that last year she seemed to have reconciled herself to using her media profile. "I have all this media, so let's take it somewhere we can use it positively," she said of the trip to Angola.

In some respects, it is extraordinary that someone in her position should have allied herself with such a radical cause. But Diana was no stranger to controversy; she had taken up issues no one else would touch and stuck with them. The human damage caused by landmines was a global issue where needless death and suffering was being inflicted. It was a cause, too, which allowed her to exercise her exceptional rapport with individuals and bring comfort to individuals in situations of extreme suffering.

Diana had been conscious of the landmine issue for some time. In 1991 she visited Sandy Gall's Afghanistan Appeal in the remote mountains of Peshawar on the borders of Afghanistan where many of the people treated were landmine victims. There she saw many landmine victims: Says Sandy Gall, "Even then one knew she was very interested in mines. I rate her contribution to the landmine issue very highly. She put it on the map. Being a journalist I realized what a tremendous influence her interest had."

Long-term friend, Lord Puttnam also remembers that her concerns about the terrible human cost of landmines predated her full involvement: "I'd been out to Cambodia in '93 and made a film which she had loved," he says. "Maybe it was one influence." Henry Bellingham, Conservative MP and friend of Diana's since her teenage years, was also aware that she was keen to work on an international issue. "I had spoken to her about her charitable work generally and I knew that she was looking for something where she would have a unique ability to kick-start something. The charities that she was dealing with in this country never fell into that category. Anyone who was in the public eye in a big way would have been able to help those charities but there was something extra that she could add to the landmine campaign and I think she saw that. It wasn't a fashionable cause within the establishment—I remember a junior defense minister at the time saying that she should do her job and ministers should do theirs. But that was the sort of challenge that she relished."

It was in 1996 that Diana finally took up the issue of landmines, in the first instance, coming back to work with the British Red Cross. Richard Attenborough's film *In Love and War* was in part about the issue. "Since the story focused on the Red Cross, I asked if the organization would care to benefit from a charity premiere with the Princess of Wales as guest of honor. As Diana was already having discussions with Mike Whitlam of the British Red Cross about the possibility of renewing her official involvement, it was agreed I should make the approach. Diana immediately said she would be happy to attend the premiere and suggested we meet to discuss the matter further. I had helped launch the first stage of the anti-landmine campaign some time previously and, as soon as we began to talk, it was evident that the idea of generating funds to aid victims appealed to her enormously. This culminated in her visit to Angola under the auspices of the Red Cross accompanied by a BBC television crew. Before she went she was concerned that she might be venturing into an area of activity that might be wrongly construed as political and we debated the pros and cons very carefully. But of one thing she was certain: The obscenity of landmines should be brought to public attention."[15]

According to Mike Whitlam, Diana's involvement unequivocally transformed the campaign. Prior to her involvement, "the landmines campaign was going nowhere. We were struggling to get anybody interested. We launched it to the advertising media and the serious press first, and it was really hard work to get anybody to take it seriously. There is no question that the Angola trip turned that around."

Lord Deedes, veteran journalist and ex-editor of the *Daily Telegraph*, who had for many years tried to draw public attention to the horrors of landmines, was asked to cover the trip. "She went to Angola in January and the press corps went off with her. Of course, as soon as she got to Angola, everybody wanted to meet her, but she was quite resolute and stuck to mines. She made it a business-like trip. I went to New York in '92 and wrote some stuff for this paper about it, but nobody took a blind bit of interest in land-mines until she came along."

Diana's trip received massive press coverage. Pictures of her walking across a landmined area and comforting landmine victims went round the world. According to Lord Deedes, "that doubled the interest in the Angola trip, and so, as a result, there were larger headlines than there would have been."

Christina Lamb, someone more used to reporting on war than royalty, was one of the journalists who followed her on that trip. "When I told my friends where I was off to, they laughed knowing me as someone more used to reporting on wars, with little patience for the media obsession with Di's latest look. Having seen first-hand the terrible effects of landmines in Afghanistan and Mozambique, I cared deeply about the issue her trip was intended to publicize, although I feared it would be a vast publicity stunt. I was pleasantly surprised when she turned up in jeans, white shirt, and no make-up. I consoled myself over how good she looked by snidely spotting the designer label. She'd come, she said, determined to work, and work she did. The Red Cross whisked us from one hospital to the next, each with ever more horrific scenes of skeletal figures with missing arms, missing legs, and half-blown-off heads, victims of the 16 million landmines scattered around the country. Many of the injuries were so gruesome that I could not look, despite years of third world reporting. But Diana never turned her head away. Instead she had something I've only ever seen before from Nelson Mandela—a kind of aura that made people want to be with her and a completely natural straight-from-the-heart sense of how to bring hope to those who seemed to have little to live for.

"The trip wiped out all my past cynicism about Diana. That lady of the lamp performance wasn't just for the benefit of the cameras. Once at a hospital in Huambo when the photographers had all flown back to their air-conditioned hotels to wire their pictures, I watched Diana, unaware that any journalists were still present, sit and hold the hand of Helena Ussova, a seven-year-old who'd had her intestines blown to pieces by a mine. For what seemed an age the pair just sat; no words needed. When Diana finally left, the small girl struggled through her pain to ask me if the beautiful lady was an angel. Could anybody have said no?"[16]

Royal correspondent Jennie Bond, more used to Ascot than Angola, was more engaged by the Angola trip than anything she'd ever done. "I thought Angola was the best trip she'd done because she got really hooked on the whole issue of landmines. It was fantastic after all these years of doing all this speculation about who was kissing who and what's going on suddenly to have a proper story with proper, meaningful statistics that mattered and a cause that seemed really to have some substance. I had great respect for her, because it wasn't an easy trip at all. And she came in for all that criticism from a government minister who said she was a bit of a loose cannon and indicated she was embarrassing the government by what she was doing."

It was Jennie Bond herself who conveyed the minister's comments to Diana on the trip and asked for her reaction. "I asked her the question; I knew she was upset. And she said: 'Jennie, don't do that to me again.' And then we got on separate planes to bounce to the next place and I wrote a note on the plane saying: 'You've got to understand, you are under attack in the national media back home and you must defend yourself. You did it; don't worry about it.' And I said, 'I know you hate being asked questions like that off the cuff, but you performed well.' And she did, because the next day her answer was in the headlines. Her answer to me was: 'Jennie, I'm only trying to help.' And all the headlines were: 'Diana says—I'm only trying to help.'"

"I'm not a political figure," Diana responded, "nor do I want to be one, but I come with my heart and I want to bring awareness of people in distress whether in Angola or any other part of the world. The fact is I'm a humanitarian figure. I always have been and I always will be."

Back home, Diana's words struck a chord with her mother. "When she was called to take up the landmines issue she called it 'working.' It was 'working,' it was looking at the whole picture in the hope that she could project it and people would identify with it. And it was suggested at various times that she was politically motivated, but she never was. She was purely for people: A humanitarian, which was what she was. She didn't know any bounds, of objects or of people. She used the word 'humanitarian.' She used it in anger when she was criticized by the politicians, and she stated in that film, the Red Cross film, that she was a humanitarian, not a politician. When I saw her in that film I thought, that's it, that's what she should say, that's what she believes. It was the first time I'd heard her use it but it was a statement of what she was."

Traveling with Diana was a small group making a film about the trip for BBC's *Heart of The Matter*. They were amazed both at Diana's consistent thoughtfulness toward them and the unprecedented level of access she gave the team. "Usually when you see the royals on these kind of occasions," says Karina Brennan, the film's producer and director, "the cameras are fairly far back and you get snatched bits of conversation but you don't really get up close to exactly what's going on, but for her to say 'Yes' to wearing a radio mic for us was fantastic and it meant we could make a very intimate documentary, the first time ever that had been done." Karina found her "absolutely delightful and her personal skills were extraordinary. I never saw her check herself in the mirror or peer in the camera to make herself look perfect. She wore a white shirt all the time and looked immaculate. Nobody was doing her hair or her make-up, she was doing it herself early in the morning and she just looked great, probably at her most beautiful."

Roger Lucas, the sound recordist who "listened in on her for the entire trip," was equally impressed. "She was fantastic in every way but especially where she thought there was a photo opportunity. She was very good at making sure that we were all in position before she did something. There were so many news people all fighting over each other that you've just got to be in that position to be able to grab it, otherwise there's no point in it happening. She had an awareness of everything that was going on, very, very sharp. The thing I noticed, as soon as I put the headphones on and started listening to everything was how her amazing giggle kept coming through. Now, bearing in mind that, obviously, it's a sober subject, she broke the ice beautifully by just being herself. She was amazingly natural. And she was getting lovely sorts of answers out of people. There were men who, quite frankly, probably didn't even know who she was, soldiers who had lost limbs or whatever who all of a sudden were surrounded by all these officials. They were sort of frightened to death, but she would just sit down on the wall with them and ask little things like, 'How do you play football now then?' And then they would say, 'Oh, we find ways, we've got sticks we can hit the ball with,' or something. It would break the ice and they would think she was wonderful.

"If they looked in any way apprehensive and she found out through the interpreter they were not happy with it, she would move on. But she was sort of directing it, if you like, in just a gentle way. I was absolutely amazed at how well she could do this thing. And you could just tell how she would win somebody round from looking like a scared rabbit one second to having her arms round them giving them a cuddle and having a smile and a laugh with them the next. It was just a pleasure to watch her work.

"The photo opportunities there, obviously, were perfect for what she was trying to achieve, which was get the press to get images which would bring the plight of the landmine victims to everybody's papers throughout the world. Watching her working the press was amazing, because she knew where all the key photographers were and, one by one, she would give them the photo opportunity. And, my goodness, I mean, she's so photogenic. It was just like watching the master at work."

Angola made a big impression on Diana. She described herself as "overwhelmed by the destruction" in the country and later told Baroness Chalker she hadn't been expecting this. "I remember when she came back from Angola, we met for lunch at Kensington Palace and she said, 'You just didn't tell me how ghastly it was going to be,' and I said, 'I tried.' But she couldn't envision it; I don't think you can until you see some of these dire situations. Certainly Angola scarred her very greatly: the number of children who were limbless, the state of the hospitals, the lack of medicines, the lack of hygiene, the lack of water, the frequency with which children were injured indiscriminately just when they were out to play. She started to think that she'd got to do much more like this. I think she wanted part of her life to be concerned with helping people in the developing world, particularly children, particularly the sick. It was important to her. 'How can I be useful?' was often her phrase."

Two pictures of Diana in Angola had incredible international impact. The first was her walk across the minefields. As Sandy Gall points out, "All the landmine stuff was jolly brave. They took her and showed her how they excavated them. I've watched Halo doing it in Afghanistan and so on and that certainly takes a bit of nerve. I'm sure she was advised not to do it by her officials because something can go wrong of course, or she could have even been hit by a piece of shrapnel so I think she was brave." Mike Whitlam was "slightly worried, because people like Chris Moon (who used to work for The Halo Trust) lost his leg, walking across an area he'd already cleared. And so even though we were walking an area that was cleared, and going to look at a live mine, which she blew up, I was just a little bit worried that, you know, they might have missed one. What would happen to me if she'd got blown up? I don't know. I did feel a hell of a lot of responsibility for that trip, because everybody was saying it's down to me."

The iconography of Diana with a mask and flak jacket on is an abiding image, says author Andrew Morton. "Of course thousands of people around the world have campaigned hard against landmines, but it's that old thing that a picture is often worth a million words. In Diana's case, that was never truer. It's beauty in a compromising position. The iconography showed someone who was making herself vulnerable. Why have you put beauty in a vulnerable position? Well, because it's man-made."

The other picture of Diana in Angola the world will always remember is of her with landmine victim Sandra Txijica on her lap. It gave the world's press the picture they had been waiting for. As always her lack of squeamishness and her ability to relate through touch and expression was remarkable. "I thought Sandra was particularly courageous," said Diana, "because we all descended on her. It's daunting to have one camera on you let alone 30 or 40, but I did reassure her that this was going to help other children around the world and she was happy. It does raise the trauma of what she is going through and it's made us much wiser. One wants to go out and help these people especially these little people because they have had part of their future taken away."

Sandra's image went round the world, forever linked to Diana, and a powerful symbol of the horrors of landmines. For one person at least Sandra was more than an anonymous African child. Peter Carrette is an Australian photographer who had photographed Diana earlier in her life in more glamorous surroundings, mainly on her Australian tours. After a press trip to Cambodia covering a United Nations High Commissioner for Refugees visit he became passionately concerned about landmines and their effect on children and devoted much time to the work of an Australian landmines group. When he saw the picture of Sandra, "it absolutely tore my heart out, because

I'd worked with landmine children before in Cambodia. Personalities I've worked with over a 30-year period don't actually like to get hands-on with people who are disabled. They don't mind shaking hands and doing all that, but when it comes to sitting on the lap, to touchy-feely stuff, most of the people you work with don't actually do what Diana did. She was really, really tender and gentle.

"My first thought after Diana died was to wonder what the people whose lives were actually touched by her thought. And I wanted to find the little girl in Angola who was for me the symbol of Diana's landmine campaigns. So I got myself to Luanda, the capital, and the Australian consul set about tracking her down. It was extremely difficult. I found out she was in San Remo up the top end of Angola which was a strictly off limits area, but I got a plane up there and I ran into some people up there who put me in touch with the United Nations who put me in touch with the Red Cross and I went out to this little village and found Sandra in a little mud hut. I took pictures with me of Diana and asked her if she remembered Diana and all this stuff. And she did a really lovely piece—written down by the interpreter— where she said that meeting Diana had changed her life. People had taken her seriously and she'd become a personality in her own local area where everybody knew her. And she had been on a stamp in Angola sitting on Diana's lap and her whole life was totally changed by a ten or 15 minute chance encounter. But an American journalist from *Time* magazine had promised her an artificial leg. He'd interviewed her a week after Diana had died and had promised to get her a leg and he hadn't come through with it. I was horrified. So I said to her, 'Look, we'll sort that out.' I took pictures of Sandra with a picture of Diana and I gave it to *Hello!* and I gave it to *Woman's Day* in Australia and I said, 'I'll give you this story exclusively but you must give me $10,000 and pay it into a trust that we keep for Sandra Txijica to use for her education,' which they did.

"A year or so later, the Australian Red Cross brought Sandra to Australia with another landmine survivor, a 13-year-old girl from Thailand who was an ambassador for the de-miners. I said to the Red Cross, if you fly her out, can you give her a week the other end of the trip and I'll take her on holiday? We took her to Byron Bay and showed her the dolphins and the Opera House and the beach—absolutely wonderful stuff. Her whole world just expanded 100 percent.

"The message she gave to me through the interpreter was that she wanted to send a message to William and Harry to say: 'If you can in any way continue Diana's work this would make a big difference because you have a voice and I don't. I'm just a little girl in a war-torn village of Angola, what can I say? But if people listen to you like they did to your mom, please speak out.'"

After Angola, Diana's involvement with campaigning against landmines gathered pace. According to Lord Deedes: "Ray McGrath encouraged her to speak for the Mines Advisory Group, which I was interested in, in the summer at the Royal Geographical Society in Kensington. It was a conference on landmines and I gave a hand with the speech." There she met Jerry White of the Landmine Survivors Network who lost his own leg in a mine accident. He heard her speak and was impressed. "She delivered a speech that was genuinely a strong statement of compassion. I thought, 'This woman gets it.' She doesn't just get, 'Oh, landmines are so awful and they blow up children.' There are many cliché speeches. I'd also by then heard scores of speeches by well-meaning wonderful activists as well as government types. Diana had the heart to it and the empowering compassion, so that it wasn't sort of talking down about victims. She had some flak from the British government, although she was trying to reassert that this was a humanitarian individual effort, not a political positioning." Jerry made contact and suggested she worked with his group.

After this conference, says Lord Deedes, "Senator Elizabeth Dole got Diana over to America to do the American Red Cross." Jerry White was surprised at how bold Diana's speech was in America. "That did turn up the volume on the ban, in a way that made her hostess, Elizabeth Dole, you know, a political animal in the United States, very uncomfortable. Diana crossed over and stepped up in a way that Mrs. Dole did not want to see. Diana became an activist in the United States and did it, in a way, without any apologies, pushing for a US government ban."

In June that year Diana spoke at a conference in London co-hosted by the Mines Advisory Group and the Landmine Survivors Network. She reiterated that she was "not a political figure. My interests are humanitarian. That is why I feel drawn to this human tragedy." And she spoke with passion about the horrors of landmines and what she had seen in Angola. "There is a chronic shortage of medicine, of painkillers, even of anesthetics. Surgeons engaged in amputating shattered limbs never have all the facilities we would expect here. So the human pain that has to be borne is often beyond imagining. The emergency medical care moreover is only the first step back to a sort of life. For those whose living is the land, loss of an arm or leg is an overwhelming handicap which lasts for life." "At this Royal Geographical meeting," says Lord Deedes, "Diana had said to me she thought we ought to do another trip, and Cambodia wasn't on, because of political kidnapping. She thought Bosnia would be safest. Well, she'd get permission to do Bosnia, in August, so I said, OK. And that worked out. And she borrowed George Soros's jet and flew into Sarajevo."

Bosnia was no blank sheet for Diana. She had been involved in the case of Irma at Great Ormond Street Hospital for Children, a victim of shelling; she had visited the Croatian refugee camp in Hungary in 1992; she had visited the home of Bosnian refugees in England. Like many in the UK at that time, the proximity and horror of what was happening there clearly engaged her. Jerry White with whom, along with Lord Deedes, she traveled, experienced a confident person with a clear sense of what she could do to raise awareness about the evils of landmines. "In Bosnia," says Jerry White, "we saw Diana at her best and most beautiful. She was emerging from the pain of her divorce and coming into her own." Lord Deedes was also impressed, perhaps even more than in Angola with the exceptional sensitivity she brought into the situation as they traveled the war-torn country. "Part of her gift in bringing comfort to those in anguish lay in this sensitive awareness of when silence is best. She was not a voluble sympathizer, quite the reverse. At some point during an outpouring of grief, she would stretch out a hand or both hands and touch the person on the arm or face. I found some of the tales we had to hear almost unendurable, yet I never saw her lose this calm. She saw dreadful wounds and heard horrifying stories while maintaining the demeanor of a professional but sympathetic nurse. Nor in the course of those three days did I see her concentration flag; and this was remarkable because the distractions were intense. She would utter a faint murmur of dismay at the sight of 40 cameramen lined up outside some humble home. Then self-discipline would assert itself. She accepted the value of photographers in her life and acknowledged the inestimable value they held for her good causes. What she found harder to stomach were the intrusive lengths to which some, in such an intensely competitive game, were ready to go.

"The emotional encounters we had with victims and the bereaved left their mark on her. What often seemed a calm, soothing response to a tale of woe took more of a toll than one at first supposed. What made it even harder were the depths of bitterness sown by this civil war in former Yugoslavia. There was an encounter in one of Sarajevo's largest cemeteries. The Princess of Wales went off alone to walk around it. As she did so, she encountered a mother tending her son's grave. There was no language barrier: The two women gently embraced. Watching this scene from a distance I sought in my mind to think who else could have done this—nobody.

"'I am a humanitarian. I always have been and I always will be,' she declared during the Angola expedition when they accused her of meddling in politics. In saying that she wrote her own epitaph, for that, I came to learn, was what she really thought about herself."

The legacy for the Landmine Survivors Network was considerable. Diana's visit launched the first amputee support work in Bosnia and The Diana, Princess of Wales Memorial Fund still supports its program there. Recently, journalist Barbara Davies traveled back to Bosnia to talk to two boys, on opposite sides of the ethnic division but united by their injuries, who famously posed with Diana on her trip there. Zarco Peric lost his leg when, aged 13, he picked up an unexploded landmine in the woods. Malic Bradaric's father was clearing mines when his son aged 15 walked across the minefield assuming, because his father was there, he was safe. Malic says, "When I was told an important person was coming to visit me I thought it must be the American helicopter pilot who flew me to hospital after my accident. But when the van pulled up outside our home I recognized her immediately. I just couldn't believe it was Lady Di." Zarco says, "When I saw who it was, my heart was beating faster than ever. She took our hands and kissed us both. She said, 'I have two sons about the same age as you.'" Diana spent two hours in Malic's home, helping make coffee, asking about the war and their injuries and especially encouraging them. "Lady Di said to us, 'You can do whatever you want to.' And I have always remembered that," says Malic. They remember vividly her last words to them: "I'll come back and see you soon. Everything will be OK. You will not be forgotten."[17]

With Lord Deedes, Diana discussed plans to take the landmine issues forward. "There was a tentative agreement that she'd go on to Oslo, I think, where there was going to be a meeting about an international ban. I was cagey about this, because the ban was political and, of course, the government were giving the armed forces what the armed forces wanted, which was landmines, and nobody had proscribed them. We briefly discussed Oslo and I warned her it was political and vaguely agreed to help with the speech that she'd make there. That was going to be in September, I think. And then within ten days she was killed."

"The last letter I got from her was all about the landmines," says Charles Spencer. "She was very proud of the landmine issue and I think if she had to have a swan song it's a wonderful one to have had because it was such an important and meaty issue. Her last letter wasn't about her summer romance or anything, it was about her landmine campaign."

In the wake of Diana's death there was a huge groundswell of popular support to sign up for the Ottawa Convention banning landmines. There is little doubt that not only did her involvement speed it up, but her memory helped push countries that were dragging their feet to ratify it. According to Mike Whitlam, "They would not have been talking at the Canadian meeting, where they ratified the Convention later that year, had she not gone to Angola. I would stake my life on that. They actually acknowledged what she'd done, at that meeting."

"She was only involved with landmines from January 1997 until her death in August, which is eight months," says Lord Deedes. "And there is no doubt at all that while she was on the job she woke the world up as nobody else has done."

"Before she engaged with landmines," says Clare Short, who became the UK's minister for overseas development in May 1997, "people like me and people like NGOs [non-governmental organizations] working in countries with landmines knew about the campaign to get the Ottawa Convention ratified, but most people had never heard of it. And by engaging, she brought it to popular consciousness across the world. So she used her beauty and fame for something that was transformed by her engagement. After that, everybody knew about landmines and everyone understood in a practical way and in an emotional way what a big issue it was and that by standing together the world could do something about it. That was fantastic.

"The other thing was that she was deadly serious about it. She wasn't just a pretty face. She had studied the facts, was absolutely on top of it, had a real grasp and knew where progress had got to in the world, what more needed doing. It was impressive. There are still an awful lot of landmines in the world, but we're far further ahead in terms of criticism of those who use them and in our determination to get them cleared. She moved it all forward and who knows how many children haven't had their legs blown off because of what she did."

"Her involvement," says Martin Bell, once a war reporter more recently an MP, "had a political effect. I do not believe that the Ottawa Convention on anti-personnel mines would have happened as soon as it did but for her charismatic involvement with the cause. She had a really interesting political effect, long after her death. It's an incredibly long shadow she cast. The Ottawa Landmine Accord was in December 1997. In 1998 along comes the enabling legislation so we can sign onto it. And we wanted to be one of the first 40 countries, at which point it has a legal effect internationally. But it was the same time as the legislation for the Welsh and Scottish devolutions was going through Parliament—a terrific log jam. So one day I was invited onto the *Today* program about it and George Robertson, the then defense secretary, was putting the line that they had run out of time. I said, 'If you don't have the time, we'll take two days out of the recess and we'll come back and mark the first anniversary of the princess's death by passing the legislation then.' That afternoon the government capitulated. They found the time. Just even the mention of her. This was nearly a year after she died."

Heather Mills McCartney, herself an anti-landmine campaigner, says, "When Diana got involved doors opened because people were interested in the subject purely because she took an interest in it. Schools started taking an interest and school children would communicate with other children, pen pals in many landmine war-torn countries. So there was this great shining light that brought all the attention to such an important cause."

"She changed the whole approach to landmines," says Sandy Gall. "And of course the fact that she spearheaded that whole thing still works today. What she did for landmines then to raise public awareness; everyone is conscious of it and now the [campaign against] cluster bombs is a sort of extension of that."

"This is why she was such an extraordinary woman," says Colonel John Mayo, former director general of Help the Aged. "High fashion one minute and deep into business the next minute. What she did for the whole question of landmines was amazing. And this is why the whole thing is so desperately sad. She was just what England needed."

Journalist Annick Cojean was the last person to talk in detail to Diana about her role. "She was becoming more and more aware of the strength she felt in herself. She felt, it seemed to me, that she had a very special connection with people through which she could express a lot of tenderness which came naturally to her, a lot of compassion. Having groped around, hesitated with her life—her private life and her status—having had moments of doubt, I think that she was more and more convinced that she had a voice with which she could both do a lot of good and also blossom. The French word is 'epanouir' and also means 'to please oneself'. A woman who is 'epanouie' means a happy woman. They become very beautiful, magnificent and mature, so they grow and blossom. And when one uses this term to describe a woman, it means that she is happy inside her own body and inside her own head. Diana knew what she was going to do. She knew which direction she was going in."

She dispensed a sort of magic, really, partly because she was very beautiful, partly because she was very famous, and partly because she just had that personal magnetism. There was no way we could guide her to carry out government policy, that wasn't the relationship at all. She was a phenomenon—but so far as Britain was concerned, overseas, a very good one.

Douglas Hurd

154

Increasingly, knowing what to say and knowing what pleasure and relief it gave people, became a way of validating herself. If no one else was telling her what a good job she was doing then, actually, ordinary people were telling her.

Vivienne Parry

During 1995 there was speculation that I might run for president and at the time, journalists were researching my ancestry. That year, I was a joint recipient, along with the Princess of Wales, of the United Cerebral Palsy Humanitarian Award. When it came to my acceptance speech, I stood up and said how delighted I was to be here and honored to be sharing the award with the princess. Then I said "because we have a relationship," I paused, looked up at the audience and raised an eyebrow. The room stirred with expectation. I went on to explain that one of the journalists researching my family history had unearthed an Earl of Coote who, it turns out, was also in Diana's family lineage. So I said that we were actually related through the Cootes. And then I explained that I wasn't going to run for president but as I was in line for the throne, I would far rather be king than president. Everyone, including the princess thought this was hilarious. Then it was the princess's turn to give her speech. She stood up, greeted all the dignitaries present, ending with "And my Cousin Colin." I was very impressed by her quick wit and good sense of humor as well as admiring enormously the way she used her glamour and global status for good causes. Diana's death was a great loss. There are few on the world stage who have the magic which Diana had and which she used so well.

Colin

March: 7th
1997.

Dearest Danielle,
     It was lovely to
hear from you & many
thanks for your letter.
     I am so happy that
you're feeling well &
perhaps on your next visit
to the Brompton you'd let
me know - 0171-937-2721
1690
(phone number)

& so I could come & see
you - I'd love that.
     I miss you very much
too & hope that your next
journey to London isn't
too far off!

     Lots of love to you &
Natasha an enormous hug,

from,

x Diana x

April: 5th
1997.

Dearest Danielle,
     I have been thinking
of you, especially as I
was in the Brompton this
week - how are you
my friend?

Please let me know when
your next visit to the
hospital is planned as I'd
love to come & see you ...
Lots of love from.
Diana. 0171-937-272

April: 29th
1997.

Dearest Danielle & Natasha,
     Thank you so much
for letting me look at
you dancing on this
video - I was very
impressed indeed!
     It was lovely to see
you all here last week &
I have no-more biscuits

left in my home ... I
wonder why!
Please take lots of care &
I hope to see you soon ...
     Fondest love
from.

Diana x

160

. . . I asked her to choose one photo which best expressed what she was about. She chose one of a little Pakistani boy whom she is holding in her arms. Her eyes are shut. It is certainly not the best photo of her—it's even out of focus and rather poor quality—but she chose this photo and it seemed to reveal more about who she was and what she wanted to do. It expressed her care for suffering children.

Annick Cojean

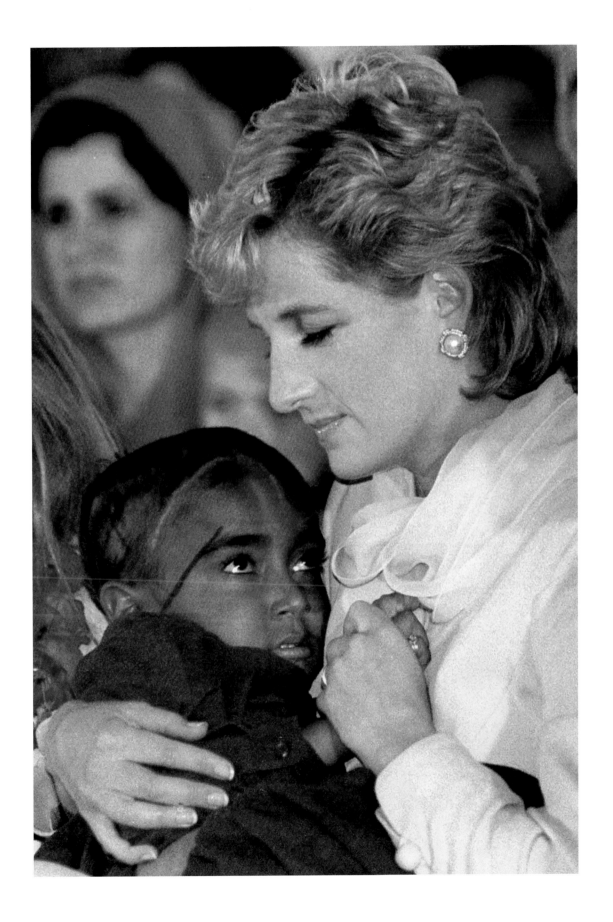

JESUS is the TRUTH
to be told;
JESUS is the LIFE
to be lived;
JESUS is the LOVE
to be loved;
JESUS is the LIGHT
to be lit.

LET us LOVE JESUS
with an undivided
LOVE,
And others, as He
LOVES
you and me.

(Mother Theresa)
1992

Even today there is a veiled prejudice toward beautiful women who are intelligent and committed. People have difficulty in accepting that it is possible to be beautiful, to have brains, and to be a person of substance.

Bianca Jagger

September 30th 1996.

Dearest Catherine,

It's impossible to put into words the thrill of wearing such a beautiful dress as your cream lace one!

I was so proud & felt very confident to stride at once & deliver my first speech since the divorce...

The comments about your design & expertise would have made your ears burn.

You gave an enormous amount of people an enormous amount of pleasure ... thank you.

My fondest love from.

Diana x

I'm not a political figure, nor do I want to be one, but I come with my heart and I want to bring awareness of people in distress whether in Angola or any other part of the world. The fact is I'm a humanitarian figure. I always have been and I always will be. . . . I have all this media, so let's take it somewhere we can use it positively.

Diana

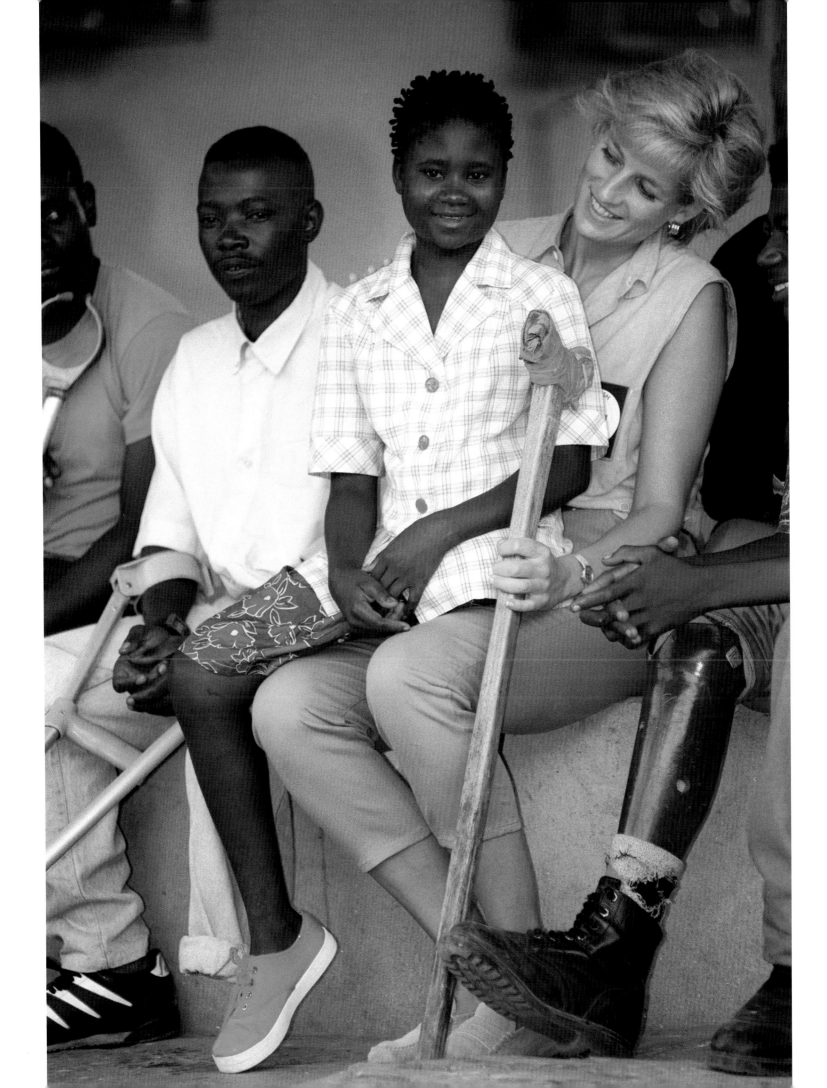

I met Princess Diana on a few occasions and was always impressed by her personal charm, sense of humor and great kindness to the people she met. From the word go, I felt as if I was a friend of hers and even though official formalities were inevitably present, her down-to-earth manner was most impressive. I think this kindness she showed as a person extended into her charity work and I believe that everybody who met her was touched by this special feeling. She campaigned tirelessly for many causes, but one especially dear to Heather and myself is the work she did to increase awareness of the atrocity of landmines. Heather had already been working in that area and I myself joined the cause later, but both of us feel that the work Princess Diana put in was invaluable in pointing up the horror of these cowardly weapons. Both of us will always remember her for her great contribution to the world, but most particularly for her special human qualities, which always shone through.

Sir Paul McCartney

The emotional encounters we had with victims and the bereaved left their mark on her. What often seemed a calm, soothing response to a tale of woe took more of a toll than one at first supposed. What made it even harder were the depths of bitterness sown by this civil war in former Yugoslavia. There was an encounter in one of Sarajevo's largest cemeteries. The Princess of Wales went off alone to walk round it. As she did so, she encountered a mother tending her son's grave. There was no language barrier: the two women gently embraced. Watching this scene from a distance I sought in my mind to think who else could have done this—nobody.

Lord Deedes

174

CHAPTER FIVE – DIANA, WHOSE BEAUTY WILL NEVER BE EXTINGUISHED FROM OUR MINDS

Few individuals have brought such widespread, popular attention and hope to millions of people, as the late Diana, Princess of Wales—to those whose lives have been touched by HIV/AIDS; to the innocent adults, children and families who have to come to terms daily with devastation caused by landmines and who live under their continual threat; to the sick and dying in the UK and abroad; and to abused, abandoned and vulnerable children throughout the world.

From hospital wards around the UK and Mother Teresa's Hospice for the Sick and Dying to the minefields of Angola and the Landmine Survivors Network in Bosnia—Princess Diana's personal warmth and genuine interest brought hope to many people during their darkest and loneliest moments; comforted families who have, sometimes needlessly and cruelly lost loved ones; and made the most vulnerable feel special.

By speaking out when others held back, she made people aware of the need to unite rather than divide, of the need to address the great issues of poverty and injustice which exist in every part of the world—believing that injustice and inequality anywhere is a threat to justice and equality everywhere.

Her personal leadership, compassion and tireless commitment has been an inspiration as we continue her work towards a brighter future for the most vulnerable around the world, and ensures that she will always be remembered as a true humanitarian.

Gordon Brown, UK Chancellor of the Exchequer

The true scale of Diana's impact on the world is best told by the impact of her death. It has been rightly described as one of the most significant events of the 20th century. As with the death of President Kennedy, everyone remembers with amazing clarity how they heard of Diana's death. They also look back in wonder at the week that followed during which Britain and the world were overcome by public grief. Led by the people who laid flowers at Kensington Palace, the media and royal family could only follow as the rest of world news was brushed aside and the scale of the mourning became news itself. The funeral was attended in London by millions, watched by many millions more on television in the UK and by an estimated three billion across the world.

Looking back on that extraordinary period, especially for those too young to remember Diana fully, the events seem baffling. How could the death of one young woman affect people so greatly? Even at the time, some people tried to dismiss the events as "mass hysteria." Yet, the accounts that follow bear witness to something deeper and more important. The scale of the grief was in part because the mass media had made Diana a global figure of interest, but it was also because her story and character had touched people in every walk of life and in every country in the world. They'd seen a beautiful young woman and vulnerable human figure whose very public struggle to cope had endeared her to them. More dramatically—something that took the British establishment by complete surprise—she really had connected with people. Her own comments that she wanted to be a "queen of people's hearts" turned out to have been based on truth: She had connected with ordinary people and meant something to them.

To ordinary people suffering from ordinary difficulties—broken marriages, physical and mental health problems, prejudices and feelings of rejection—Diana was a rarity. She was a person from the highest strata of society who appeared to care about their difficulties and even seemed to understand them. She didn't hide that she, too, knew unhappiness, rejection, loneliness and feelings of inadequacy. Yet, however low she was feeling herself, people saw that she tried to use her position for good. As David Ireland, appeals and PR director of SeeAbility, says, "They saw her as a friend in high places." When Diana died, many people felt as if they had lost a friend.

"She spoke to a constituency who is not represented—and never will be represented—by the mass media," says author Andrew Morton. "The mass media is there to pander to the great and the good, and the little people occasionally get a look in to boost circulation figures. But essentially that outpouring of emotion—and it was dignified emotion, it was never hysteria—was because people felt that she spoke to them about the concerns and conditions in their lives."

Diana's death seemed exceptionally cruel. It was unfair that someone who had used touch and gentleness should die such a brutal death and particularly unfair that someone who had sought out the dying to console them should die alone and uncomforted. Above all, it was unfair that an attentive and loving mother who desperately wanted to be there as a good and normal influence on her sons was now removed from their life.

Diana was someone people had expected to be around forever so they could comment on her life and pore over her appearance. The shame that followed the realization that such voyeurism linked people to the paparazzi who had chased her to her death and flashed bulbs in her face as she died, was intense.

The great and the good had often judged her and found reasons to dismiss her or belittle her; but among the ordinary people of the world, no one begrudged her quest for personal satisfaction. The compassion she had shown to others, her unwillingness to judge, and her readiness to love those whom others condemned as architects of their own misfortunes, was recognized by a public that adored her. Everyday more and more flowers were brought until the air around Kensington Palace was filled with a sweet and heady scent. Queues formed—the mighty and the humble—to write words of love and appreciation in the condolence books. People wept publicly, grieving for her, for themselves and for the cruelty and tragedy of life. Ordinary life pretty well came to a standstill.

A humanitarian is someone who, regardless of race, class and creed, understands people's need for dignity, respect and love. The non-judgmental love that Diana had advocated was paid back in full. "Of course she realized the effect she had on people, but she would never expect the kind of funeral she had," says her friend, Lucia Flecha de Lima. "I bet from where she is, she was amazed to see what was going on."

❈ ❈ ❈ ❈

HEARING THE NEWS ~ "I was in South Africa in my house, there with my four children, and the telephone went in the middle of the night," says Charles Spencer. "It was the manager who runs this place [Althorp] and he said, 'We've heard that there's been a car crash in Paris and Dodi Fayed's dead but your sister's just injured. We thought you should know straight away.' I went downstairs and I flicked between the various satellite news stations. They were saying much the same actually. They were saying that she'd been seen walking away and I thought, well, I'd better stay up and just see how bad it is and then my sister Sarah rang me and she said, 'Look, I'm afraid it's really bad news. It looks like she's got brain damage.' I was totally shaken. I couldn't believe it. And then I rang my sister Jane, whose husband worked for the Queen. He was on another line in the background and he went, 'Oh, no,' and then my sister Jane said, 'I'm afraid that's it, she's died.' And it was an incredible shock. I sat up, obviously in shock, for the rest of the night and then my children came running through in the morning and I said, 'I've got some appalling news for you. I'm afraid Aunt Diana's been killed.' And one of my daughters, who was aged three or so at the time, just smiled at me and said, 'Not in real life, Daddy.' And I said, 'Yes, I'm afraid it is true.' And I turned on the television and at that moment they're pulling the Mercedes out of the tunnel."

Dickie Arbiter was a press officer for Buckingham Palace by that time, having formally worked for Diana and Charles. 'I used to live at the Old Barracks, Kensington Palace, and my radio pager went off at about 12:35, and it was someone from CNN paging me from Atlanta. I phoned him back and he said, 'Can you tell me about the crash?' I said, 'What crash?' He said, 'Diana's been in a crash in Paris.' And while he was talking, I went over to the television set and as I flicked onto CNN and watched, I said, 'Look, I really can't tell you anything about it. All I can say is phone Buckingham Palace press office and get the person on duty.' By which time I was wide awake and watching things unfold. I called Paul Burrell, and brought him in to watch it. I then got a message at 2:40 Saturday night, Sunday morning, that she'd gone, and at 3:50, I was in Buckingham Palace press office."

Daniel Jones, one of the young dancers from English National Ballet, five minutes away, was one of the first to arrive with flowers. "I was with a guy in the company when we heard at five o'clock in the morning and we came here. We put flowers on the gate before anyone else because we knew her. It was kind of like I felt I had to do something. We *knew* her."

The following day Diana's sisters and Prince Charles flew to Paris to accompany the coffin back to England. The decision was to fly into the military airport Northolt, to the west of London. Dickie Arbiter had to brief the press there. "I had to tell them to be respectful, but I didn't need to . . . you could have heard a pin drop. I suppose I saw the coffin for the first time and I tried to convince myself that it was the wind blowing into my eyes making them water, but it wasn't. And I remember watching this and again not quite believing but, you know, you see a box, you see a royal standard over it and you have to believe and then you see the family coming out. Jane and Sarah. And then you know it is true. And when the hearse left Northolt with its police escort I sort of followed on because there was a lot of work to do in London. And I was amazed at how the westbound side of the A40 was at a complete standstill and people were actually out of their cars. There was an enormous crowd lining all the way back into London. People had heard."

Members of Diana's household who traveled back from Northolt were amazed. There were crowds several deep lining the whole route back to London. Her sister Sarah recalls that "people were lining the pedestrian bridges over the road and all along the central reservation." They realized then that the funeral could never be a private matter.

At the perimeter fence of Northolt along with many others was Kirsty Lawley and her mother, who lived on the estate adjoining the airport. Kirsty, who has suffered from serious illnesses throughout her life, had first met Diana when she visited Great Ormond Street Hospital for Children on one of Kirsty's many stays in the hospital. "She flew into Northolt at the end of our road," says Kirsty's mother Tina. "Kirsty made me walk through the fields onto the Western Avenue. We saw the RAF plane come in and we saw the coffin. We were choked. Kirsty clung to the fence and sobbed." "It was kind of shocking because I didn't believe it," says Kirsty. "It was pretty upsetting because some people there got very upset—but I'd met her, and I've seen her and stuff, and it upset me quite a bit."

Back in London, "the crowds were sort of making a beeline for Buckingham Palace and Kensington Place to lay flowers," says Dickie Arbiter. "And all through the night you could hear this buzz of people. It was very still, very hot those few days. The weather didn't break until the end of the week and then it only broke momentarily before the sun came out again. In fact I went into Kensington Gardens one morning about half-past four and there were so many people there. There were people just sitting weeping and people putting flowers and passing on. I stayed a bit later one morning and there were people with suits and the great British umbrella and a briefcase, just sort of laying flowers and then going off to work. There was this constant stream of people and a blanket of flowers stretching down the bank towards Kensington Road. It was one of those weeks that I will never, ever forget. People used to say, where were you in November 1963? Now they say, where were you on August 31, 1997?"

"I live in Kensington, very near Kensington Palace," says Christopher Balfour, who only weeks before had been invited by Diana to the palace with Christie's staff to say thank you for helping with the dress auction, "so I know what those flowers were like and what flowers were left up against the railings there. And I remember, with a friend, coming back after dinner one night and we'd sort of just go and just look to see what it was like, people with candles doing a vigil. The park between Kensington Gore and Kensington Palace was completely jammed."

Diana's friend Lucia Flecha de Lima set off for England the minute she heard of Diana's death. Outside all the palaces the flowers were mounting up, laid by the gathering crowds, but inside the chapel in St James's Palace, Lucia found Diana's coffin without a single flower. "The first day when I arrived at the chapel there was not one single flower on her coffin. Then I said to the chaplain that if he didn't allow flowers in, I would throw open the doors of the chapel so everyone could see her there without a single flower and all the flowers outside that people had brought. I said: "Tomorrow I'll come back with my flowers for her," and I came every day. And from then on, every day I brought flowers, not only mine but from friends and people who knew her. And I went to a flower van outside the Michelin restaurant and he said: "What are they for?" And I told him, and every day after that he insisted I take flowers to her for nothing. Who am I to do it on my own behalf? I did it on behalf of all the people.

"I was able to go to the chapel every day and take my flowers to her and flowers from friends who were not able to be there. And they were around her, over her coffin representing the flowers of the world, and I said that to Prince Charles. "These flowers represent the people, thousands and millions of flowers all around the world that people want to give to Princess Diana." I've never felt like that in my life. I have experienced personal loss so I understand it, but the public's reaction was extraordinary. It was the most extraordinary event."

For Jayne Fincher, who had spent the last 17 years photographing Diana, there were professional decisions to take. "At first I was completely shocked by it. We didn't know whether we should issue pictures or not, or what we should do. The flower thing started a few days later and then I heard that William and Harry were coming down to walk by the flowers and my father said, "We have to do this. If you've got the archive, it's an historic thing. It's like when Churchill died, you have to cover the event." I said I would come with him and take some flowers from my garden, but I would not take any pictures. We got out of the car down at Kensington Palace, and walked up to the flowers and—I'll never forget this—as soon as the smell of the flowers hit me, I just started to cry. I was really embarrassed, because there were all my colleagues and the television crews were there, but I just felt overpowered by it. From that point on I must have cried for two weeks, it was awful."

Across the country there were others who had met Diana only once, or had never met her, who felt the same way. Julie Watton-Butler, from Walsall Hospital where Diana had only visited once, said, "The day after she died, my boss called me in and said, "I want you to get some silk and drape it over the photo she signed when she came, like a little memorial." We have a very stable workforce here so a lot of the people who'd been here on the day of her visit were still here. A lot of them had met her. So it was extremely powerful—people you didn't know were stopping you and talking and you could see the grief in their faces. Nothing like that has ever happened in my lifetime. The shock. I mean, I can remember exactly what I was doing when I found out she died."

Back at Kensington Palace a committee was set up to handle the funeral arrangements. Dickie Arbiter found himself at the center. "I was there right at the very beginning. Contrary to speculation at the time, contrary to anything that's been written afterward, it was always going to be treated as a royal death. Let's not forget that she might have lost her HRH title, but she was still a member of the royal family. She was still expected on major occasions to come out. Which she did, because of the children. I was there at the meetings right at the very beginning, on the Monday morning. The lord chamberlain who chaired the meetings sort of metaphorically rolled his sleeves up. Now we knew that we had various plans for other members of the royal family and we took, initially, the plans for the late Queen Mother's funeral from the Chapel Royal to Westminster and we worked off the basis of those. And I remember very well at the end of that day getting all the television companies in and saying, 'Right, this is what we're doing. Coffin will travel from St James's Palace, Chapel Royal, to Westminster Abbey via the Mall,

Horseguards Approach Road, Horseguards Parade, Whitehall and round Parliament Square to Westminster Abbey. After the service it will go out by road down Whitehall, the Mall and out to Althorp.'"

In the days following, the police warned that the route was too short to cope with the numbers expected to pour into London. Some people suggested the cortege should go twice around Trafalgar Square but eventually the committee hit on the idea the funeral should set out from Kensington Palace. Robert Fellowes phoned the Queen and cleared it. "I was really pleased that she should set out from her home," said one of the committee.

Whatever officials were planning, the behavior of the royal family was causing some concern to the public. William and Harry had been taken to church the morning they had heard the news, but their mother had not been mentioned in the service, the royal family had sealed themselves away in Balmoral since, and the Union Jack flying high over Buckingham Palace had not been lowered. The mood among the public, echoed by the tabloids, was as critical of the royal family as it has ever been in England. "Show Us You Care" was the headline in the *Daily Express*, openly challenging the Queen for the first time in post-war Britain. "They were in deep trouble because they didn't realize they were in trouble," says royal journalist James Whitaker. "For just about the only time in her entire reign, the Queen was not aware of what people were thinking and, of course, that flag became the focal point of people's anger."

Just before the funeral Charles returned to London with William and Harry who appeared outside Kensington Palace to see the millions of bunches of flowers laid at the gate. "There is an old saying within royal circles," says Dickie Arbiter, "that you do not wear private grief on a public sleeve and we saw that when the Prince of Wales, William, and Harry came down and did that walkabout in Kensington Gardens. And they were very good. You had a lot of public wailing there. Yes, those people had lost somebody who had done tremendous good, but they didn't know her. They'd seen her. So I thought in the circumstances the boys were very, very good and very brave, given that, you know, William was 15 and Harry was 12."

Coincidentally, Jerry White co-founder and director of the Landmine Survivors Network emerged from Kensington Place as the boys arrived. He had been in Bosnia with Diana just a few weeks before and felt he should come straight to London on hearing of her death. He brought a basket of pears because one of his vivid memories of traveling in Bosnia was of how much Diana liked fruit. "Being a soppy American, I did these little things that just meant something to me, so bringing pears or making sure that Landmine Survivors Network sent flowers, was important. I took them to Kensington Palace. Paul [Burrell] greeted us and said, 'It would mean so much to Diana that you're here.' Sarah [McCorquodale] was there. I had never met her before or had anything to do with the Spencers or royalty, but I gave her a sloppy American hug, and said, 'I am so sorry. And then we went into the room where Diana's coffin was going to be on the last night. They were going to sing her favorite hymns and light candles that night. I suddenly felt moved to pray." By coincidence as they left the palace, William and Harry arrived with their father. "The crowds were sort of seven or eight deep, surrounded by all the flowers, and they said, 'William and Harry are coming.' I didn't feel close enough to be there, so we left and walked out of the gates just as William and Harry, and Graham [one of the bodyguards], and Prince Charles were coming in. The crowd was crying out to Prince William: 'We loved your mother.' I could feel the energy of this moment, and I thought, 'Oh, shit, I'll just go and introduce myself, and say, like you would to anyone, 'William, I'm sorry, I knew your mother, and she was just with us in Bosnia.'"

Jim Fletcher from English National Ballet was also there at that moment. "That was the moment where William says, 'Thank you, thank you.' Well, the minute he opened his mouth, of course I just fell to pieces and I ran away from the place, it was so frightening. They'd just lost their mum, I mean what professionals. Really a chip off the old block those two."

❊ ❊ ❊ ❊

THE NIGHT BEFORE ~ The night before the funeral, crowds gathered in Kensington Place and many stayed there all night. Others slept the night outside Westminster Abbey. Ruth Rudge, Diana's old headmistress from West Heath, came to stay the night before with Kay King who had employed Diana at Young England Kindergarten and had also been a pupil at West Heath herself. "Ruth Rudge stayed with us and we gave her a lift to the funeral. I said to her that I really felt there was something she should see. And standing up above Kensington Palace, looking down on the sea of flowers, I said to her, 'Can you believe that shy teenager has been responsible for this incredible outpouring of emotion?' It was the most extraordinary scene, it really was."

Daniel Jones, from English National Ballet who had met Diana many times, said, "I spent the night before the funeral in the park. I'm not religious, but that was the most spiritual experience that I will ever have in my life. I went with a couple of friends, we took a book, just a blank notebook and we just went around asking people to write down what they felt and why they were so affected by it. And the things that people were writing were just so beautiful. Even Liam Neeson [the actor], people like that and from the poorest to the richest. I think it was something that was brought about by her generosity and how genuine she was. The environment that she was in was unfortunate, but then at the same time we wouldn't have known her as well if she hadn't been in the situations she was in. I think there was a huge spiritual side to her."

"Some people say hysteria swept the nation," says Sister Barbara Smith of The Passage Day Centre. "I don't think it was hysteria. It was love. One of my colleagues said he went just to walk the streets of London at night, to see what was happening. He's an Irishman, and he said he was just so taken by the silence and the candles and the people. People just wanted to be there and express their grief, and express it visibly, because they felt for her and she felt for them. There's no doubt about it."

Diana's mother anonymously joined the crowd. "To see so many people lined up, who felt they knew her, who had come long distances, spent long hours, there was a lot of that. I was staying with my daughter, Jane, who lived there at that time. And I just joined the people in Kensington Palace Gardens. I don't think she did know how much she was appreciated. I don't think anyone does. I don't think she knew how much she was loved and admired. But I do know those same people fueled her, they kept her going, it was a two-way thing, they made her smile."

The late Reverend Dr Tony Lloyd, former executive director of The Leprosy Mission, said, "Somebody who was in a sleeping bag, in Trafalgar Square on the night before the funeral said that when Big Ben struck 12:00, a girl stood up and said, 'I am not religious, but I think we all need to pray.' And she led them in the Lord's Prayer."

❊ ❊ ❊ ❊

THE DAY OF THE FUNERAL ~ The day of the funeral was another hot day and the crowds came early and spread out along the route. Police took flowers from the crowd and laid them where the coffin would pass. Diana would be carried from Kensington Palace on a gun carriage, along beside Hyde Park, through to St James's where Prince Charles, Princes William and Harry, Prince Philip, and Charles Spencer would join up and walk behind the coffin. Those attending the funeral could not get through the crowds to the church. Christopher Spence, of The London Lighthouse and now chair of the Memorial Fund remembers, "When we got to Trafalgar Square the crowds were so thick there was no way we were going to be able to walk along the pavements, so we went to a policeman and he said, 'There's only one way. You'll have to walk in the road down Whitehall.' It was an extraordinary experience walking from Trafalgar Square to St James's with these banks of people lining the road. It's hard to describe, except the grief was absolutely palpable. It was not hysterical or prurient; it was real people feeling real grief. They were there because this person meant something to them. For all her difficulties, they felt she was beside them. She walked with the people." "I think your senses in a situation like this are all very attuned," says Siobhan Fitzpatrick of the Northern Ireland Pre-School Playgroups Association, one of Diana's charities. "The smell of flowers was nearly overpowering. That literally hit us. In the morning we walked up to the Abbey together and it was quite eerie in many ways. People were waiting on the pavement and it was practically silent except for the sobbing, which was very, very moving." "There are moments in history that are almost cosmic," says Jerry White, "where the world stands still for a breath, and this is one of them. You cannot explain it. You had to have seen it. You cannot explain what that was like—the crowds of British citizens, silent, embracing, sort of lining the streets, and you felt eerie. All I heard was our shoes hitting the cobblestones on the way up to the church."

As the coffin, draped with the royal standard and mounted on a gun carriage, left Kensington Palace there was an eerie silence with only the sound of the soldiers' feet on the road. A sudden wail broke the silence. For Charles Spencer his loss hit home: "When, I think, I saw her coffin on the day of the funeral on the gun carriage. The shock of seeing that, you know, it was all so public and it was so appalling. That walk was just a nightmare really. The worst experience of my life was walking behind my sister's body to Westminster Abbey. Worrying about the boys and thinking, you know, this is all so horrendous and so public and having to keep your eyes straight ahead and not look either side. I can still hear the horses' hooves and the grinding of the gun carriage and see the coffin in front and the crunch of our steps.

Walking behind the chief mourners came representatives from the many charities of which Diana had been patron. According to Pat Baron from Help the Aged, "The colonel in charge said, 'Right. We're now going to walk round to St James's,' and so we did and we slowly walked around in front of a silent crowd, absolutely silent. We went round the back and the smell of the flowers was extraordinary. We came off Pall Mall and went round the back of St James's Palace and then we came back and waited by the Queen Mother's residence, by Clarence House, to pick up as they came past. It was the smells, it was fantastic and the silence was fantastic as well. And somebody said, 'Do you mind if I walk with you?' and it turned out to be one of Prince Charles's security squad. He said, 'Oh, they've arrived,' because he had the phone. And up walked the men, the royal men and came and stood in front of us. I can remember the way Prince Philip was superb with William. Poor William. Anyway, the hearse arrived and they said, 'Right, off we go.' And it was the crunching to the guardsmen's feet on the gravel that was extraordinary. Anyway we walked through and there were these flowers being thrown and I was so worried I might tread on a flower. I managed to hold it until the end when they brought the coffin out and then I did cry. I went home and just

went to bed. I was drained, absolutely drained and I never dreamed it would affect me so much.'"

Sarah Thomas is the mother of Oliver, a child who suffered from the debilitating skin condition epidermolysis bullosa and whom Diana had visited in Great Ormond Street Hospital. "Oliver and I were in the front row of her funeral procession. It was awful. I don't know how it happened but a few of us from the charity, with our kids, were put in the front row of that enormous procession. To be honest, it was the most awful thing I've ever gone through other than family funerals, because it was so, so moving. We were right behind William and Harry. I didn't look at the crowds. It was awful. All you could hear were soldiers' footsteps, people literally wailing, the bells, and we were just following, looking at William's head. And poor William didn't once look up, he just walked on with his head down; I felt so much for him and Harry. It seemed totally unreal that we were all there following Princess Diana."

"I walked behind the coffin and her two boys," says landmine victim Zarko Peric, whom Diana had befriended in Bosnia only a month before. He was the same age as Harry. "They had their heads bowed and I felt so bad for them. I couldn't really believe I was there. I felt so lost and I couldn't really take in that the Diana who had come to see me and Malic [Bradaric] was now lying in that coffin."[1]

Caroline Duprot from English National Ballet described how the company as a whole went into mourning for a long time. "To be honest I've had some deaths in my family, but I was as moved as if she was really someone from my family. The day she died I had been in France at home for the weekend. My mom came to me—it was like five o'clock or four o'clock in the morning—to wake me up because it was such a shock, even in France. I knew the funeral was going to be incredible but I wasn't expecting the reaction. It was hard. A lot of us were crying as well but the procession was beautiful."

Inside the church Patricia Wood, head of Riddlesworth School at the time, and Ruth Rudge from West Heath School had been placed beside each other. "Ruth turned to me when she saw the churchmen coming in from all the denominations and said, 'Just look at all these churchmen for that little girl.' You tend to think of the children you've taught as children. To see what they do afterwards is often a great surprise. You look at children and you think: Well, fancy her developing in that way."

The late Reverend Tony Lloyd was moved by how much the congregation reflected the woman he had known. "Diana had so much compassion for the important people as well as the little people and the funeral was an example of this. I sat next to the mother of a boy who was in the hospital at the same time as Prince Charles, and I said to this lady, 'Did you know the princess?' She told me she didn't, but that the princess visited Prince Charles one night and then did the ward rounds. And she took the name and address of this boy and wrote to him every month until she died. Which was staggering. There were two punk rockers behind us, and still I don't know what their story was. So the next row was army, Queen, the punk rockers, the ladies from the bowling clubs. I have never felt people so moved in this country. The funeral was the most extraordinary event I have ever been to in my life. The soldiers came along, hobnail boots on them, and they carried this very weighty coffin. I was sitting about 12 rows behind the Queen. And Charles was very upset. And I could just see him, the side of the head, and these soldiers walked past me and the sound of their hobnail shoes."

"The funeral was really a harrowing experience," says Sarah Jane Gaselee, one of Diana's bridesmaids. "I was really embarrassed because I kept crying and her children were all crying and it was like, I was ashamed. When they came past me and I saw the coffin with the flowers that said 'Mummy' I was overcome. We were sitting quite near Elton John and the piano, and when he sang that song I was in bits, and so was everybody else, absolutely in bits. I went up to Kensington, obviously, and had a look at all the flowers, put some there myself and I was like absolutely amazed by the people."

"It was like a movie," says Derek Deane, former artistic director of English National Ballet. "I was four seats away from Elton John who was bashing it out on a piano and then the whole family paraded past and then she came by. And all I could think were these poor men carrying her were going to faint. One looked like he was about to faint, he was sweating profusely and I thought he was going to die. So I was more worried about him. It was surreal; my sadness came out a long time after she died. During that whole period of all these flowers and then the funeral and all of that, I just couldn't take it all in."

"It was very, very emotional for me," says designer Jacques Azagury. "I was right there in the front row and I was OK until I actually saw the coffin, and that's when I broke down. And, quite frankly, I didn't remember very much after that until I actually got home and my friends were watching it on television, and I had to watch the whole thing on television again, to remind me of it. You know, the whole thing was kind of so surreal. At one stage, two feet away, I had the Queen and Prince Philip and Prince Charles and the whole of their family, and the next second I'd have, like, Hillary Clinton next to me. And the whole thing was just completely unreal, and with the choir and with the grandness of the hall and everything. It was just an utterly surreal experience for me."

"During the funeral," says Kay King, who ran the Young England Kindergarten where Diana once worked, "I was just in such a state of complete shock. The children's things on the coffin, the flowers and the letter and everything, and then, of course, Charles Spencer making that speech. Talk about sitting there in a state of shock—and then hearing the applause. It was literally like a tidal wave. You heard it in the distance, and it was as if it was bursting through the doors of the church. It was one of the most amazing things. Again, I remember comparing it to the wedding when they said, 'I do,' and again, the applause rippling through the church. It was a very powerful speech. I've listened to it so many times. It was remarkable to be able to make that speech."

"It was awesome," says singer Chris de Burgh. "Even now I'm getting choked up thinking about her, and thinking about walking around the silent streets of London the night before, packed with people. And then, in the Abbey itself, when Elton had finished singing, you could hear the clapping outside, but nothing happened inside. But when Earl Spencer got to that bit about the boys, the tears, I can feel them pricking my eyes. Christ, he just did it full on—it was absolutely spine-tingling. And then when the applause started outside and then it swept in through the open doors . . . I'll never forget that."

"I was going to do a sort of classic eulogy where you just say really nice things," says Charles Spencer, "and I thought, well, that's really not right. And then I went to bed and, as I'm sure that anyone who's lost someone very close knows, you don't sleep at all well, so I suppose you're in shock. I woke, I think at about 4:30 the next morning and I wrote it in an hour and a half. I've never found anything easier to write in my life. I think what I was really saying in the speech was that this was a real woman with her own real issues to deal with and I was very keen in the speech not to picture her as someone who was perfect. But as somebody who despite being very human had done their best, and that's what I was really saying. I wasn't angry, I was just trying to keep it together. It was emotional, but I was trying to just hold it together so I could get through it, because I knew how difficult it would be. So it probably

came across as anger, but it was just me trying to get from the first word to the last one without breaking down."

"I was also proud," says Diana's mother, Frances Shand Kydd, "because all the family were steady, in public view, at any rate. And the boys were, and they walked, which I don't think they should have. And the girls were solidly safe for reading their readings. And my son, unfortunately, has been criticized greatly for his oration, but the people in Hyde Park rose to a man and a woman and cheered. The press thought the worst—and they were keen to find a scapegoat, and so they pilloried him, for evermore, it seems. But he spoke for the nation."

"The majesty of Westminster Abbey, the dignitaries who were there, we felt so honored to be part of that," says Siobhan Fitzpatrick. "The hairs on the back of my neck did rise when Earl Spencer gave his oration, but certainly the experience was one of those experiences that one would never forget."

John Young, former chair of the Development Foundation for the National Hospital for Neurology and Neurosurgery (formerly called the National Hospital for Nervous Diseases), was with his wife who was in a wheelchair. "We had been pushed up into three rows in front of Mr. Al Fayed and only two rows behind the prime minister and everybody else. It was amazing. It was like a great wave at the end of Spencer's speech. It started right outside. For the Queen and the royal family, it was absolutely dramatic, because it was like a wave that was going to engulf you, you could hear it start outside, and then it came right at the bottom, and it came up and up and up and up. The applause was absolutely overwhelming. It gave you sort of goose pimples. It was marvelous—oh, marvelous. So spontaneous."

"It was completely extraordinary," says Rachel Thomson of the Pre-School Learning Alliance. "The whole thing—going into the Abbey, being surrounded by the great and the good. Clive James and Ruby Wax stood in the queue in front of us, Wayne Sleep sat next to us, and the editor of the *Guardian* was sitting in the next row to us. And it was hearing the silence inside, hearing the quietness of the crowd outside while the service was going on. I think two things stand out, one was hearing Elton John's rendition of the song, which, on an acoustic basis, was just extraordinary and kind of spine-tingling. The other was Earl Spencer's speech being so close, and it being very, very quiet, and then hearing from the silence of the Abbey the crowd outside clapping, almost like an echo, growing stronger. And coming out afterwards: we, of course, had been almost trapped in a bubble, not knowing what the reaction of people would be, what the crowds were like, and it was extraordinarily silent, coming out."

"The music and the service was just incredible," says Derek Bodell of the National AIDS Trust. "It was such an eclectic group of people in there. The music was incredibly powerful and of course then there was Earl Spencer's speech, I've never been in a church where people applauded before. But I think it was the John Tavener bit at the end—you've got this very haunting music, very evocative and we were towards the west door. They had TV cameras hidden behind the pillars so you can see, but if you didn't look at that, all you could hear were the soldiers' footsteps, the steel tips on their boots hitting the stone. Within the Abbey it was very, very audible as they were coming from the altar and you've got this steady beat as they get closer and it started somebody off crying next to us. He didn't just cry, he sobbed which started off the whole crew around us. It was a very, very sad moment."

By the end of the service, many of those attending were overcome. "I was sobbing by the end, quite spontaneously and uncharacteristically," says David French, former director of Relate. "We'd all been through this colossal build-up, but it was a deeply moving experience."

"I went to the Abbey for the funeral," says Jean Pike, who had been a lady-in-waiting for many years, "and when I came out what really struck me was the crowds outside were still there. They were standing in total silence, it was really moving, coming out a good ten minutes, maybe quarter of an hour after the others had gone, and they were still lining the streets in complete silence. And that was very emotional, very dramatic."

"It's funny how her persona seemed to kind of pass through the media and come out the other side unscathed. People felt that they knew her who'd never met her," says Louise Halliday from English National Ballet. "All of us had our own kind of perceptions of her and it was completely reflected in the public response to her death. It was such a true response, wasn't it."

It was not just a London-based phenomenon. All around the country people watched television. "Because she was so liked, people didn't easily accept her death," says Marilyn Griffiths, a worker from Walsall Hospital that Diana had once visited. "The day that she died I came in on the lunchtime and it was just deathly quiet everywhere, nobody spoke, nobody said hardly anything. And then on the day of the funeral they all brought tellies in—well, they weren't supposed to but they did—and then they sat and they watched and they wept. We sorted out some black bows ourselves and sold them and people bought them as they come up to the dining room. We made about a hundred pounds and we just put that aside for the Diana Memorial Fund/Jayne Fincher."

"The day of the funeral, we'd gone to Blackpool," says Julie Watton-Butler, another worker from Walsall Hospital. "And there was not a soul about. We'd gone on the coast and from the south of Blackpool right up north to where we stayed, there was not a person about. The three piers were closed, and it was just eerie, because everybody just wanted to be around a television. And when we got into the hotel, the manager had made sandwiches for lunch, and everybody just wanted to be together and sharing, you know, it was such a dreadful thing."

"I remember watching her funeral," says Belinda Knox who had been at West Heath School at the same time as Diana, "and feeling profoundly moved by it. I had one of those lasting thoughts, insight if you like. I felt she had made so much of her life. She had been involved in some of the most challenging issues of our time—her marriage propelled her into a position of authority and she helped raise the profile of several issues—HIV, landmines to name but two and she touched the hearts of many people. I thought, I'm still here; I've still got opportunities. Look at what you can do with your life—Diana was incredibly courageous."

Across the world, millions watched the funeral. Many places erected public screens. People wept openly in the street. One public figure on holiday in Jamaica at the time said, "It was incredible. I have never seen grown black men crying openly on the streets, but they did for Diana." Diana's death affected people across the globe in quite unprecedented ways. In Cairo, the BBC's Jim Muir experienced a community in shock, particularly as many had hoped to see Diana offer a bridge between Islamic and Western cultures.

The British embassy in Washington was heaped high with floral tributes. In Chicago where Diana had been so triumphantly only a few months before, the British consulate was overwhelmed by the reaction. Caroline Cracraft, head of public affairs, comments, "She was like a ray of sunshine in a rather gloomy world and the emotion after her death was just amazing. The other thing that was fascinating was how very few people of high standing asked us to make special arrangements for them to come in and sign the books of condolence without having to stand in line. I was amazed at the sorts of people who stood in that line for hours and hours. When we asked what we were to do with all this, the instructions were to dump the books and we ignored that. We thought her boys should have the opportunity to hear the ordinary people." "When she died," says Dr Stephen Nicholas, Harlem Hospital's director of Pediatrics, "the lobby of Harlem Hospital, was just like the British consulate down the way. You couldn't get in for all the flowers, the books, the candles. And Harlem genuinely wept for Princess Diana."

In Delhi BBC correspondent Mike Wooldridge, looking for responses to the death of Princess Diana, found himself unprepared "for an event that happened quite spontaneously in a narrow back street." One of the buildings was the home of a pioneering project designed to increase HIV and AIDS awareness among prostitutes or sex workers. "Discovering we were asking about Princess Diana and her death they emerged from the house and standing as a group in the bustling street they observed a minute's silence. After-ward, they explained that they thought she cared for people like them."[2]

Others abroad who could not be at her funeral found themselves choked and overwhelmed as they tried to pay tribute to her. "The night of her funeral," said musician and composer Jean-Michel Jarre, "I was in Moscow for one of the biggest concerts I've ever made in my life. It was in front of three million people, in front of the university for the 800th anniversary of the city of Moscow. And suddenly, on stage, I said: "I want to pay tribute. I want to say a few words about Princess Diana." I said, "I would like to dedicate this next song to Diana, because she told me always she loved it very much. It's called *China*, and it's a song I wrote when I was in China for the first time." It's a quite moving, slow piece. I said that and suddenly, on a Saturday night in Moscow, where you have a lot of vodka, and the crowd was quite noisy, suddenly you had such a silence. You had three million people—it was amazing, three million people—and they suddenly were all quiet, and they held up thousands of small lights, lighters, matches. Believe me or not, I was so overwhelmed I couldn't move. No one on stage could move. We were totally petrified. Even in Moscow, in a place where you don't have the BBC every day, where you don't have the British press, suddenly she was an extraordinary symbol of peace and just like a friend. Even talking about this, I'm still very emotional about it. I don't know, maybe for two or three minutes, no one could start, I couldn't start. No one said a word. The whole city of Moscow, I mean, half of the city, became totally quiet."

"I was in Sweden when the accident occurred," says Mary Baker who knew Diana through the Parkinson's Disease Society. "I had to come through the airport and every time I showed the English passport everybody said, "I'm so sorry about Diana." I remember buying something and when I went to pay, the girl burst into tears and said, "How on earth can you manage without Diana?" This was Sweden.

"The charity world absolutely adored her. When we heard she'd died, Leslie Finlay and I were both asked to the funeral and we couldn't go because we had a big meeting in Denmark. At the conference we asked for two minutes' silence and I was asked to say a few words. I thought I could do it, because one of the things that I'm lucky with is I can usually speak to the public. I'd read about this phrase in many books, that your throat 'constricts' but it happened to me. I could not get one word out and Leslie Finlay was in the front row, so he came out onto the stage to help because we'd got an audience of about 300 Danes and we both broke down. Then I managed to pull myself together and talk about happier times with her and both of us managed then to get on the stage, but it has never ever happened to me before. I had never, ever, ever, behaved like that before, so she really got under my skin. I thought the world of her."

"We had a huge number of calls to the charity," says Julia Samuel,

Diana's friend who founded The Child Bereavement Trust. "And I don't know exactly what happened, but certainly some of it seemed to be that people felt they knew her personally. They'd seen her every day in the newspapers, and people certainly felt they identified with her and knew her. And when she died, it certainly felt like a very personal loss to people whether they'd known her or not. When people have experiences of loss, when they have a sister or brother or friend die, our natural response is to try and protect ourselves against the feelings of pain. We work through that pain. We go in and out of it, moving between loss and restoration. Often people don't fully do the loss work, which doesn't fully allow them to do the restoration work. All of us want to not feel that pain, so when we expect it to come we can defend ourselves against it. It seemed to me because Diana wasn't actually a personal loss to them, her death could get to people in a way that they didn't defend against, so they could express that feeling of pain, which was actually as much to do with their own losses as with her."

"Before Diana died I'd felt increasingly uncomfortable about my trade," says photographer Jayne Fincher. "I'd already quit the royal rotation, because of the intrusiveness of the paparazzi. Then, when the accident happened, I felt completely shamed, I wouldn't tell anyone what I did for a job. The average person in the street doesn't understand the difference between the photographers and they just automatically assume that you're all like the paparazzi. There were perhaps half a dozen of us who had been in it all the way through and generally had a great affection for her, and we were all absolutely devastated by it."

Tim Graham, royal photographer, was also affected deeply. "She was a story I covered from the first moment she was known to be linked with the prince, obviously right through to her death and her funeral. My wife and I were both invited to the funeral. It sounds ridiculous now, but I felt I just wanted to finish this story, I felt I wanted to photograph the funeral and I couldn't do that if I became a guest inside the Abbey. I wrote to the lord chamberlain and explained that. We gave the money from any sales from that day to charity, because I didn't want to earn money out of it. I just felt I wanted to end the story."

❊ ❊ ❊ ❊

LEGACY ~ Diana's death was a traumatic event for the whole country—perhaps even the whole world. Her funeral bore witness to the sorrow felt at such a sudden and untimely death. Even the most skeptical, who distanced themselves from the public expression of grief, have always accepted that the events around her death were of great social significance. The British abandoned their customary reserve and wept in the streets, and the monarchy was criticized openly in the press in an unprecedented way. But how will the person who caused all this be remembered?

It is always difficult to assess someone's historical significance soon after they die, but it is especially difficult in Diana's case. This is partly because some commentators have disparaged Diana as if the world must really have been mistaken about a woman having such a powerful effect. It is also partly because her contribution cannot be quantified and measured against more tangible human achievements. She did not accomplish any heroic feats; she did not build bridges or find cures for diseases. She did not mastermind military battles or create timeless works of art. With the exception of landmines, where there was the tangible outcome of the Ottawa Convention, her contribution to history is harder to pin down. It is a contribution to styles of behavior and to attitudes and understanding. This is the stuff traditional historians eschew.

Yet what Diana achieved in her short life is arguably as significant as more obvious historical contributions. On a surprising number of issues Diana brought about a steep change in how a problem was seen—from a local small-scale impact on forgotten charities to the world-wide issue of landmines. On the small scale she improved incomes and profiles of struggling charities, bringing the world's attention to unfashionable, unattractive conditions and the unsung heroes who give their time day after day to caring for the disadvantaged. For many of these charities, she was quite simply irreplaceable. "We've never had a replacement," says a representative of the charity DEBRA (the charity supporting epidermolysis bullosa sufferers). "She was a huge loss. I know all the charities she worked with suffered. There's no one like that with the children any more."

More visible is Diana's legacy on global health issues. "Her intervention on AIDS was incredibly important because of the timing of it and the way she was prepared to come out as she did. It can't be underestimated," says Baroness Jay. This change might have come eventually without Diana. But she sped things up, and for those dying of AIDS at the time it was crucial, gaining them the care and dignity they needed from friends and family in the last moments of their lives. "She made a unique contribution to probably one of the most socially challenging issues of the last century really, and had a consistency and a loyalty to it that was quite remarkable really," says Derek Bodell, of the National AIDS Trust.

The same could be said for all those other "unfashionable" issues Diana took up. She transformed perceptions of leprosy and insisted on treating with compassion people who society sneered at: the homeless, those suffering from mental health issues like eating disorders or drug addiction. "I can't think of anybody in public life who contributed as much as her to raising awareness of the issues," says Colonel John Mayo, former chief executive of Help the Aged. "The impact she had worldwide was phenomenal." "She woke people up," says Sister Barbara Smith formerly of The Passage Day Centre. "The good she has done through her work has been immeasurable." "She had the ability to get things changed," says Nigel Clark, executive chairman of Great Ormond Street Hospital Children's Charity. "Her contribution to the landmine situation and her ability to break the stigmas of leprosy and of AIDS, was enormous. Now, I don't know how much you can quantify that, but it certainly shattered misconceptions."

Diana's approach to issues was also unique. Perhaps because she had gone through her own battle to speak out when many would have preferred her to remain silent, she understood the importance of facing issues openly. "I think in a way she taught a lot to your nation," says her friend Lucia Flecha de Lima. "If you are not happy you have to say so." Dickie Arbiter, former palace spokesman, agrees. "That's one of the legacies from Diana—bringing things out into the open, rather than keeping them under wraps." "Her death and funeral," says Christopher Spence, chair of The Diana, Princess of Wales Memorial Fund, were "a resounding demonstration of the kind of world people everywhere long for: A more open world, in which we face up to real issues affecting our lives without denial or pretense; a more expressive world, in which we are unafraid to make real connections with one another and to show our true feelings; a more diverse and inclusive world, in which no one is left out, most especially those who for one reason or another find themselves on the margins of society and without a strong voice."

What Diana also showed in abundance was compassion and love. She never seemed to judge people for their misfortunes. Mark McGreevy of the Depaul Trust, who saw her in action with the homeless, believed this kind of non-judgmental love is what makes a true humanitarian. "To me, a humanitarian is someone who does things without motive, for the good of humanity. People don't deserve charity; they deserve justice, and I think Diana understood that. Maybe her legacy is that the way that we approach things should be non-judgmental, that what we must ask is: 'Let me hear what's happening from the grass roots and let me articulate your story, because I have got the platform to do it—and then let's try to bring people together who can actually resolve it.' Maybe the legacy is to reflect that this process is much simpler than we think."

Diana is seen by some as one of the very few modern figures who was able to see the human being through the different cultures or the different symptoms. She genuinely seemed to relate to the person or the child she was holding, able to ignore the barriers politics and religion put between people. "She was completely color blind," says her lawyer, Anthony Julius. Journalist and broadcaster Yasmin Alibhai-Brown says, "She was absolutely exceptional in this. There has never been another member of the British establishment who related to people from other cultures, including Muslims, completely on their own terms. She simply accepted them as people and embraced them. And she did it without any effort. It came completely naturally to her." There are some who believe that with her interest in Islam—expressed in her visits to Pakistan—she could well have become a leading force for peace and understanding between two worlds.

Peter Sandford, who knew Diana as patron of ASPIRE, saw this non-judgmental concern as one that would reach out and touch when others stepped backwards. "She pioneered that style of intimacy. I went on a trip recently to look at development work in Angola and I was part of that terrible thing of being a white journalist taken into a hospital where children were dying of malaria and malnutrition. We walked in and all these mothers were standing there with their dying children in their arms. What can you do? You can't speak the language. You can't change the situation. As I was walking around, I thought of Diana. And as the mothers held out their babies towards me, I actually took them and held them. It sounds ridiculous: I didn't make their children live because I can't change the world, and neither could she—but I think just from watching her perhaps we've all learned how you respond in that situation. At its most basic, it was about touch. When I first walked into the hospital, I was horrified by what I saw—it was like walking into hell. My initial reaction was I wanted to cry. And as I stood back for a moment, a man who was showing me around said, 'Don't worry, you won't catch anything,' although it hadn't really been about that. That thing of touch is very important, because that's what she was doing when she held babies with AIDS. She was saying, 'You won't catch it,' and I realized how important that must be to people who are stigmatized in that way, touching people who are somehow untouchable."

"I have always felt that Princess Diana was a true humanitarian, in the fullest meaning of the word. In spite of her lofty position, she had the ability to stand in the shoes of ordinary people who were confronted by illness, poverty, repression, or danger beyond their control, and she had the courage and purposefulness to extend herself to do what she could to help them. Her tragic and untimely death cut short what might have become one of the most powerful voices of her generation for world peace and humanitarian aid," says Henry Kissinger.

Heather Mills McCartney, who herself has been very involved in campaigning against landmines for many years, saw Diana as someone whose concern has motivated others. "She could have been 'a lady who lunches,' going shopping and meeting her friends and doing very little else, just the odd appearance. She didn't need to go to the extremes she went to. I don't believe

she did things to feel more loved. Those who did criticize Diana did very little for anyone else. Monuments are not built for the critics but for those who are criticized. Diana helped millions of people, we need to remember that about her. She motivated so many people to start doing things for others and making a difference to their lives and realizing that life isn't just about what you can do for yourself, it's about what you can do for others. That really is the only reason that we're here as far as I'm concerned."

When people describe Diana's legacy they often describe intangible emotional elements. "She brought hope," says royal journalist James Whitaker. "For all her problems and, of course, they were myriad, she achieved so much more good in life than she did bad. She gave hope to utterly hopeless people. She made them feel good, and that's a hell of a good legacy to have left." "The biggest gift she left behind," says Jim Fletcher of English National Ballet, "was her gift of loving people, of being close to people. She had this very special gift of knowing what to say to total strangers, which I think is something very special. There's something really precious, a spiritual gift, left behind following the princess's death. She has left us something—I don't know precisely what it is—but it's something that's very warm and something that's missing now. I can't think of another person alive today from whom that same sense emanates."

Trying to sum up this emotional legacy it is often said that: "Diana touched people's hearts." The cynics scoff; this is pure sentimentality. But what people mean is that Diana's very human problems and her desire to overcome these difficulties and do her best by her children and other less advantaged people touched them. Her difficulties didn't belittle her, they endeared her especially to many who recognized their own dreams and difficulties. "She symbolized what every American female between the ages of 12 and 13 was brought up to dream of as true happiness," said one American.[3] "She was Cinderella plucked from the masses, driven to her wedding in a glass coach and kissed on the balcony by Prince Charming. Then when she died we realized she summed up all our troubles too—the young wife plagued by eating disorders, the lonely single mother, the divorced woman who struck out on her own."

In all aspects of her life and death Diana embodied the poignancy—and greatness—of the human condition, her feelings of love, passion, rejection and grief, her struggle with bulimia, her attempt to make a new life for herself, her desire to put her exceptional talents with people to good use—all snuffed out in an untimely death. She touched human hearts because people saw her own struggles, her empathy for theirs and her attempt to focus on what mattered. She taught people what mattered.

"It was an education of the human heart watching her," says The Body Shop's Anita Roddick. "From the first movement of kindness—and she made kindness tenacious—it was never wishy-washy. From those first days of always talking to people—and they'd never been talked to before, never—she used touch. If you look at the photos of her hugging people, it's not phoney, it's not false, that's exactly how it was with her. She was learning to articulate and she was getting stronger. She was also an authentic spirit. Very few people who represent causes are authentic. They do one or two events a year or they raise money by partying. I loved the way the experience changed her values. She was very focused and very tenacious and she raised the profile of issues, not because she was a famous beautiful celebrity or queen-to-be, but because she was emotionally attached. She immersed herself in the reality of the thing and I don't think celebrities do that."

Many still mourn Diana's loss as the loss of a bright star, someone who had she lived could have been a powerful humanitarian voice in this troubled world. "We should remember she was only 19 when she first became a public figure," says Bianca Jagger. "Public opinion was sometimes severe and intolerant towards her even though she was a normal young woman of that age. People assume you should always have known what you know later in your life, but life is a long process of maturing and learning. We saw a shy young woman beginning to evolve into a woman of substance, into someone dedicated. I admired her evolution into someone acquainted with, and knowledgeable about, serious issues. It is a great tragedy that she died so young as we were only just beginning to see a person reaching her potential. Even so her concrete contributions were quite considerable especially in the two areas of landmines and AIDS."

"There's not a week goes by," says Lord Puttnam, "when I don't think in some situation where something needs to be done . . . 'If only Diana was around.' There's no one else even remotely in the same league. Everyone connected with AIDS or developing world health issues is convinced that Diana could have been the most extraordinary ambassador for the plight of the growing number of AIDS orphans around the world. There's no one even on the horizon with the same stature, and level of international interest to raise concern about global health."

At a tribute event in November 2002, hosted by The Diana, Princess of Wales Memorial Fund, Nelson Mandela spoke of the contribution Diana would have made on HIV/AIDS. "I was devastated [when she died] because she would have turned the tables around, but we are still faced with that problem . . . I urge the world at large to learn from her example and embrace her legacy. Her inspiration must continue to change lives now and in the future."

Whether Diana's legacy endures will depend to some extent on how Diana herself is remembered. Her life and death still excites interest in the public and the media is keen to keep that very lucrative interest alive. Inevitably the more scandalous and sensational the memories the more money is to be made. It means the uncontroversial good works can easily be overlooked for the sensationalist angle. Diana's legacy is also at risk from the hostility with which she is viewed by the traditional courtier class who appear to blame her for the unpopularity that has haunted the royal family since Charles and Diana's relationship fell apart. Although, as composer Jean-Michel Jarre says, "the way Diana was perceived, all over the world, was probably the most important positive influence in how England itself was viewed," there are elements of British society who do not want her remembered now. They see her memory as standing in the way of restoring a good feeling towards the monarchy. There are others too—a minority but a powerful minority—who were uncomfortable with the public show of grief at her death, dismissing it as mass hysteria.

Yet, paradoxically one of Diana's most immediately tangible legacies is the impact she has had on the British royal family, in the way she brought up her children. There's widespread agreement that Diana introduced "normality" and "modernity" into the upbringing of the boys. "We've got to look at the way William now will take the monarchy into this century and beyond, if it survives," says Ken Wharfe, Diana's former bodyguard. "The influence that Diana had is crucial to that." "Maybe," says Hereward Harrison, co-founder of ChildLine, "she's left us a future king who, if he gets there, is going to be a bit more with it all around."

Many approve of the way Diana tried to bring her children out of an ivory tower to face, at the earliest possible age, the realities of other people's lives. "I know she wanted them to have concern and care for other people," says Sister Barbara Smith. "She wanted them to grow up and know there was another side of life to having what you wanted when you wanted." "Her true

legacy, obviously, is her boys," says former BBC royal correspondent Jennie Bond. "There's an awful lot of Diana in them and she brought them up in a different way to royal princes before—taking them around the homeless and making them see the other side of life." "William himself," says Henry Bellingham, MP, "has said that his mother motivated and inspired him to take interest in the poor and down-and-outs in London, for example. I think that her style of charitable work has made a lasting impression on him and I think the royal family see only good coming from that."

Diana appears to have fully understood that there was a huge gap between the remote traditions of British royalty and contemporary Britain and adopted an entirely new style. The vast majority of the population saw her determination to bring up her children differently as entirely admirable. Jean-Michel Jarre heard her speak quite explicitly about the importance of finding a new way for royalty. "She told me, 'I don't want to be superficial. I want to use my power for others, and to invest myself, to be involved in some action. I want to build something on my own, for me, and for my children.' She never said, 'for me, it was always 'for me and for my children.' That was the main thing: Getting her children ready for the future."

"She wanted her boys to see real life," says Diana's hairdresser and friend Sam McKnight, "and experience it first hand. One of her biggest goals was to learn from past mistakes in the family and have those boys buy a magazine in a shop, simple as that. Go to Boots, go to Marks and Spencer's, be nice to the lady who serves you and that kind of thing." "They had a beautiful human being as a mother," says Jim Fletcher, "and if they have a spark of that they'll be very lucky individuals. The people that come into their lives will be very lucky too."

"Largely she's changed royalty through being the mother of William and Harry," says Richard Kay of the Daily Mail, "because they're going to be very different royals. But, yes, she's managed to change some of the approach, the formality, the stuffiness of royalty. The royals had to respond to Diana, because she reached people in a way that the rest of them, frankly, didn't, and so they looked at what she was doing. She made royalty so approachable: She shook people by the hand, she cuddled children. OK, we're not going to see the Queen do that, but I've been on tours with the Queen since Diana's death, and suddenly you find the Queen approaching jobs in an entirely new way. She will now meet the people that a charity is trying to help, rather than just meeting the people who run it."

"The royal family have followed her lead," says Anita Roddick. "I think that we've seen very much more contact between senior members and the public. And I think they've understood that when they are seen to do good publicly, then we appreciate it and we follow their lead." "She had this affinity and this charisma and this way of being able to talk to people, in a very touching manner," says relative Anthony Duckworth-Chad. "And a quick wit, too, a very nice quick wit. She was a real role model of how it should be done." "Now, ten years on," says Ken Wharfe, "everybody's doing what the princess was doing. We're getting the Queen having tea with council house tenants in Newcastle and the prince going to the local pub and hostels. This is something that Diana cracked 12 years ago."

In her address to the nation when Diana died, the Queen said that lessons were to be learned from Diana's life and death. Although the sentiment has not been reiterated publicly, few doubt that Diana's life and death have affected forever more the history of the monarchy in this country. Constitutional historian Ben Pimlott says, "Diana's death was a huge trauma, and it's a trauma that won't go away. I don't think it rocked the monarchy in the sense that I think the monarchy was about to collapse like the French Revolution.

But it was a kind of deep embarrassment. Diana's death removed a difficult player: The sense of there being two rival courts would have gone on. Prince Charles has had a much easier time after her death, but the funeral was the first public mass demonstration to have elements of hostility to the monarchy since the 19th century. Once you get that kind of scar tissue, it's always there to be reactivated. The idea of sort of a million-strong crowd turning out against the monarchy would have been unimaginable in the middle of the 20th century. I've talked to courtiers since, and there was a very conscious Buckingham Palace attempt to take what the Queen said about lessons to be learned seriously."

The seismic threat to elements of the British establishment may be why Diana's reputation is so at risk. Yet across the spectrum of Diana's life—the fashion world, the celebrities, the intellectual heavyweights, and the charity world, people wish to remember the complex person who struggled with her own difficulties to give help to others. "There's a lot written about Diana that tends to be a bit negative," says Sir Cliff Richard. "Nobody's perfect, we all know that, but if we can leave behind something that's a positive memory, it's far more beneficial. The negative parts won't improve anything at all."

"Mixed with the excellent qualities she had," says Lord Deedes who so admired Diana's involvement with the landmines campaign, "there was a certain amount of folly. This is where people are so stupid. They either dress her up as a saint or an angel or they dress her up as a bitch. The truth is, she was a proper human being. She had these great virtues and this gift of being able to be incumbent to people who were in distress. At the same time, she was capable of being ineffably silly. Well, this is a human right: We all are, to some degree, two personalities. Bear in mind no individual has ever been so exposed. She got the Beckham [famous UK footballer and celebrity] treatment to the power of ten. Very difficult to live normally when that is done to you and this is why I'm sympathetic. Nobody, until they experience it, can understand the weight of the pressure of the media when they're on the hunt.

"When you assess the character, bear in mind that because of television and photography and the modern media, people have come to invent unshakeable opinions about people without having ever met them. Diana was very much a victim of this: without knowing her, people formed a judgment. In fact, she was a mixture of the virtues and vices that most of us have got but it was her misfortune that every bloody thing she did was scrutinized by a thousand cameras. She had no privacy whatever.

"Within the last period of her life she was on a new track, for the better, no question. And she could have done much more. It was a very great tragedy, her death in Paris."

What might have been will be a question forever more attached to Diana. "Great usually comes with time," says Anita Roddick. "If the media don't trivialize her I think she has a bloody good chance of it. The narrative needs to be about this not academically bright person who was shoved into this role, who changed it amazingly, stood up for issues that no other member of the royal family had stood up for, and had a real sense of love for her kids. She was humanizing the whole process and I don't think that could be celebrated enough."

"If you look at it in one sense you say a wasted life, but it wasn't, because she has achieved so much," says Jim Fletcher of English National Ballet. "You only had to look at the stream of flowers to see how many lives she touched. She was one of the bright, bright stars that shine and that go out, but always stay in your memory."

For Diana's mother, Frances Shand Kydd, as well as the pride in her daughter's public achievements, there are, of course, her own private memories.

"In fact, little does the public know that it's not the anniversaries and birthdays that trip your heart. It's something unusual, unexpected, you know, when you hear a bit of music or see a picture or something. Those are the things that trip your heart."

❋ ❋ ❋ ❋

THE DIANA, PRINCESS OF WALES MEMORIAL FUND ~ One of the crucial ways in which Diana's legacy continues is through the work of The Diana, Princess of Wales Memorial Fund set up to handle the huge amount of money which poured in from the public when Diana died. "The Fund was a response to the situation we found ourselves in," says Michael Gibbins, Diana's private secretary. "We were sitting in Kensington Palace with all this money pouring in. There was a point when we gave up counting the bags and started counting the vans. We had 50 bags at a time in the room. It was amazing what people gave. One envelope had £5,000 in cash; another was from a child with 20 pence taped to a card. When all the money arrived, at first we thought we would just give it to one or two charities but we didn't realize then what an enormous amount it would be."

"I went to Kensington Palace that morning to meet Michael Gibbins," says Anthony Julius, the princess's lawyer and one of the founders of the Fund, "and he said that even then, within hours of the news of her death, people were coming with five pound notes and coins to the palace. He asked me: 'What shall we do with this money? Should we give it to the charities she supported?' I said 'No, let's set up a charity of our own.' He then said 'What shall we call it? and I answered, 'The Diana, Princess of Wales Memorial Fund.' I had a very strong sense even then, on that first day, that her name and her memory would be under attack and that it was necessary to establish something which would reflect the nature of her commitment and give a sense of what she wanted to do with her life. If we'd just given it to the charities they would have spent it perfectly wisely of course, but the actual memory of Diana would be dissipated. We need institutions in order to carry memory. My sense was in those last months she was moving toward something that was quite radical and new. And I'm very happy that the Fund is not just about giving money, but also has a kind of campaigning aspect to it."

One of the first things The Diana, Princess of Wales Memorial Fund did after Diana's death was to give a million pounds to each of the six charities of which she had remained patron until her death: English National Ballet, The Leprosy Mission, National AIDS Trust, Centrepoint, the Royal Marsden Hospital NHS Trust, and Great Ormond Street Hospital for Children. All spent the money on projects that would continue the kind of work that drew Diana to their charities. The Leprosy Mission, for instance, spent the money on a new enterprise in Delhi providing employment for leprosy sufferers. "It was a wonderful initiative," said former executive director the late Reverend Tony Lloyd, "a stunning piece of technology making audio cassettes, because while very few people die from leprosy, many die from not having a job. So her work goes on."

Other charities that Diana had been involved with as patron received £60,000 grants. The Tushinskya Trust, for instance, a small charity supporting pediatric medicine that Diana had visited in Moscow, established a memorial scholarship to bring young Russian pediatricians to the UK for specialized training. At the Northern Ireland Pre-School Playgroups Association, money from the Fund helped build a community garden. "She often commented on how great it was to meet women who were working in local communities providing cross-community early years provision. It was like a hidden

Northern Ireland, it didn't hit the media headlines, but it was critically important in terms of building the new future. We had this dream of having an interactive outdoor garden area, because most of our children don't have gardens, and the Fund actually funded the gardens. It is beautiful now, a mix of plants, herbs, fruit trees, raspberries, strawberries, apples. And the children who use the center really enjoy it. To us it's a perfect and lasting memory of the princess."

Other charities of which Diana was not a patron but had some direct personal connection also benefited. Diana had visited the Sandy Gall Afghanistan Appeal in Pakistan in 1991 and money from the Memorial Fund came at a critical moment for the charity. "It saw us through a very crucial time. It was extremely difficult getting funding when the Taliban were in power in Afghanistan, and the Fund came in just when we were really at a very low ebb."

The Landmine Survivors Network (LSN), which organized Diana's trip around Bosnia to see the devastation wrought by landmines, received a grant with which they are able to pay for amputee workshops and support groups. "You want to know Diana's legacy?" says co-founder and director Jerry White. "Her visit launched the first amputee support work in Bosnia. It launched LSN and we are now in seven countries around the world, reaching thousands of survivors and their families." Two of the young men who have benefited from these workshops are Zarko Peric and Malic Bradaric, the land-mine victims Diana met in Bosnia and who came over to Diana's funeral.

Andrew Purkis, the chief executive of The Diana, Princess of Wales Memorial Fund, says that the Fund has tried to build up a distinctive identity based on the principles Diana stood for her in her life. "The charity is built on the inspiration of Diana. In the early years we felt it was appropriate and right for the Fund to make gifts to all the organizations with which she had a formal association during her lifetime. Once that was done, the trustees always intended to focus on funding the kind of people and projects that we think embody Diana's values. In the UK we have decided mainly to fund young people on the verge of adulthood, a group that can sometimes be off-putting, inspiring fear and distaste. We felt it was in keeping with Diana's approach that we should try to support people who are often the most vulnerable. It's also an age where if young people are given support and interest, it can turn their whole lives around. These are the kind of projects we feel would be a fitting memorial to her."

Although Diana did not have any contact with the charity Hear Our Voice while she was alive, it now receives money from the Memorial Fund, reflecting the way Diana took on marginal and unfashionable causes, particularly where children and young people were affected. The charity offers services and support for young people experiencing mental health problems in relatively isolated rural communities in Cornwall. By chance, Diana did actually meet one of the young people who now benefits from the charity when she visited Camelford in Cornwall. Clare was then an awestruck child who had the enormous pleasure of receiving Diana's attention when she singled her out in a rain-soaked crowd. Later Diana also touched Clare's life. As a sufferer with epidermolysis bullosa, a severe skin disorder, she became aware that Diana had embraced this little known, unpopular cause. "Diana was the royal who really cared and she'll be remembered as long as the Diana Fund's going. I've found Hear Our Voice very helpful for my problems. This is what Diana's legacy is about."

While young people have been the focus in the UK, internationally there has been a different emphasis. In Africa the Fund supports numerous initiatives for families devastated by AIDS or genocide, and projects to ease the plight of the dying. "Internationally," says Andrew Purkis, "the Fund has followed other principles from Diana's life. We have tried to build on her concern with AIDS and also reflect the special empathy she had with the dying and bereaved. That led to palliative care—caring for people for whom there is no cure—emerging pretty early on as a key area of concern. We've not only funded specific projects but we've also used her name and reputation to try and raise the status of palliative care. There are signs now that attitudes towards care of the dying, especially in places like Sub-Saharan Africa, are beginning to change and we are playing a really important role in that. It's a very good example of where Diana's Fund might be able to change, in quite a fundamental way, attitudes towards a major source of human suffering."

Professor Miriam Were, chair of the National AIDS Control Council, has spoken of how palliative care is now of overwhelming importance in Africa given the presence of the AIDS epidemic. "With most of the world I appreciated the compassionate Princess Diana. Lovingly she held on her lap children in Angola whose legs had been blown off by landmines and hugged sick children in Indonesia and elsewhere. Her death devastated me in a very personal way, but what gave comfort was the thought that Princess Diana has left the world her children. It seemed as if death was the end of her compassionate contribution, but through the Fund, Diana lives on. It is such a joy each time I realize that death need not be the end."

One initiative which epitomizes the Fund's response to caring for the dying and bereaved, is the Memory Box project, run through South Coast Hospice in the heavily AIDS-affected province of KwaZulu-Natal, South Africa. Working through a specialist children's community care team, the project uses memory boxes to help parents break the news to their children that they have HIV/AIDS, and may soon die. Children decorate the small aluminium boxes and put photographs, identity cards and other mementos from their parents inside. Kath Defilippi, director of South Coast Hospice says, "Because HIV disease is breaking up so many families, the memory boxes at least give orphaned children a chance to save some memories of their parents, and survive in the knowledge that they were loved."

Diana's special abilities with the dying are also reflected in support for charities like the Acorns Children's Hospice in the UK. When she visited this hospice, its chief executive John Overton recognized her as someone able to cope with and comfort the dying. "Not everybody, even in the caring professions can cope with what a children's hospice is about. It is a special skill that enables nurses, doctors, and caregivers generally to be able to cope. The nurses become almost surrogate moms to their charges and when they die, as they inevitably will, they feel a great loss. Because of her station in life Diana perhaps exhibited this special gift in a different way, but she was never fazed by it and you can see that by her relationships and her close proximity to people suffering with AIDS and children with limbs badly affected by landmines. Even coming in here she would sit and kneel and talk. There is something spiritual about it, but I don't think it's any particular faith. In fact very often there's a pragmatism as well."

The Memorial Fund has since Diana's own death supported a project at Acorns to help support siblings of dying children. The project provides support groups for the children to talk to each other, to have outings and to make their own magazine. Charles Spencer, Diana's brother, has taken a particular interest in this project. "It is a really good project to support. Diana was passionate about children, particularly unwell children. They were close to her heart." "She had empathy," says John Overton, "with all the youngsters who had gone through or were going to go through this tragedy of losing a sibling." "Diana did not die of a prolonged illness," says Charles Spencer. "Her death was very sudden. Therefore the grief came very quickly. Most of the country was also grieving for Diana so it was almost like sharing the grief with many other people. It would perhaps have been better if I could have been given more time to grieve personally; personal grief is absolutely vital. The death of a young sibling must be particularly awful because you share your childhood with them and then they are taken away from you. Diana and I had a chance to grow up together."

Acorns Hospice is a very special place. It offers respite for families whose children are dying but it also provides accommodation for whole families to stay with a dying child. The hospice also has a garden and a pond where children can place a pebble with their sibling's name and come back whenever they need to think about that child. "I liked the garden especially," says Charles Spencer, "the pond and the stones, because you can quietly remember someone. You are welcome to be part of the surroundings long after the death of your sibling, which is wonderful: You know that there is somewhere to go and remember. Diana is buried on an island with a lake around and I often wander down and remember things that we used to do together; they represent very private thoughts."⁴

According to Andrew Purkis, the Fund is also seeking to develop Diana's work on landmines by funding de-mining groups and amputee support. "We think it is right that we continue Diana's campaigning on the issue of landmines and other 'explosive remnants of war,' which is why the Fund has been working jointly with Landmine Action, the UK arm of the international campaign to ban landmines, to launch the 'Clear-Up Campaign,' and more recently, help set up the Cluster Munitions Coalition. This could potentially do for cluster bombs what the Ottawa Convention did for land-mines. The trustees always felt that she was prepared to stick her neck out for things she believed in and so should we."

One of the most striking accounts of Diana's legacy comes from Andrew Morton whose own career was made by the biography *Diana: Her True Story*. "After she died in 1997, we were faced with a dilemma. The book, which she co-operated with, was a number one best-seller in America and in Britain. It was predicated not on a lie, but on the fact that we had said that she was not involved. The first few obituaries, notably in *The Times*, ironically, were saying it was an aberration, that it wasn't part of her life and so on. I knew instinctively that her memory and her legacy would be systematically denigrated by those people who were opposed to her in her lifetime who would redouble their efforts in her death. And, at the same time, one felt that she was a historical figure now.

"I had always intended to put the conversations I had with her in my will for my old university. But she died 40, 50 years prematurely and we were faced with the decision of what to do. It wasn't a commercial decision, but I felt that we had to reissue a revised edition and acknowledge that Diana had, in fact, co-operated with it. At the same time we decided to make a substantial donation to a small charity, the kind of charity that she would have liked, we thought, that went to the places that were unfashionable and unrec-ognized and dealt with people who were outsiders. We funded this scheme in north-east Angola which effectively helped the local population go into their fields, or down to the river and get some water each morning, without having their feet blown off by a landmine. The money helped to rebuild a hospital; it helped to fund landmines awareness and to drive a few corridors into fields, roads and rivers so that basic human life could exist for these people.

"I've recently become a trustee of this charity, HMD Response, and it has now worked in Chechnya, in Bosnia, in Angola, and the Lebanon. It got a £300,000 grant from The Diana Memorial Fund/Jayne Fincher to fund work in the northwest frontier, the interface between Afghanistan and Pakistan, which is the most god-forsaken place in the world. When the Russians invaded Afghanistan, they just parachuted landmines into the area. The literacy and life expectancy rate is among the lowest in the world. We are enormously grateful for that kind of grant because people's lives will be genuinely transformed."

Not unlike Diana herself, her Fund has never been far from controversy and publicity, sometimes even appearing to fulfill critics' prophecy that it would bring with it all the expectations, drama, and controversy Diana herself attracted. The Fund has indeed been at the center of real dramas. The most serious has been the on-going saga of a lawsuit with the Franklin Mint, an American company specializing in collectables and memorabilia. "It's a very unusual and complex situation," says the Fund's director, Andrew Purkis, "and one that baffles a lot of people. But the base line is that when Diana died, a decision was taken that there was value in her name and that her image should be protected from inappropriate uses. It was realized that a lot of goods and memorabilia would be produced and that a lot of people would be making money out of them and it was felt at the time that it would be better if charity benefited from that and a free-for-all was avoided. Of course it has led us into some very difficult decisions and no doubt with hindsight we'd have done some things differently. But in spite of all the difficulties, and a legal counter-suit launched by the Franklin Mint, it has meant that a whole lot of new money was created for charity, not by fund-raising and competing with other charities, but from commercial activities. In seven years the Fund has raised 36 million pounds this way. That's one reason why the Fund has been able to give away between 8 and 12 million pounds a year which makes the Fund a major and special grant-giving body in the UK. There is surely no better way of remembering Diana than continuing her work."

"All these people who attack The Diana Memorial Fund/Jayne Fincher," says Andrew Morton, "should actually go out in the field and see the work that is being done. I genuinely believe Diana would approve, because these are people who are society's outsiders. And society's outsiders were drawn to her and she was drawn to them. Her legacy is this Fund. It's unsung; it's often criticized. Obviously it started off in a rush and mistakes were made. But the fact that they've done so much in such a short period of time is great credit to them."

Hundreds of people have contributed to this book on Diana's humanitarian life and legacy. Countless others continue to benefit from work carried out in her name. The princess's own words, as penned to her friend Lisa Yacoub, will touch many people across the world who continue to be inspired by her memory: "The biggest disease today is the feeling of being unwanted. People need to be loved. Without love, people die."

She spoke to a constituency who is not represented—and never will be represented—by the mass media. The mass media is there to pander to the great and the good, and the little people occasionally get a look in to boost circulation figures. But essentially that outpouring of emotion—and it was dignified emotion, it was never hysteria—was because people felt that she spoke to them about the concerns and conditions in their lives.

Andrew Morton

It was with profound shock that I learnt of my sister's serious injury, and subsequent death, in Paris, early this morning.

All those who have come into contact with Diana, particularly over the past 17 years, will share my family's grief: she was unique; she understood the most precious needs of human beings, particularly those that suffered; and her vibrancy and sparkle, combined with a very real sense of duty, are now gone forever. It is heart-breaking to lose such a human being, especially when she was only 36. ✳

My heart goes out to the families of the others killed in this incident. Above all, my thoughts are with William and Harry, and with my mother and two sisters, who are showing tremendous bravery in the face of senseless tragedy.

I would ask you please, at this time, to respect the fact that Diana was part of a family, and, amongst the general mourning at her death, realise that we too need space to pay our final respects to our own flesh and blood. For that, we will need privacy.

Finally, the one consolation is that Diana is now in a place where no human being can ever touch her again.

I pray that she may rest in peace.

✚ This is not a time for recriminations, but for sadness. However, I would say that I always believed the press would kill her in the end. BUT NOT even I could imagine that they would take such a direct hand in her death, as seems to be the case. It would appear that every proprietor and editor, of every publication that has paid for intrusive and exploitative photographs of her, encouraging greedy and mindless individuals to risk everything in pursuit of Diana's image, has blood on his hands today.

The crowds were sort of making a beeline for Buckingham Palace and Kensington Palace to lay flowers. And all through the night you could hear this buzz of people. It was very still, very hot those few days. The weather didn't break until the end of the week and then it only broke momentarily before the sun came out again. *Dickie Arbiter*

She was the people's princess and that's how she will stay, how she will remain, in our hearts and in our memories forever.[5]

Tony Blair, UK Prime Minister

The crowds were sort of seven or eight deep, surrounded by all the flowers, and they said, "William and Harry are coming." I didn't feel close enough to be there, so we left and walked out of the gates just as . . . (they) were coming in. The crowd were crying out to Prince William, "we loved your mother."

Jerry White

Lady Diana was the most beautiful symbol of humanity and love for all the world. She touched my life in an extraordinary way. She can never be replaced and I will always remember her with deep love and joy.

Luciano Pavarotti

Westminster Abbey

FUNERAL
of
DIANA
PRINCESS OF WALES

Saturday 6 September 1997
11.00 a.m.

I have never felt people so moved in this country. The funeral was the most extraordinary event I have ever been to in my life. The soldiers came along, hobnail boots on them, and they carried this very weighty coffin. I was sitting about 12 rows behind the Queen. And Charles was very upset. And I could just see him, the side of the head, and these soldiers walked past me and the sound of their hobnail shoes.

Reverend Tony Lloyd

I stand before you today, the representative of a family in grief, in a country in mourning, before a world in shock. We are all united in trying to cope terms with the events of last Sunday morning, when the brutal destruction of the girl we loved transformed all our lives, just as it ended hers.

We are all united in paying our respects to Diana, whether as mother, daughter, sister, friend, or the very essence of duty and compassion. We are to acknowledge her unique qualities; to thank her for bringing magic into our lives; for sharing us issues that really matter; for inspiring us, whether in action or in fantasy. Today is our chance to say thank you, for all you have done for us. I ask you to remember her as she was: A girl who lived by the "Hugging has no harmful side effects"; a beautiful — and by that !

mean, do not rush to canonise her. There is no need. She stands tall enough as one of the most great, rounded, women of this century. She had beauty. She had glamour. She was elegant. Compassion was hers — as was humanity. But her greatest gift was intuition, and she used it wisely.

Without her God-given sense of who needs our love and attention, now, would we know that it is safe to touch a leper, kiss an AIDS victim, or that innocent civilians are having their legs ripped off by the abomination of landmines?

Without her instinctive maternal touch, could we have two young princes whose experiences and tastes range healthily wide, secure in the love

I STAND BEFORE YOU TODAY, THE REPRESENTATIVE OF A FAMILY IN
GRIEF, IN A COUNTRY IN MOURNING, BEFORE A WORLD IN SHOCK.

WE ARE ALL UNITED, NOT ONLY IN OUR DESIRE TO PAY OUR
RESPECTS TO DIANA, BUT RATHER IN OUR NEED TO DO SO. FOR, SUCH
WAS HER EXTRAORDINARY APPEAL, THAT THE TENS OF MILLIONS OF
PEOPLE TAKING PART IN THIS SERVICE ALL OVER THE WORLD, VIA
TELEVISION AND RADIO, WHO NEVER ACTUALLY MET HER, FEEL THAT
THEY TOO LOST SOMEONE CLOSE TO THEM IN THE EARLY HOURS OF
SUNDAY MORNING. IT IS A MORE REMARKABLE TRIBUTE TO DIANA
THAN I CAN EVER HOPE TO OFFER HER TODAY.

DIANA WAS THE VERY ESSENCE OF COMPASSION, OF DUTY, OF STYLE,
OF BEAUTY. ALL OVER THE WORLD, SHE WAS A SYMBOL OF SELFLESS
HUMANITY; A STANDARD-BEARER FOR THE RIGHTS OF THE TRULY
DOWNTRODDEN; A VERY BRITISH GIRL WHOSE CONCERNS
TRANSCENDED NATIONALITY; SOMEONE WITH A NATURAL NOBILITY,
WHO WAS CLASSLESS, AND WHO PROVED, IN THE LAST YEAR, THAT
SHE NEEDED NO ROYAL TITLE TO CONTINUE TO GENERATE HER
PARTICULAR BRAND OF MAGIC.

TODAY IS OUR CHANCE TO SAY THANK YOU FOR THE WAY YOU
BRIGHTENED OUR LIVES - EVEN THOUGH GOD GRANTED YOU BUT
HALF A LIFE. WE WILL ALL FEEL CHEATED, ALWAYS, THAT YOU WERE
TAKEN FROM US SO YOUNG; AND YET WE MUST LEARN TO BE
GRATEFUL THAT YOU CAME ALONG AT ALL. ONLY NOW YOU ARE
GONE DO WE TRULY APPRECIATE WHAT WE ARE NOW WITHOUT. AND
WE WANT YOU TO KNOW THAT LIFE WITHOUT YOU IS VERY, VERY,
DIFFICULT. WE HAVE ALL DESPAIRED AT OUR LOSS OVER THE PAST
WEEK, AND ONLY THE STRENGTH OF THE MESSAGE YOU GAVE US
THROUGH YOUR YEARS OF GIVING HAS AFFORDED US THE STRENGTH
TO MOVE FORWARD.

THERE IS A TEMPTATION TO RUSH TO CANONISE YOUR MEMORY.
THERE IS NO NEED TO DO SO. YOU STAND TALL ENOUGH AS A HUMAN
BEING OF UNIQUE QUALITIES NOT TO NEED TO BE SEEN AS A SAINT.
INDEED, TO SANCTIFY YOUR MEMORY WOULD BE TO MISS OUT ON
THE VERY CORE OF YOUR BEING - YOUR WONDERFULLY
MISCHIEVOUS SENSE OF HUMOUR, WITH A LAUGH THAT BENT YOU
DOUBLE; YOUR JOY FOR LIFE, TRANSMITTED WHEREVER YOU TOOK
YOUR SMILE AND THE SPARKLE IN THOSE UNFORGETTABLE EYES;
YOUR BOUNDLESS ENERGY, WHICH YOU COULD BARELY CONTAIN.

BUT YOUR GREATEST GIFT WAS YOUR INTUITION, AND IT WAS A GIFT
YOU USED WISELY. THIS IS WHAT UNDERPINNED ALL YOUR OTHER
WONDERUL ATTRIBUTES. AND IF WE LOOK TO ANALYSE WHAT IT WAS
ABOUT YOU THAT HAD SUCH A WIDE APPEAL, WE FIND IT IN YOUR
INSTINCTIVE FEEL FOR WHAT WAS REALLY IMPORTANT IN ALL OUR
LIVES.

WITHOUT YOUR GOD-GIVEN SENSITIVITY, WE WOULD BE IMMERSED IN
GREATER IGNORANCE AT THE ANGUISH OF AIDS AND HIV SUFFERERS,
THE PLIGHT OF THE HOMELESS, THE ISOLATION OF LEPERS, THE
RANDOM DESTRUCTION OF LANDMINES.

DIANA EXPLAINED TO ME ONCE THAT IT WAS HER INNERMOST
FEELINGS OF SUFFERING THAT MADE IT POSSIBLE FOR HER TO
CONNECT WITH HER CONSTITUENCY OF THE REJECTED. AND HERE
WE COME TO ANOTHER TRUTH ABOUT HER - FOR ALL THE STATUS,
THE GLAMOUR, THE APPLAUSE, DIANA REMAINED THROUGHOUT A
VERY INSECURE PERSON AT HEART, ALMOST CHILDLIKE IN HER
DESIRE TO DO GOOD FOR OTHERS SO SHE COULD RELEASE HERSELF
FROM DEEP FEELINGS OF UNWORTHINESS, OF WHICH HER EATING
DISORDERS WERE MERELY A SYMPTOM.

THE WORLD SENSED THIS PART OF HER CHARACTER, AND CHERISHED
HER FOR HER VULNERABILITY, WHILST ADMIRING HER FOR HER
HONESTY.

THE LAST TIME I SAW DIANA WAS ON JULY 1ST, HER BIRTHDAY, IN
LONDON, WHEN, TYPICALLY, SHE WAS NOT TAKING TIME TO
CELEBRATE HER SPECIAL DAY WITH FRIENDS, BUT WAS GUEST OF
HONOUR AT A FUNDRAISING CHARITY EVENING.

SHE SPARKLED, OF COURSE. BUT I WOULD RATHER CHERISH THE
DAYS I SPENT WITH HER IN MARCH, WHEN SHE CAME TO ~~SPEND TIME~~ VISIT
~~WITH~~ ME AND MY CHILDREN ~~AT~~ OUR HOME IN SOUTH AFRICA.
                                        IN

I AM PROUD OF THE FACT THAT, APART FROM WHEN SHE WAS ON
PUBLIC DISPLAY MEETING PRESIDENT MANDELA, WE MANAGED TO
CONTRIVE TO STOP THE EVER-PRESENT PAPARAZZI FROM GETTING A
SINGLE PICTURE OF HER. THAT MEANT A LOT TO HER.

THESE WERE DAYS I WILL ALWAYS TREASURE. IT WAS AS IF WE HAD
BEEN TRANSPORTED BACK ~~IN TIME~~ TO OUR CHILDHOOD, WHEN WE
SPENT SUCH AN ENORMOUS AMOUNT OF TIME TOGETHER, THE TWO
YOUNGEST IN THE FAMILY. FUNDAMENTALLY SHE HAD NOT
CHANGED AT ALL, FROM THE BIG SISTER WHO MOTHERED ME AS A
BABY, FOUGHT WITH ME AT SCHOOL, AND ENDURED THOSE LONG
TRAIN JOURNEYS BETWEEN OUR PARENTS' ~~HOUSES~~ WITH ME, AT
WEEKENDS.   HOMES

IT IS A TRIBUTE TO HER LEVEL-HEADEDNESS AND STRENGTH THAT, DESPITE THE MOST BIZARRE LIFE IMAGINABLE AFTER HER CHILDHOOD, SHE REMAINED INTACT, TRUE TO HERSELF.

THERE IS NO DOUBT THAT SHE WAS LOOKING FOR A NEW DIRECTION IN HER LIFE AT THIS TIME. SHE TALKED ENDLESSLY OF GETTING AWAY FROM ENGLAND, MAINLY BECAUSE OF THE TREATMENT THAT SHE RECEIVED AT THE HANDS OF THE NEWSPAPERS. I DON'T THINK SHE EVER UNDERSTOOD WHY HER GENUINELY GOOD INTENTIONS WERE SNEERED AT BY THE MEDIA; WHY THERE APPEARED TO BE A PERMANENT QUEST ON THEIR BEHALF TO BRING HER DOWN.

IT IS BAFFLING. MY OWN AND ONLY EXPLANATION IS THAT GENUINE GOODNESS IS THREATENING TO THOSE AT THE OPPOSITE END OF THE MORAL SPECTRUM. ~~THOSE WHO INHABIT THE MURKY SWAMPS OF MALEVOLENCE, AND WHO NEED TO SUCK THEIR VICTIMS DRY OF THEIR SOULS.~~

TO SAY SHE MANIPULATED THE MEDIA IS TO MISS THE POINT. YES, SHE QUITE RIGHTLY HARNESSED THE INTEREST IN HER TO HIGHLIGHT HER CHARITIES' AIMS; AND, THROUGH SHEER NEED TO SURVIVE, SHE HAD TO DEFEND HER INNER SELF BY BOWING TO THE JUGGERNAUT STRENGTH OF THE PRESS OCCASIONALLY. BUT 'MANIPULATION', WITH ITS IMPLIED SLYNESS AND CUNNING, I REJECT AS A CHARGE AGAINST HER. FROM WHERE I STAND, THE ONLY PEOPLE I SEE 'MANIPULATING THE MEDIA' ARE THOSE WHO OWN LARGE CHUNKS OF IT.

IT IS A POINT TO REMEMBER THAT, OF ALL THE IRONIES ABOUT DIANA, PERHAPS THE GREATEST WAS THIS: A GIRL GIVEN THE NAME OF THE ANCIENT GODESS OF HUNTING WAS, IN THE END, THE MOST HUNTED PERSON OF THE MODERN AGE.

SHE WOULD WANT US TODAY TO PLEDGE OURSELVES TO PROTECTING HER BELOVED BOYS, WILLIAM AND HARRY, FROM A SIMILAR FATE, AND I DO THIS HERE, ON BEHALF OF YOU, DIANA. WE WILL NOT ALLOW THEM TO SUFFER THE ANGUISH THAT USED REGULARLY TO DRIVE YOU TO TEARFUL DESPAIR.

AND, BEYOND THAT, ON BEHALF OF YOUR MOTHER AND SISTERS, I PLEDGE THAT WE, YOUR BLOOD FAMILY, WILL DO ALL WE CAN TO CONTINUE THE IMAGINATIVE AND LOVING WAY IN WHICH YOU WERE STEERING THESE TWO EXCEPTIONAL YOUNG MEN, SO THAT THEIR SOULS ARE NOT SIMPLY IMMERSED BY DUTY AND TRADITION, BUT CAN SING OPENLY, AS YOU PLANNED. WE *FULLY* RESPECT THE HERITAGE INTO WHICH THEY HAVE BOTH BEEN BORN, AND WILL ALWAYS RESPECT AND ENCOURAGE THEM IN THEIR ROYAL ROLE; BUT WE, LIKE YOU, RECOGNISE THE NEED FOR THEM TO EXPERIENCE AS MANY DIFFERENT ASPECTS OF LIFE AS POSSIBLE, TO ARM THEM

SPIRITUALLY AND EMOTIONALLY FOR THE YEARS AHEAD. I KNOW YOU WOULD HAVE EXPECTED NOTHING LESS FROM US.

WILLIAM AND HARRY, WE ALL CARE DESPERATELY FOR YOU TODAY. WE ARE ALL CHEWED UP WITH SADNESS AT THE LOSS OF A WOMAN WHO WASN'T EVEN OUR MOTHER. HOW GREAT YOUR SUFFERING IS, WE CANNOT EVEN IMAGINE.

I WOULD LIKE TO END BY THANKING GOD FOR THE SMALL MERCIES HE HAS SHOWN US AT THIS DREADFUL TIME: FOR TAKING DIANA AT HER MOST BEAUTIFUL AND RADIANT, WHEN SHE HAD ~~AT LAST REDISCOVERED~~ JOY IN HER PRIVATE LIFE - ~~AND WE THANK DODI AL-FAYED FOR MAKING HER LAST WEEKS ONES OF HAPPINESS. BUT~~ ABOVE ALL, WE GIVE THANKS FOR THE LIFE OF A WOMAN I AM SO PROUD TO BE ABLE TO CALL MY SISTER - THE UNIQUE, THE COMPLEX, THE EXTRAORDINARY AND IRREPLACEABLE DIANA, WHOSE BEAUTY - BOTH INTERNAL AND EXTERNAL - WILL NEVER BE EXTINGUISHED FROM OUR MINDS.

Charles Spencer

Candle in the Wind

Goodbye England's rose
May you ever grow in our hearts
You were the grace that placed itself
Where lives were torn apart
You called out to our country
And you whispered to those in pain
Now you belong to heaven
And the stars spell out your name

And it seems to me you lived your life
Like a candle in the wind
Never fading with the sunset
When the rain set in
And your footsteps will always fall here
Along England's greenest hills
Your candles burned out long before
Your legend ever will

Candle in the Wind

Goodbye England's rose
May you ever grow in our hearts
You were the grace that placed itself
Where lives were torn apart
You called out to our country
And you whispered to those in pain
Now you belong to Heaven
And the stars spell out your name

And it seems to me you lived your life
Like a candle in the wind
Never fading with the sunset
When the rain set in
And your footsteps will always fall here
Along England's greenest hills
Your candles burned out long before
Your legend ever will

Loveliness we've lost
These empty days without your smile
This torch we'll always carry
For our nations golden child
And even though we try
The truth brings us to tears
All our words cannot express
The joy you bought us through the years

Goodbye England's rose
From a country lost without your soul
Who'll miss the wings of your compassion
More than you'll ever know

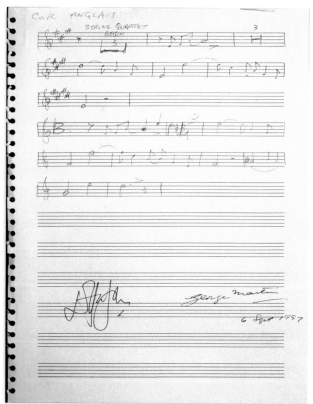

The funeral was really a harrowing experience. I was really embarrassed because I kept crying and her children were all crying and it was like, I was ashamed. When they came past me and I saw the coffin with the flowers that said "Mummy" I was overcome. We were sitting quite near Elton John and the piano, and when he sang that song I was in bits, and so was everybody else, absolutely in bits.

Sarah Jane Gaselee

I went to the Abbey for the funeral, and when I came out what really struck me was the crowds outside were still there. They were standing in total silence, it was really moving, coming out a good ten minutes, maybe quarter of an hour after the others had gone, and they were still lining the streets in complete silence. And that was very emotional, very dramatic.

Jean Pike

Diana is buried on an island with a lake around and I often wander down and remember things that we used to do together; they represent very private thoughts.
Charles Spencer

The world has lost one of its most compassionate humanitarians,
and I have lost a special friend.   *Sir Elton John*

I distinctly remember her caring; That is how I remember her best;
And let it be that only good; Surrounds her in her rest.   *Barry Gibb*

She highlighted neglected causes. She reached out to people on the margins of society. She made even the most humble people feel special. Her inspiration must continue to change lives now and in the future. I am glad that her work continues through her Memorial Fund.

Nelson Mandela

I thought she was so great not to be consumed by everything that had happened to her and to keep giving and giving. I thought she was a very strong person—the Elvis of compassion. Our generation has grown up with so much cynicism about humanity and she made you think again. I really believe that she was a beacon of compassion and hope.

George Michael

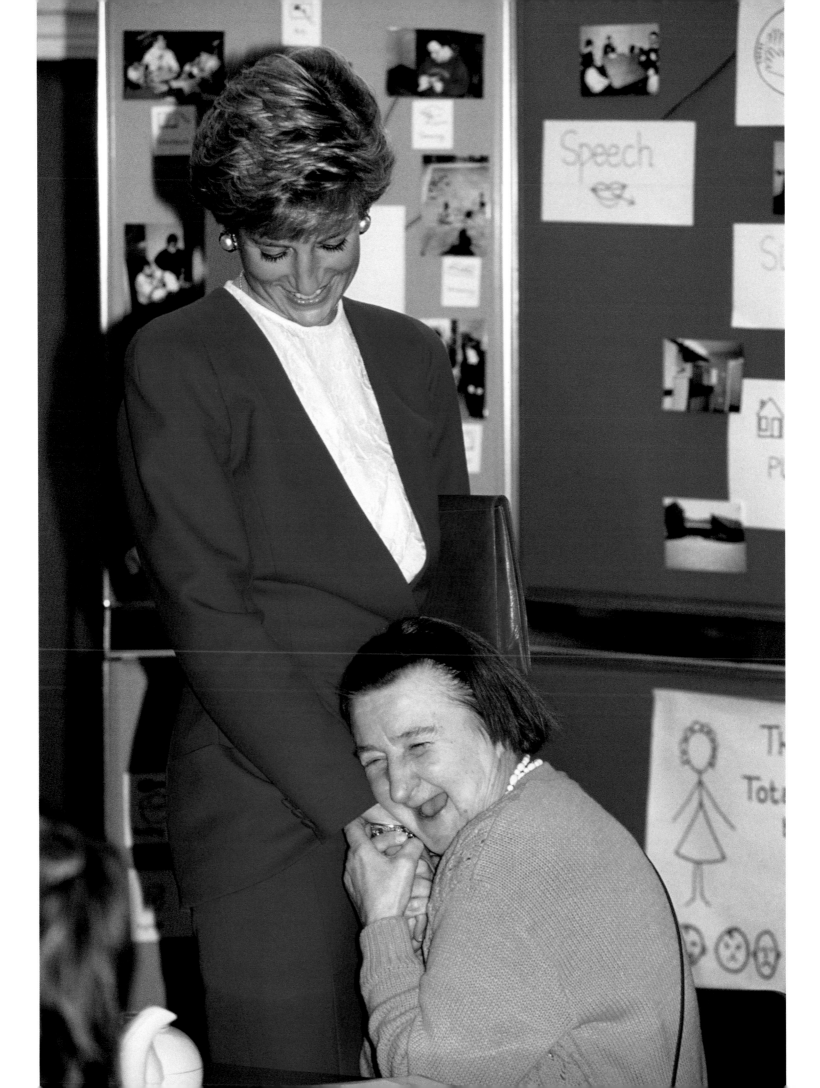

The biggest disease today
is the feeling of being
unwanted.

People need to be loved,
without love. people die

———

Here endeth another lesson of
wisdom from the Kensington arena !!
x

Diana.

THE WORK CONTINUES

FACES OF THE FUND

Diana's mission to help and champion those most in need lives on in The Diana, Princess of Wales Memorial Fund. It helps people to change their lives for the better, by giving grants to charities in the UK and around the world, campaigning on issues close to the princess's heart and raising new money for humanitarian work. Its work has helped bring hope and encouragement to organizations trying to change the world for the better; and to many individuals who, but for the Fund, would have been marginalized and unable to realize their full potential.

Here are just six people who have been touched by Diana's Memorial Fund in different ways.

JOHN PROCTOR, 20, is reading politics and international relations at Sussex University. He is also a volunteer at the Allsorts youth project.

"I was aware that I was gay from around 14, but I didn't really believe it myself until I was 16. I ended up being outed by one of my friends at school. It was quite scary. The school didn't know how to deal with it; they hadn't had anyone come out before.

"When you've got 40 people in your boarding house calling you 'poof,' you know there's only so much of that you can take with a smile on your face. You certainly find out who your real friends are. I don't mean to make it sound all bad; I really enjoyed my time there. But it was quite odd being the only gay one in the school, so coming to Allsorts relieved that.

"Allsorts supports young gay, lesbian and bisexual people and those questioning their sexuality, in Brighton and Hove. They provide one-to-one support and a weekly drop in, workshops in schools and colleges, run residentials, lots of stuff.

"I started coming along to the drop in aged 18. I was living in a country town in Sussex. Being young and gay there was a pretty isolating experience. There wasn't anyone else who I knew who was gay or out and I didn't really know that many people my age as I went to boarding school. So I started coming to Allsorts. It made a huge difference. It certainly ended the isolation, being able to meet young people who'd been through some of the

problems I had. Meeting people who'd come out and dealt with it.

"Allsorts offered me somewhere safe to make new friends. A place where I could be myself. It certainly helped build my self-confidence and made me feel more at ease with who I am.

"After a year, I wanted to put something back, so I'm now a young persons' representative. I help out with workshops in schools and colleges in the local area.

"It's a case of raising awareness of issues and making people think about things that they wouldn't do otherwise. The effects people saying things can have on people, is one of the things we highlight and trying to get people to think about perceptions of being gay, lesbian, and bisexual.

"We certainly wouldn't have been able to achieve the things we have without the money, advice and encouragement from The Diana, Princess of Wales Fund.

"Diana gave vulnerable people a voice that wouldn't have otherwise been heard. She certainly touched on issues that lots of other so called celebrities would have been scared of and wouldn't have got involved in. She didn't have prejudice, she just treated those people like they should be treated, like people."

Landmine Action is a campaigning organization that tries to influence government policy that will improve the lives of people threatened by landmines, cluster munitions, and other unexploded ordinance. They also work with groups in affected countries to tackle the problems caused by these lethal remnants of war. RICHARD LLOYD, 38, is their director.

"I joined Landmine Action in 1998 because I had spent some time in Laos, where I witnessed the effects of landmines literally on the streets. I'd already become aware of the problem because of the massive public attention that Diana brought in the UK and internationally.

"Diana had a very obvious ability to connect with people, and for us she made our issue one that ordinary people care about. She seemed to have a talent for spotting very important but difficult issues and throwing her weight behind them. I suspect she liked taking on difficult issues in the same way that the Memorial Fund does now. The British government were really unhappy about Diana's stance on banning landmines.

"It's been a continual battle to get resources for what we do. It's been a continual struggle to keep the issue on the public agenda in countries like the UK which don't have a landmine problem themselves. But it's been the most interesting and exciting five years that I can remember.

"Diana's legacy is really important to us because most people still now associate

what we do with Diana. She backed our international campaign against landmines and very often the first time people heard of the issue was when Diana got involved. The Fund has been our biggest backer financially and as a champion of what we do. So our connection with the memory of Diana and the Memorial Fund itself is inextricable.

"The funding was massively important after Diana died and after the British government signed the Ottawa Treaty which bans anti-personnel landmines. Public perception was that the problem was solved. And of course that wasn't and still is far from the case. At a time when public and political interest was starting to diminish, the Fund helped keep the campaign going. They have really backed a lot of the things that we've done and that have had a big impact in a lot of countries. So the Fund's been instrumental in not only keeping us going and growing but in keeping the issue on the political agenda and moving forward.

"I'd like to have shown Diana the dramatic changes in the worst affected countries. For example, in Cambodia, the casualty rate has been massively reduced since the mid '90s. In many other countries there's now the real prospect of getting rid of the worst of the mine problem within the next five to ten years, if enough resources are put in. And also to see that two thirds of the world have banned anti-personnel mines. I think she would be rather pleased by that and the fastest growing arms control treaty in history. A fairly impressive legacy, I would say."

Caregiver CECELIA NKULULEKHU MSOMI, 40, lived through the ethnic violence of KwaZulu-Natal, South Africa, in the late '80s and early '90s. Today she sees her community, friends and family in another state of war— the war against HIV/AIDS.

"Becoming a hospice worker has made a big difference in my life. I have had a lot of death in my family and being a hospice worker has helped me to cope with all this. My mother, father, brother, and two sisters have all passed away. I think all my siblings died of HIV/AIDS and they called me earlier this year to say my brother is sick and probably dying of it too.

"As a caregiver, I am involved in helping HIV/AIDS patients, cancer patients and children who are sick at home. The people we visit are very, very poor. We cook for them, give them medication, and food parcels. If there is a need, we also spend an hour with a lonely person to console them and assess if they need counseling, which I sometimes do myself. We start each visit with a prayer. We do a lot of praying in this work.

"Being funded by Diana's Memorial Fund takes a lot of the stress off of us. The Memory Box project [which gives children who face the death of a parent the opportunity to collect things to remember them by] was formed through this Fund and it has helped us a lot and has given us and the community more hope.

"Diana loved people very much. She didn't want to see people suffering, especially if that person was hungry, she wanted to give them a better life. Diana was a champion for the vulnerable and underprivileged. She did a lot for landmines victims, she was there for them. If she was alive today, I think she would be helping with the issues we deal with.

"Helping to carry on Diana's work means a lot to me. Sometimes I come across a person who has been infected by her husband and has to live with the consequences. I just want to help knowing that this is what Princess Diana would have done."

In 1998 FATOS DERGUTI, a straight 'A' student from Kosovo arrived in the UK knowing little English but with big ambitions. Albanian Youth Action (AYA) helped him on the road to achieve them.

"At 17 I had a choice—head for the mountains and fight, or flee. I'd not left my country before. I am the youngest and the only boy in my family, so I was very protected, and not allowed to go out that much. But I had to leave my home town in '98 as the war was coming nearer. My best friend and I smuggled ourselves out on the back of a truck to Hungary and got a plane to England.

"The most important thing is education because it keeps you away from bad things that you can easily get into, and it helps you realize your potential. Albanian Youth Action found us a school where we could do our A-levels.

"It was alienating at first. We didn't know the language, we didn't know the place. I've come from a small town where you know everybody and say 'hello' 70 times on your way to get bread in the morning, to here, where everyone looks at you strangely. It was really difficult.

"I taught myself English by reading Physics books with a big dictionary. AYA kept us busy with arts and drama workshops, mixing with English speaking people, making friends. Now I am a peer tutor for them on health issues.

"I am in my third year at Imperial College, London, reading material science and engineering. After that I will either move into industry or become an academic. I come from a family of teachers, so I think, why be original? It's in my genes!

"I remember when AYA got the money from Diana's Fund in '99. The Fund is giving an opportunity for people who are less fortunate and who have to face up to so many difficulties. Its helping people who cannot think of aims in life because they are too busy thinking about their immediate problems. The Fund is in fact Diana. She died, so the only thing left of her is the Fund and that's what keeps going and that's what keeps us going. We don't need to have known Diana to appreciate the Fund. When you talk about calculus in physics you don't talk about Newton just because he created it, you talk about calculus. Subconsciously, we know he did it. So when we talk about the Fund we think about Diana all the time, helping people."

MARK KEENAN turned up at Fairbridge on his 21st birthday, homeless, helpless, not long out of prison and with no job. Or rather, statistically speaking, his prospects were predictable and bleak. A well-worn route of alcohol or drug abuse, reoffending and imprisonment is the future for most young people who have repeatedly been in prison. But Fairbridge doesn't deal in statistics. It deals with individuals with potential. With young people who can make changes in their lives for the better, given support and the opportunity to believe in themselves. The Fund supports courses for offenders prior and after release, giving them the confidence to break the cycle of reoffending.

"I got fond of the old alcohol at 17 and it wrecked things for me. I was on a downward spiral and I knew I had to put the brakes on sooner or later or end up doing a life sentence or being six feet under. I had an erratic lifestyle from 16 to 20. I've been in prison five times. Mainly for assault and robbery. I was quite violent and I kind of lose my rag sometimes, fueled by alcohol. That's what caused most of the problems. I knew that, so I stopped it.

"I'm quite a different person today. I've got rid of all the anger that I used to have. People don't believe that somebody can change, but I have. I don't even drink anymore.

"Life in prison is boring, isolated, lonely. Basically, everything's taken away from you, everything that you take for granted

on the outside and it's just a waiting game 'till they let you out again. I participated in the Fairbridge course just before the end of serving five months in a young offenders' institution. I loved it. I'd been in prison previous to that and nothing like that ever happened. You know, you've got your work everyday, but this was something different. Something that prisoners aren't used to. I really enjoyed the course, it gave me confidence, and if you don't have confidence then you won't do anything.

"I thought,' God this is something I could really enjoy on the outside, given a bit of focus to think about things when I got out.' I think I've just grown up a little bit. Realized that I don't want to be locked up for the rest of my life. So I've done something about it. Fairbridge helped me get my own flat, it's a palace. It's my pride and joy. I'm getting things back again, I'm getting on with my family again. My girlfriend thinks she's met a new man because I've changed that much. People are surprised, so am I. I'm more surprised than anyone, to be honest.

"I was not a big supporter of Princess Diana when she was alive, but I do respect what she did do and what she stood for. The landmines and stuff, cancer and young people, yeah. I also want to work with youth. I'd like to pass on the benefit of my experience. If I can help anybody else, if it helps just one person then it will have been worth it.

"I admire the stuff that the Fairbridge people do. The way they devote their time to young people. Prison doesn't address issues for young people.

"You're there, you serve your sentence, you get out, and that's all, basically. No help or anything, but Fairbridge is trying to change that. I considered it a privilege that week previous to me getting out, working with groups and stuff, getting a bit of confidence. I started coming here when I got out. I've done the bike project. I learned how to build a bike from scratch, how to cycle properly, everything to do with bikes and bike safety. I've still got to put on the brakes, then I can take it home."

Heart 'n Soul is a south London arts organization which offers young people with learning disabilities the opportunity to realize their talents and personal potential through music, theatre and club culture. For the past five years, LIZZIE EMEH, 25, has been singing soul, funk, and R&B songs at their Beautiful Octopus and Squidz club nights, which are run by and for people with learning difficulties.

"If Diana didn't do the things that she did, Heart 'n Soul wouldn't have been born. We wouldn't have a voice. Diana made sure that we had a voice, so when I think of Diana I think of a very unique person. The person that put Diana on this earth knew what they were doing. They said: 'You're gonna go and change some lives.'

"If I didn't get involved in Heart 'n Soul, I would be sitting at home twiddling my thumbs right now. I'd still be singing, but nobody would notice me. It made me feel empty inside—I didn't like it at all. But it's not like that anymore. Heart 'n Soul has made people notice me and I've got their respect now. It's been a long time coming but I've eventually got peoples' respect.

"When I was singing before, they didn't used to listen to me but now they come and see the shows and say to me, 'You're really, really good,' and 'Wow that was amazing; your voice is just amazing.' I turn around and say it's a gift and I use that gift. Everyone else has got a gift. Diana gave us this gift—a voice— and Heart 'n Soul has given us a voice as well.

"In the future I would like to do other things. I have a really big ambition for a person who has learning disabilities. I would like to be presented with a Music of Black Origin Award for my work—I could really see myself up on stage. But I wouldn't be picking up the award just for myself; I'd be picking up the award for people with learning disabilities too. Diana did things to help other people. If you can do things to help other people the world would be a better place.

"Although Diana has gone now, people like me are still spreading her word. We're still doing all of her work although she's not here anymore. I remember Princess Diana as being very loving. Very loving. She was really caring. How can you sum up a woman that's changed so many lives and changed so many points of view? But the thing is she won't ever be forgotten because we're still doing her work for her."

2001 World Congress on Family Law
42nd Street
Aberdeen Foyer
ACORD
Acorns Childrens' Hospice Trust
Acta Community Theatre
Action for Children in Conflict
Action for Disability
Action for Prisoners' Families
Action Group
Action Mental Health (VOTE)
Action on Disability and Development (ADD)
ADFAM National
Afghanaid
Africa Educational Trust
After Adoption
Albanian Youth Action Ltd
Albert Kennedy Trust
Allsorts Youth Project
American Friends of Covent Garden
Anglo-European College of Chiropractic
Ann Craft Trust
APT Enterprise Development
ASPIRE
Association For Real Change (ARC)
Association of Charitable Foundations
Australian Council on Smoking
Australian Junior Red Cross
BAAF (British Agencies for Adoption and Fostering)
Barnardo's Australia
Barnardo's New Zealand
Barnardo's UK
Beacon of Hope
Beavers Arts
Benesh Institute of Choreography
Bereaved Families of Ontario
Bereavement Care
Bibini Centre for Young People
Black Health Agency
Bloorview Macmillan Rehabilitation Centre
BOC Covent Garden Festival
British Deaf Association
British Lung Foundation
British Red Cross Society
British Red Cross Youth
British Youth Opera
BUILD Nottingham Mentor Programme
CADMAD
Cambodia Trust
Cambridge Female Education Trust (CAMFED)
Canadian Red Cross Youth Services
CARE Canada
Centrepoint
Changemakers
Chester Childbirth Appeal

Chester Summer Music Festival
Chicken Shed Theatre Company
Child Accident Prevention Trust
Child Bereavement Trust
Child Witness Preparation Program of Peel
Childhood Bereavement Project (NABS)
ChildLine
Children in Scotland
Children of the Andes
Children's Express
Children's Legal Centre
Children's Rights Officers and Advocates
Chinese Information & Advice Centre
Chinese Mental Health Association
Chipangali Wildlife Trust
Christian Aid
Church of England Children's Society
Citizen Advocacy Information and Training
Citizenship Foundation
City Ballet of London
Cleveland Arts
Coalition to Stop the Use of Child Soldiers
Commonwealth Society for the Deaf
Community Service Volunteers
Concern Worldwide London
Conflict Development and Peace Network
Council for Disabled Children
Cruse Bereavement Care
Dadihiye Somali Development Organization
DEBRA
Deptford Albany
Disability Awareness in Action
Disability Sport England
Displaced People in Action
Douglas Bader Foundation
Down's Syndrome Association NI
Dunfermline Advocacy Initiative
Eating Disorders Association
Edinburgh Development Group
Edinburgh Young Carers
Education Action International
Education for Development
Ellen Gee Foundation
Elton John Aids Foundation
Enable
English National Ballet
Escape Artists
Ethiopian Community Centre
Eureka!
Faculty of Dental Surgery
Fairbridge in Scotland
Families Outside
Family Planning Association
Family Rights Group
Family Service Units

Family Welfare Association
Firefly Youth Project
FOCUS
Foundation For Conductive Education
Freshfield Service
Friends of the Imperial War Museum
Gloucestershire County Cricket Club
Good Shepherd Centre Hamilton
Grahamstown Hospice
Great Ormond Street Hospital NHS Trust
Greenwich and Lewisham Young Peoples' Theatre
Groundwork Northern Ireland
Guinness Trust
HALO Trust
Handicap International
Headway – Nottingham
Health Unlimited
Healthlink Worldwide
Healthy Gay Living Centre
Hear Our Voice
Heart 'n Soul
Helderberg Hospice
Help Age International
Help the Aged
Help the Hospices
Home Start UK
Honourable Society of the Middle Temple
Hope for Children
Hospice Africa Mbarara
Hospice and Palliative Care Association of South Africa
Hospice Durham
Hospice Uganda
Hoxton Hall Outreach Video Project
Huntingdon's Disease Society
INQUEST Charitable Trust
Institute for Study of Drug Dependence
Intermediate Technology Development Group
International Childcare Trust
International Spinal Research Trust
Jaipur Limb Campaign
Just World Partners
Kara Counselling and Training Trust
Kingwood Trust
Kurdistan Children's Fund
Landau Consultants Ltd
Landmine Action
Landmine Conference Washington
Landmine Disability Support
Leap Confronting Conflict
Leonard Cheshire Foundation
Leprosy Mission
Leukaemia Research Appeal for Wales
Lifeline Network International Nehemiah Project
Lighthouse Project
Llamau Housing Society Ltd

London African Volunteers Network
Lyford Cay Foundation
Macintyre Care
MacRobert Arts Centre
Malcolm Sargent Cancer Fund for Children in Australia
Manic Depression Fellowship London
Maua Methodist Hospital
Maya Centre
Medical Foundation for the Care of Victims of Torture
Medical Missionaries of Mary, Uganda (CAFOD)
Mencap
Mental Health Foundation
Mental Health Media
Mercy Corps Scotland
Midlands Refugee Council
MIND In Tower Hamlets
Mines Advisory Group (MAG)
Mother of Mercy Hospice for Terminally Ill Home
    Based Care
Motivation
Nacro Cymru Swansea
Nairobi Hospice
Naledi Hospice
National Aids Trust
National Children's Bureau
National Children's Orchestra
National Council for the Welfare of Prisoners Abroad
National Development Team (NDT)
National Hospital for Neurology and Neurosurgery
National Information Forum
National Institute of Adult Continuing Education
National Meningitis Trust
Natural History Museum Development Trust
Ndola Ecumenical Hospice Association
Nelson Mandela Children's Fund
Newport International Competition for Young Pianists
North of England Refugee Service (NERS)
Northern Ireland Pre-School Association
Northern Refugee Centre
Nsambya Home Care Services (St Francis)
Ocean Road Cancer Institute
Off The Record – Bath and North East Somerset
Ontario AIDS Network
Opportunity International
Osteopathic Centre For Children
Oxfam
Pakistani Resource Centre
Parkinson's Disease Society
PASADA
The Passage
People and Planet
People in Partnership
PhotoVoice
Pied Piper Appeal
Post-Adoption Centre

POWER
Prader-Willi Syndrome Association
Pre-School Learning Alliance
Prince's Trust (The)
Princess of Wales Children's Health Camp
Prism Arts
Prison Reform Trust
Project for Advocacy Counselling and Education
PSS
Queen Elizabeth Central Hospital
Rainbow Project
Refuge
Refugee Action
Refugee Council
Refugee Education and Training Advisory Service
Refugee Lifeline
Refugee Resource
Refugees Arrival Project
Relate (Head Office)
Response International (HMD)
Rethink
Roadpeace
Roma Support Group
Rowcroft Hospice
Royal Academy of Dramatic Art
Royal Academy of Music
Royal Anthropological Institute of Great Britain
    and Ireland
Royal Australian College of Dental Surgeons
Royal Highland Yacht Club
Royal Marsden NHS Trust
Royal New Zealand Foundation for the Blind
Royal NZ College of Obstetricians and Gynaecologists
Rural Media Company
Saferworld
Sandy Gall's Afghanistan Appeal
Sargent Cancer Care for Children
Save the Children Fund (HQ)
Scope
Scottish Catholic International Aid Fund
Scottish Chamber Orchestra
Scottish Council for Research in Education
Scottish Pre-School Association
Scottish Refugee Council
SCOVO
SeeAbility
Send a Cow
Serpentine Gallery
Shaftesbury Homes and Arethusa
Skill National Bureau For Students With Disabilities
Skills for Southern Sudan
South Sudanese Community Association
Southall Black Sisters
SOVA (Welsh Office)
St Bernard's Hospice

St Francis Hospice Association
St Luke's Hospice
St Matthew Housing Ltd
Stop AIDS Campaign
Survivors Fund (Surf)
Swansea Festival of Music and Arts
Tara Counselling and Personal Development
    Company Ltd
The Centre for Crime and Justice Studies
The Hereford – Muheza Link Society
The Presswise Trust
THT Lighthouse
Transrural Trust
Trust for Sick Children in Wales
Turning Point
Tushinskaya Children's Hospital Trust
Ty Hafan Children's Hospice
Uganda Community Relief Association
UK Youth
Ulster Quaker Service Committee
UN Year of Volunteering
UNITE Ltd
University of Hertfordshire
University of Wisconsin Medical School
Variety Club of New Zealand
VERTIC
Victim Services of Peel
Victim Support National Association
Village Aid
Voluntary Service Overseas
Wales Pre-School Playgroups Association
War on Want
Wave
Welfare Association (UK)
Wellbeing
Welsh National Opera
Welsh Refugee Council
West Glamorgan Forum
West Lothian Youth Action Project
WHIP
Who Cares? Trust
Winston's Wish
Women in Prison
Women's Health
World Piano Competition
World Vision
World Vision Canada
Wyre Forest Advocacy
Y CARE International
YMCA Scotland
Young Minds
Young Voice
Young Women's Christian Association of Great Britain
Youth Assisting Youth

ACKNOWLEDGMENTS, BIBLIOGRAPHY AND INDEX

This authorized portrait of Diana, Princess of Wales has been shaped by the words and memories of family members, friends and other individuals who came into contact with the late Princess through her humanitarian work. We wish to acknowledge and thank the following people:

Victor Adebowale
Mike Adler
Yasmin Alibhai-Brown
Chris Anderson
Dickie Arbiter
Maureen Ashton
Richard Attenborough
Jacques Azagury
Catherine Baker
Mary Baker
Christopher Balfour
Simon Barnes
Nicholas Barrington
Pat Baron
Carol Beardsmore
Martin Bell
Henry Bellingham
Pollyanna Benjamin
Jane Bennett
Michael Bennett
Helena Best
Henry Bienen
Manolo Blahnik
Tony Blair
Derek Bodell
Christine Bodkin
Jennie Bond
Peter Bowring
Malic Bradaric
Karina Brennan
Gordon Brown
Peter Carrette
Paul Chadwick
Lynda Chalker
Caroline Charles
Jimmy Choo
Louise Chunn
Clare
Nigel Clark
Jo Clarke
Roger Clarke
Jean-Paul Claverie
William J Clinton
Annick Cojean
James Colthurst
Caroline Cracraft
Phil Craig
Alice Crawford
Phyllis Cunningham
Barbara Daly
John Dart
Barbara Davies
Colin Dawson
Chris de Burgh
Derek Deane

Bill Deedes
Kath Defilippi
Patrick Demarchelier
Clark Denmark
Fatos Derguti
Maria Dorrian
Bridie Dowd
Anthony Duckworth-Chad
Caroline Duprot
Arthur Edwards
Maureen Edwards
David Emanuel
Elizabeth Emanuel
Lizzie Emeh
Oliver Everett
Janet Filderman
Jayne Fincher
Siobhan Fitzpatrick
Lucia Flecha de Lima
Jim Fletcher
David French
Eleanor Gall
Sandy Gall
Sarah Jane Gaselee
Peter Gautier-Smith
Frank Gelli
Barry Gibb
Michael Gibbins
Anne Giscard D'Estaing
Arpad Gonz
Katharine Graham
Tim Graham
Norman Grant
Malcolm Green
Marilyn Griffiths
Anne Grindrod
Ian Grindrod
Heather Hall
Lucinda Hall
Louise Halliday
Clementine Hambro
Nick Hardwick
Hereward Harrison
Margaret Harrison
Anna Harvey
David Harvey
Bob Hawke
Victoria Hemphill
Geoff Henning
India Hicks
Brian Hill
Susan Hill
Juliet Hindell
Imogen Holt
Richard Horton

Valerie Howarth
Douglas Hurd
David Ireland
Bianca Jagger
Jean-Michel Jarre
Margaret Jay
Patrick Jephson
Robert Jobson
Elton John
Paul Johnson
Brian Johnston
Daniel Jones
Anthony Julius
Tokuo Kassai
Susie Kassem
Richard Kay
Mark Keenan
Kay King
Henry Kissinger
Belinda Knox
Noboru Kobayashi
Mick Lacey
Christina Lamb
Kirsty Lawley
Tina Lawley
Ken Lennox
Bunty Lewis
Patrick Lichfield
Harald Lipman
Marguerite Littman
Richard Lloyd
Tony Lloyd
Christopher Long
Jean Lowe
Roger Lucas
Yad Luthra
Malcolm Macnaughton
Gill Maguire
John Major
Nelson Mandela
Claudia Marquis
Hannah Marvelley
Pat Mason
Ed Matthews
John Mayo
Margaret McAllen
Paul McCartney
Sarah McCorquodale
Mark McGreevy
Sam McKnight
Jeff McWhinney
George Michael
Verona Middleton Jeter
Heather Mills McCartney
Teresa Mitchell

Rosa Monckton
Andrew Morton
Cecelia Nkululekhu Msomi
Debbie Newberry
Stephen Nicholas
Julie O'Hare
Bruce Oldfield
John Overton
Fiona Page
Walter Page
Peter Palumbo
Judith Parnell
Vivienne Parry
Luciano Pavarotti
Nancy Pearce
Maudie Pendry
Zarko Peric
Elaine Phillips
Jean Pike
Ben Pimlott
Brenda Polan
Colin L Powell
Barbara Pratley
John Proctor
Andrew Purkis
David Puttnam
Esther Rantzen
William Rees-Mogg
Cliff Richard
Elizabeth Ridsdale
Sarah Robeson
Anita Roddick
Rebecca Roman
Les Rudd
Julia Samuel
Peter Schaufuss
Mona Shaker
Frances Shand Kydd
Harry Shapiro
Clare Short
Muriel Simmons
Roger Singleton
Katie Slater
Wayne Sleep
Barbara Smith
Louise Smith
Kate Snell
Mair Spargo
Christopher Spence
Charles Spencer
Robert Spencer
Peter Stanford
Tomasz Starzewski
Danielle Stephenson
Denise Stephenson

Richard Stott
Pat Street
Andrew Sutton
Reginald Sweet
Elizabeth Taylor
Mario Testino
Maartin Teterissa
Paul Theobald
Sarah Thomas
Rachel Thomson
Wendy Thomson
Anthony Tippett
Anne Tomkinson
Lynn Tory
Sue Tuckwell
Sandra Paulina Txijica
Ted Unsworth
Valentino
Anne Wake-Walker
Catherine Walker
Penny Walker
Andrew Ward
Charlene Warrender
Makoto Watanabe
Julie Watton-Butler
Ann Webster
Miriam Were
Guy Whalley
Ken Wharfe
James Whitaker
Jerry White
Mike Whitlam
Janet Winfield
Patricia Wood
Dean Woodward
Jane Woodward
Mike Wooldridge
Lisa Yacoub
Magdi Yacoub
John Young
Jayne Zito

234

EDITORIAL CONTRIBUTORS

The Diana Memorial Fund Editorial Team:
Writer: Rosalind Coward
Project Management: Jo Bexley, Lucy McCredie
Project Administrator: Sharon Wilson
Picture Researcher: Christine Cornick
Researchers: Liz de Planta, Joanna McCathie

PQ Editorial Team:
Publisher: Geoff Blackwell
Editorial Director: Ruth Anna Hobday
Production Manager: Jenny Moore
Editor: Kate Parkin
Research Assistant: Birgitta Nilsson
Index: Diane Lowther

We wish to acknowledge the following organizations:

Acorns Children's Hospice Trust www.acorns.org.uk
Albanian Youth Action www.albanianyouthaction.org.uk
Allsorts Youth Project Ltd www.allsortsyouth.org.uk
Althorp www.althorp.com
ASPIRE (Association for Spinal Injury Research, Rehabilitation and Reintegration)
    www.aspire.org.uk
Barnardo's www.barnardos.org.uk
The Benesh Institute/Royal Academy of Dance www.benesh.org/www.rad.org.uk
British Deaf Association www.bda.org.uk
British Lung Foundation www.lunguk.org
British Red Cross www.redcross.org.uk
Centrepoint www.centrepoint.org.uk
Chain of Hope www.chainofhope.org
The Child Bereavement Trust www.childbereavement.org.uk
ChildLine www.childline.org.uk
Children with Leukaemia www.leukaemia.org
The Commonwealth Society for the Deaf www.soundseekers.org.uk
Crusaid www.crusaid.org.uk
DEBRA UK www.debra.org.uk
Depaul Trust www.depaultrust.org
DrugScope www.drugscope.org.uk
Eating Disorders Association www.edauk.com
Elton John AIDS Foundation www.ejaf.org
English National Ballet www.ballet.org.uk
Fairbridge in Scotland www.fairbridge.org.uk
Foundation for Conductive Education
www.conductive-education.org.uk
Freshfield Service www.freshfieldservice.co.uk
Great Ormond Street Hospital Children's Charity www.gosh.org
Harlem Hospital Center, USA www.ci.nyc.ny.us/html/hhc/html/harlem.html
Headway the Brain Injury Association www.headway.org.uk
Hear Our Voice www.hov.org.uk
Heart 'n Soul www.heartnsoul.co.uk
Help the Aged www.helptheaged.org.uk
Henry Street Settlement, USA www.henrystreet.org
Homestart www.homestart.org.uk
Hospice of the Good Shepherd www.hospiceofthegoodshepherd.com

Incarnation Children's Center, USA www.icc-pedsaids.org
Landmine Action www.landmineaction.org
Landmine Survivors Network www.landminesurvivors.org
The Leprosy Mission www.leprosymission.org.uk
Little Company of Mary, Zimbabwe http://sthafrica.lcmglobal.org
London Lighthouse/Terrence Higgins Trust www.tht.org.uk
National AIDS Trust www.nat.org.uk
National Center for Child Health and Development, Japan www.ncchd.go.jp
The National Hospital Development Foundation www.uclh.org/donation/nhdf.shtml
The Natural History Museum www.nhm.ac.uk
Northern Ireland Pre-School Playgroups Association (NIPPA) www.nippa.org
Parkinson's Disease Society www.parkinsons.org.uk
The Passage www.passage.org.uk
Pre-School Learning Alliance www.pre-school.org.uk
Relate www.relate.org.uk
Royal Academy of Dramatic Art www.rada.org.uk
Royal Academy of Music www.ram.ac.uk
Royal Australasian College of Dental Surgeons www.racds.org
The Royal Marsden Hospital www.royalmarsden.org
Saltash Handicapped and Disabled Organization
Sandy Gall Afghanistan Appeal www.sandygallafghanisatanappeal.org
SeeAbility www.seeability.org
South Coast Hospice, South Africa Email: schospkz@venturenet.co.za
St Matthew Housing www.stmatthewhousing.org
Sunrise (Child Bereavement Centre – Edward's Trust)
www.edwardstrust.org.uk/sroverview.asp
Trinity Hospice www.trinityhospice.org.uk
Turning Point www.turning-point.co.uk
Tushinskaya Children's Hospital Trust Email: tushinskaya@aol.com
United Cerebral Palsy (UCP), USA www.ucp.org
WellBeing www.wellbeing.org.uk
Welsh National Opera www.wno.org.uk
Wilson Stuart School www.wilsonst.bham.sch.uk
The Zito Trust www.zitotrust.co.uk

BIBLIOGRAPHY

Clayton, Tim and Craig, Phil, *Diana: Story of a Princess*, Hodder and Stoughton, London, 2000

Fincher, Jayne, *Diana: Portrait of A Princess*, Callaway, London, 1998

Fried, Natasha and Katrina, *The People's Princess: A Memorial*, Stewart, Tabori and Chang, New York, 1997

Graham, Tim, *Diana: A Tribute*, Weidenfeld and Nicholson, London, 1997

Heaton, Trevor, ed. *Diana: Our Norfolk Princess*, Eastern Counties Newspapers, Norwich, UK, 1998

Hill, Susan, *The Day I Met Diana, Princess of Wales: The People's Stories*, Long Barn Books, Ebrington, Gloucestershire, 1997

Howell, Georgina, *Diana: Her Life in Fashion*, Pavilion Books, London, 1998

Jephson, P.D., *Shadows of A Princess: An Intimate Account by her Private Secretary*, HarperCollins, London, 2000

MacArthur, Brian, ed. *Requiem: Diana Princess of Wales 1961-1997*, Pavilion Books, London, 1997

O'Mara, Michael, ed. *Diana: Her Life in Photographs*, Michael O'Mara Books, London, 1995

Morton, Andrew, *Diana: Her True Story - In her Own Words*, Michael O'Mara Books, London, 1997

Morton, Andrew, *Diana's Diary: An Intimate Portrait of the Princess of Wales*, Michael O'Mara Books, London, 1990

Pimlott, Ben, *The Queen: Elizabeth 11 and the Monarchy*, revised edition, HarperCollins, London, 2002

Snell, Kate, *Diana: Her Last Love*, Grenada Books, London, 2000

Spencer, Charles, *Althorp: The Story of an English House*, Viking Penguin Books, London, 1998

Spoto, Donald, *Diana: The Last Year*, Harmony Books, New York, 1997

Wharfe, Ken, *Diana: Closely Guarded Secret*, Michael O'Mara Books, London, 2002

Walker, Catherine, *An Autobiography by The Private Couturier to Diana, Princess of Wales*, Universe Publishing, New York, 1998

FOOTNOTES

Chapter 1: The Unique
1 *Tonight* Programme *'Diana, My Sister'*, 14 June 2001 (this and all subsequent quotes from Charles Spencer unless stated); 2 Heaton, Trevor, ed. *'Diana: Our Norfolk Princess'*, Eastern Counties Newspapers, 1998; 3 *The Mail on Sunday*, 27 July 2003

Chapter 2: The Complex
1 MacArthur, Brian, ed. *Requiem: Diana, Princess of Wales 1961-1997*, Pavilion Books, London, 1997; 2 ibid; 3 *'The Princess and the Press'*, Channel 4 television, 16 November 1997; 4 *'Story of a Princess'*, ITV, 1991; 5 MacArthur, Brian, ed. *Requiem: Diana, Princess of Wales 1961-1997*, Pavilion Books, London, 1997; 6 *British Deaf Association Newsletter*, Summer 1992; 7 Harvey, Anna, *Vogue* magazine, October 1997; 8 Walker, Catherine, *An Autobiography by The Private Couturier to Diana, Princess of Wales*, Universe Publishing, New York, 1998; 9 *Vogue* magazine, October 1997; 10 ibid; 11 MacArthur, Brian, ed. *Requiem: Diana, Princess of Wales 1961-1997*, Pavilion Books, London, 1997

Chapter 3: The Extraordinary
1 MacArthur, Brian, ed. *Requiem: Diana, Princess of Wales 1961-1997*, Pavilion Books, London, 1997; 2 ibid; 3 *'Story of a Princess'*, ITV, 1991; 4 Walker, Catherine, *An Autobiography by The Private Couturier to Diana, Princess of Wales*, Universe Publishing, New York, 1998; 5 *San Francisco Examiner*, 1997; 6 Fried, Natasha and Katrina, *The People's Princess: A Memorial*, Stewart, Tabori & Chang, New York, 1998; 7 Fincher, Jayne, *Diana: Portrait of A Princess*, Callaway, London, 1998; 8 MacArthur, Brian, ed. *Requiem: Diana, Princess of Wales 1961-1997*, Pavilion Books, London, 1997

Chapter 4: The Irreplaceable
1 William J. Clinton from: The Diana, Princess of Wales lecture on AIDS, 13 December 2001; 2 Walker, Catherine, *An Autobiography by The Private Couturier to Diana, Princess of Wales*, Universe Publishing, New York, 1998; 3 *Panorama*, BBC TV, 1995; 4 MacArthur, Brian, ed. *Requiem: Diana, Princess of Wales 1961-1997*, Pavilion Books, London, 1997; 5 *Express on Sunday* magazine, August 1998; 6 Hill, Susan, *The Day I Met Diana, Princess of Wales: The People's Stories*, Long Barn Books, Ebrington, Gloucestershire, 1997; 7 ibid; 8 MacArthur, Brian, ed. *Requiem: Diana, Princess of Wales 1961-1997*, Pavilion Books, London, 1997; 9 *Hello* magazine, 4 November 2003; 10 MacArthur, Brian, ed. *Requiem: Diana, Princess of Wales 1961-1997*, Pavilion Books, London, 1997; 11 Polan, Brenda, *'Diana, Her Own Woman'*, *You* magazine, London, 1996; 12 Walker, Catherine, *An Autobiography by The Private Couturier to Diana, Princess of Wales*, Universe Publishing, New York, 1998; 13 BBC website, 1998; 14 Walker, Catherine, *An Autobiography by The Private Couturier to Diana, Princess of Wales*, Universe Publishing, New York, 1998; 15 MacArthur, Brian, ed. *Requiem: Diana, Princess of Wales 1961-1997*, Pavilion Books, London, 1997; 16 ibid; 17 *The Mirror*, 21 August 2002

Chapter 5: The Memory
1 *The Mirror*, 21 August 2002; 2 BBC website, 1998; 3 Juliet Hindell, BBC website, 1998; 4 *Basil*, Acorns Children's Hospice Trust Magazine, Winter 2001; 5 Speech, 31 August 1997

The Diana, Princess of Wales Memorial Fund is particularly grateful to Patrick Demarchelier, to Mario Testino, and to all those other contributors who have supplied their images for this book free of charge.

Legend

AP: Alpha Press
CP: Camera Press
DC/AP: David Chancellor/Alpha Press
DMF/JF: Diana Memorial Fund/Jayne Fincher
ES: Earl Spencer
PC: Private Collection
PD: Patrick Demarchelier

All images are listed left to right from top unless otherwise stated.

[Page no...©Copyright]

Introductory pages

Endpapers...Mario Testino; p.1...Patrick Demarchelier; p.2...PD; p.4...PD; p.6...Mario Testino; p.8...Earl Spencer; p.9...ES; p.10...ES; 11...Snowdon/Camera Press; p.12...ES

Chapter One – The Unique

p.29...ES, except center right and bottom center...Earl Spencer/Artist Lela Pawlikowska; p.30...Alpha Press; p.31...ES; p.32...Earl Spencer/Artist Lela Pawlikowska; p.33...ES, except center left...*Eastern Daily Press* and bottom left...Private Collection; p.34...ES; p.35...ES; p.36...PC, except bottom right...ES; p.37...ES; p.38...AP, ES, ES, PC, PC, PC, PC, ES, PC, AP, PC; p.39...AP; p.40...PC; p.41...Diana Memorial Fund/Jayne Fincher, Bridget Wheeler Photography, PC, PC, DMF/JF, David and Elizabeth Emanuel, Elizabeth Emanuel, ES, David and Elizabeth Emanuel, David and Elizabeth Emanuel; p.42...DMF/JF, John Scott/Alpha Press, John Scott/Alpha Press, DMF/JF, PC, DMF/JF, John Scott/Alpha Press, DMF/JF, DMF/JF, Lichfield/Camera Press; p.43...ES; p.44...John Scott/Alpha Press, John Scott/Alpha Press, DMF/JF; p.45...DMF/JF; p.46...Lichfield/Camera Press; p.47...Lichfield/Camera Press; p.48...Snowdon/Camera Press

Chapter Two – The Complex

p.64...DMF/JF; p.65...DMF/JF, except top right...Rex Features; p.66...DMF/JF; p.67...DMF/JF; p.68...DMF/JF; p.69...DMF/JF; p.70...DMF/JF, DMF/JF, DMF/JF, DMF/JF, Rex Features, DMF/JF, DMF/JF, AP, AP, AP; p.71...DMF/JF; p.72...DMF/JF; p.73...DMF/JF; p.74...DMF/JF; p.75...DMF/JF, except top right and second-from-right center...AP; p.76...AP, except top left and top right...DMF/JF; p.77...DMF/JF; p.78...AP; p.79...Donovan/Camera Press, DMF/JF, AP, DMF/JF, DMF/JF, AP, AP, DMF/JF, DMF/JF, AP, AP, PC; p.80...Help the Aged/Private Collection; p.81...DMF/JF; p.82...PD; p.83...PD; p.84...DMF/JF, DMF/JF, AP, AP, DMF/JF, AP, AP, DMF/JF, DMF/JF, AP, DMF/JF; p.85...PD; p.86...PC, except center left...DMF/JF; p.87...PD; p.88...PD

Chapter Three – The Extraordinary

p.110...PD; p.111...Courtesy Ronald Reagan Library, Rex Features, DMF/JF, Sherlock Robinson/Courtesy Harlem Hospital Center, DMF/JF, DMF/JF, DMF/JF, DMF/JF, DMF/JF, Sherlock Robinson/Courtesy Harlem Hospital Center, DMF/JF; p.112...DMF/JF; p.113...AP, DMF/JF, DMF/JF, AP, AP, AP, AP, DMF/JF, DMF/JF, DMF/JF; p.114...AP; p.115...PD; p.116...AP, Nicolas Richter, Rex Features, DMF/JF, DMF/JF, DMF/JF, DMF/JF, DMF/JF, AP, PC, AP; p.117...PD; p.118...PC; p.119...PC; p.120...AP; p.121...AP; p.122–23...Nicolas Richter, p.124...AP, DMF/JF, DMF/JF, DMF/JF, DMF/JF, DMF/JF, Paul Hackett/English National Ballet, AP, AP, Times/News International; p.125...DMF/JF; p.126...Private Collection/Patrick Demarchelier; p.127...PD; p.128...Jayne Fincher/*Hello*; p.129...PD; p.130–31...Rex Features; p.132...PD

Chapter Four – The Irreplaceable

p.153...DMF/JF, DMF/JF, DMF/JF, Mark Lloyd, PC, PC, DMF/JF, DMF/JF, PC, Courtesy The Arab Republic of Egypt; p.154...DMF/JF; p.155...DMF/JF; p.156...DMF/JF, DMF/JF, AP, AP, AP, DMF/JF, DMF/JF, DMF/JF, DMF/JF, DMF/JF, Private Collection/Chain of Hope; p.157...Private Collection/Aprica; p.158...DMF/JF; p.159...DMF/JF, AP, AP, AP; p.160...PC, except bottom right...AP; p.161...AP; p.162...AP, Private Collection/Chain of Hope, Private Collection/Chain of Hope, Private Collection/Centrepoint, Présidence de la République Française; AP, DMF/JF, DMF/JF, DMF/JF, DMF/JF, DMF/JF; p.163...Reuters; p.164...AP; p.165...ES, Rex Features; p.166...DMF/JF; p.167...AP, DMF/JF, AP, AP, AP, AP, David Chancellor/Alpha Press, DC/AP, DC/AP, DC/AP, Camera Press, CP; p.168...CP; p.169...CP, except bottom row...DC/AP, DC/AP, PC, PC; p.170...DC/AP, DC/AP, DC/AP, Rex Features, Rex Features, DC/AP, Rex Features, DC/AP, DC/AP, DC/AP, DC/SP, AP, DC/AP; p.171...DC/AP; p.172...Private Collection/Yad Luthra, except bottom right...Rex Features; p.173...Private Collection/Yad Luthra; p.174...DC/AP; p.175...DC/AP; p.176...Mario Testino

Chapter Five – Diana, Whose Beauty Will Never Be Extinguished From Our Minds

p.190...AP; p.191...DMF/JF, CP, AP, DMF/JF, CP, AP, Henry Dallal, AP, AP; p.192...ES; p.193...DMF/JF; p.194...DMF/JF; p.195...Henry Dallal; p.196...AP; p.197...DMF/JF; p.198...Henry Dallal, Henry Dallal, DMF/JF, DMF/JF, Henry Dallal, CP, DMF/JF, CP, CP; p.199...DMF/JF; p.200...DMF/JF; p.201...AP; p.202...PC, DMF/JF, AP, DMF/JF, CP, CP, DMF/JF, AP; p.203...ES; p.204...DMF/JF; p.205...ES; p.206...DMF/JF; p.207...ES; p.208...ES; p.209...ES; p.210...Elton John; p.211...CP; p.212...CP; p.213...AP; p.214...CP; p.215...PC; p.216...PC; p.217...PA Photos; p.218...AP, AP, AP, DMF/JF, DMF/JF, David Rose/Panos Pictures, Caroline Penn/Panos Pictures, Roger Allen/*Daily Mirror*, Acorns, Caroline Penn/Panos Pictures, Paul Weinberg/Panos Pictures; p.219...Tim Graham; p.220...DMF/JF, DMF/JF, DMF/JF, Rex Features; p.221...DMF/JF; p.222...PD; p.223...PC; p.224...DMF/JF

Diana – The Work Continues

p.226...AP; p.227...Charlotte MacPherson, Steve Forrest/Panos Pictures; p.228...Paul Weinberg/Panos Pictures, David Rose/Panos Pictures; p.229...Murdo MacLeod/Panos Pictures, Marc Schlossman/Panos Pictures

Published under license from The Diana, Princess of Wales Memorial Fund in 2004 (and this edition in 2007) by PQ Blackwell Limited, 116 Symonds Street, Auckland, New Zealand
www.pqblackwell.com

This edition published in 2007 by Andrews McMeel Publishing, LLC, 4520 Main Street, Kansas City, Missouri 64111

Library of Congress Control Number on file

ISBN-13: 978-0-7407-6955-9
ISBN-10: 0-7407-6955-3

Design by Carolyn Lewis

Printed by Everbest Printing International Limited, China

www.andrewsmcmeel.com